HISTORY REPEATING

HISTORY
REPEATING

WHY POPULISTS RISE
AND GOVERNMENTS FALL

SAM WILKIN

PROFILE BOOKS

First published in Great Britain in 2018 by
Profile Books Ltd
3 Holford Yard
Bevin Way
London
WC1X 9HD

www.profilebooks.com

1 3 5 7 9 10 8 6 4 2

Printed and bound in Great Britain by
Clays, Bungay, Suffolk

A CIP catalogue record for this book is available from the British Library.

ISBN 978 1 78125 9689
eISBN 978 178283 4106

The paper this book is printed on is certified by the
© 1996 Forest Stewardship Council A.C. (FSC).
It is ancient-forest friendly. The printer holds FSC
chain of custody SGS-COC-2061

Contents

CONTENTS

for Caroline

Introduction

Let us imagine, dear reader, that you wish to topple the establishment. Imagine you are an outsider political candidate, despised in Washington or Westminster; or perhaps a campaigner for democracy in an authoritarian country like China or Cuba; or even a revolutionary militant, seeking to depose a corrupt and unjust regime. Imagine that you have been seized by an overpowering vision of yourself leading the people to a better future, swathed in robes of white cotton walking forth upon rose petals scattered by youths singing songs in your praise.

Or perhaps that is just me. Regardless, I have bad news. Let me put it bluntly: your fellow citizens are sheep. 'Let's remake this great nation!' you will cry. 'Baa,' they will bleat contentedly, distracted by salty snacks and Instagram. They neither know nor care that the system is failing them. Someone could burst through their front door and shave them, and they would stagger hairless to their feet and return to snacking on the sofa. Such ovine complacency is a problem for those who seek to rally mass movements against the political establishment; indeed, it has been a problem for all leaders who dream of political change, from those who fought to end racial segregation in the American South to those who toppled the Russian government in 1917: there is just not much net gain for the common man in undertaking political action. Struggling against the status quo entails personal effort for a widely shared reward. We all want a better world, but no one wants to give up their weekend for it.

But do not lose hope: the people can be mobilised. When the UK's referendum on Brexit was held, for instance, some 2.8 million people turned out to vote who had not voted in the previous election; many of them had never voted in their lives. Whether one was appalled or elated by the referendum outcome, it was an extraordinary surge in political participation. And it was no less extraordinary when, in the first post-Brexit general election, turnout among eighteen to twenty-four-year-olds rose by 16 percentage points; and turnout among ethnic minorities rose by six points. What force could compel millions of hitherto uninterested people to rise up from their sofas and participate in politics?

These participation surges are examples of what I will call 'mobilisation politics', and they can produce a very different politics than that to which we have become accustomed. It is the politics of Brexit, of Donald Trump's victory, of the movements against them, and of great political uprisings throughout history. This book explains how such moments of turmoil come about, by telling the stories of leaders who wanted rebellions, mass uprisings, or votes against the establishment, and got them – occasionally to their own great surprise. We have all heard about a butterfly flapping its wings and causing a hurricane. In politics, it is far more common that the hurricane was already building, and a butterfly that happened to be flapping around nearby has loudly claimed credit. Political leaders put a face on events, but it is underlying social, political and economic conditions that give mass movements their strength. The leaders who have led momentous political changes tend to draw conclusions about the size of their wings, but even the most delicate flutter can produce a great storm if conditions are right.

But only if conditions are right. The sexiest revolutionary of all time, Che Guevara, once claimed that 'The revolution is not an apple that falls when it is ripe. You have to make it fall.' He then disproved his own thesis by dying while attempting to overthrow the government of Bolivia. Today's political leaders, no matter how much we love or hate them, are no less the victims or beneficiaries of broader conditions. Many people no doubt spent 2017 chanting incantations in magic Latin (*egomanius incarcerus! referendi reverso!*). But would such magic really fix politics? Take the case of Italy, where, during the early 2000s, a wealthy businessman became prime minister and then proceeded to alienate much of the country's political establishment. During the Eurozone debt crisis, the Italians got rid of him. A few years later, the most popular opposition party in Italy was led by a former professional comedian who wanted a referendum on leaving the Euro. Unless underlying conditions are addressed, *plus ça change ...*

But what kinds of conditions produced the turmoil of 2016? Two types are most frequently mentioned, but neither is sufficient to explain these surprising political events. The first is economic distress. But, as we shall see, the link between economic hardship and political unrest is not that simple. If hardship caused uprisings, it would have been peasants who led the Russian Revolution rather than comparatively well-off urban workers. If hardship caused uprisings, there would be a rebellion attempted in North Korea every day (perhaps unsuccessfully, given the North Korean government's willingness to oppress its people). As we shall see, even the extremes of personal hardship do not, on their own, cause people to rise up against the political establishment.

The other underlying condition that is often mentioned is psychological distress. It is said that people who turned out for the Brexit vote or supported Donald Trump were enraged by an assault on their values; or were reacting to a perceived threat from ethnic or religious minorities; or perhaps longed for a more authoritarian leader. But if disputes over values were the cause of recent political events, surely the non-voters who voted for Brexit would have turned out to vote in the previous UK general election as well?

3

Presumably, people's values did not change that much between the 2015 general election and the 2016 Brexit referendum. Hence conflicts over values cannot, on their own, explain why 2016 was such an unusual year.

But if economic distress, psychological angst, and the size of Boris Johnson's wings cannot explain the surprising events of 2016, what can?

Social science

I began thinking about this book some time ago, because in my profession of political risk analysis, it has long been apparent that beneath the apparent dullness of modern politics – the all-but-interchangeable parties and policy platforms – the wheels have slowly been coming off. Perhaps, I thought, people will want to read a book about why this happens.

Take, for instance, the country risk ratings compiled by the financial journal *Euromoney*. In the 1980s and 1990s, the US ranked among the least risky countries in the world, perhaps unsurprisingly, given its long history of democracy, stability and general richness. By 2012, however, the United States had dropped to 15th place, eclipsed by, among others, Hong Kong and Singapore. At the time of writing, *Euromoney* ranks the United States one place ahead of Chile. Good for Chile, which only became a democracy in 1989. The country risk rankings of BlackRock, a leading asset management firm, are even more startling, rating France as more risky than Thailand, a country under military rule. It would be tempting to dismiss BlackRock as a bunch of cranks, but the company's annual profits of more than $11bn suggest that these cranks understand a thing or two about the world economy.

Of course, such trends, while striking, have many causes, including benign factors such as improved conditions in developing economies. Yet one cause is the deterioration of political stability in

Europe and the United States. When America lost its triple-A rating from Standard & Poor's in 2011, the agency specifically attributed the downgrade in part to attempts by Congress to use the threat of a sovereign default to wrest concessions from the White House. Not since 1860, when Standard & Poor's was founded, had the United States been downgraded. A triple-A rating that had survived two world wars was undone partly by political polarisation.

I was personally impacted by the turmoil of 2016 – particularly the post-Brexit crash in the value of the pound. And yet, as I have spent much of my career studying political turmoil in other countries, I was not only shocked but more than a little intrigued to see political risk come home. I am reminded of the reaction of my father, a professor of anatomy and physiology, after he cut his arm badly while attempting some home repairs. He was so fascinated by his examination of the subcutaneous fat layer that it took him a while to realise he was in a lot of pain. Most of this book is about the history and science of what causes stability to crumble, rather than assigning blame for what happened, point-scoring against people who hold different political views than I do, or making fun of Boris Johnson. Still, in the final chapter I will let fly with some personal views.

What is in this book?

In this book, I will introduce some of the more extraordinary political leaders in history – some familiar, some largely unknown – and explain how their delicate flapping toppled governments. Each chapter assembles a piece in the puzzle of political instability. Throughout the book, I will reference the events of 2016 – a historical case that we can all remember, despite many people's best efforts to forget it. I will identify hidden patterns in history; conditions and events that echo in different time periods and on opposite sides of the globe. Some of these patterns offer insight into the root causes of political turmoil. Others, I assume, are mere coincidence. Take for instance the tendency of anti-establishment leaders to have iconic hats – Trump's baseball cap is only the latest version; think of Mao, Fidel or Che Guevara. The trend was, arguably, started by Lenin, who for some reason began wearing a painter's cap he had picked up in Sweden. I cannot think of any reason why revolution requires a great hat. Perhaps you can.

Chapter 1 introduces the characters: the charismatic populist, the old-school politico, the rising middle class. I will tell the story of Thailand's turmoil and a poodle named Foo Foo. In the wake of a punishing financial crisis, Thailand elected a billionaire populist. The Bangkok middle class rose up against him, but the outcome was not what one might have expected.

Chapters 2 and 3 lay out the causes of political instability. I begin with one of history's most epochal and improbable mass uprisings, in which a group of Russian workers toppled a ruthless czar. They also reshaped the globe: within a few decades, one third of the world's people would be living under communist governments. Did the workers' uprising spring from intolerable suffering? Personal economic distress? Collective insanity? None of the above, it turns out; and from this case I suggest what those forces are that make mobilisation politics possible.

Chapter 3 tells the story of another uprising that reshaped geopolitics: the Islamic revolution in Iran, which, as most people have forgotten, started with a poetry reading. I address the question of why regimes fall (for one thing, it helps if the leader is out of his mind) and how uprisings of the right succeed. At one time, social scientists thought that revolutions were the result of exceptionally powerful rebellions. There is more to it than that, as we shall see.

Neither Russia nor Iran were democracies; so what does it take for a rich democracy to fail? I tackle that question in chapter 4, which tells the story of Argentina – arguably the only country in the modern era to become rich and then become poor again. The antihero of the chapter is Juan Perón, perhaps the purest populist of all time, a man so superbly gifted in the populist dark arts that he became, like Voldemort, *he who must not be named*. For years, after his downfall, it was a crime to print his name or image in Argentina until, like Voldemort, he made his untimely return, with the help of a sinister accomplice.

For a story with a happy ending, try chapter 5. In the 1930s and 40s, the United States overcame many of today's challenges, including populism and political polarisation. I recount the tale of Huey Long, a man whose charisma was almost a superpower; a natural revolutionary who started his first mass uprising in high school. Did Long threaten American democracy, or inadvertently save it? It is a question with great relevance today.

Which brings us to chapter 6: a handy guide to assessing whether your country is doomed. I explain why social science predicts that we will all be living in the world of Blade Runner, and why in actuality things will probably be worse, and I provide some pointers on assessing political risk. Also, there is a sex scene.

The life of Foo Foo: a populist tail

'A company is a country ... They're the same.
The management is the same.'

Thaksin Shinawatra, billionaire prime minister of Thailand,
November 1997

Meet Foo Foo

Thai royals love their dogs. King Bhumibol wrote a book about his dog, Tongdaeng, which reportedly became the best-selling book in Thai history. Tongdaeng, an adopted stray, is introduced in the book as a 'common dog who is uncommon'. Tongdaeng can be seen chasing other dogs around trees (always clockwise), eating coconuts (with difficulty), sitting obediently at the king's feet with paws crossed, and calling her pups telepathically. Everyone in Thailand loved Tongdaeng. One person who posted an insult about Tongdaeng on a Facebook page was charged with sedition and faced a possible prison sentence of thirty-seven years.

The king's son, the crown prince Maha Vajiralongkorn, also loved his dog, a white poodle named Foo Foo. While Tongdaeng enjoyed simple pleasures, Foo Foo lived large. The US ambassador to Thailand was surprised to see Foo Foo attending a November 2007 gala dinner 'dressed in formal evening attire complete with paw mitts'. At one point Foo Foo leapt up on the table and began lapping water from the guests' glasses, to general amusement. Eventually, it emerged that the prince had awarded Foo Foo the rank of Air Chief Marshal in the Thai Air Force. Everyone saw the humour of it, although for members of the Thai military who were now outranked by a poodle, it may have taken some time.

And then a video of the birthday party for the crown prince's third wife was leaked on to YouTube. Everything about the party seems normal – the uniformed staff, the stacked presents, the floral arrangements, the balloons, the trees festooned with lights – aside from one detail: the prince's wife is almost naked. She wears a straw boater, killer heels, a thong and nothing else. The prince smokes a pipe and looks at ease. Even his wife looks relaxed. Then Foo Foo makes his appearance, living large, getting a kiss from this nearly naked Thai woman, and helping to blow out the candles. 'Careless Whisper' plays in the background.

To be fair, princes often misbehave at parties. Most Thais probably ignored the crown prince's antics, and focused on the wise counsel of their revered king. With the benefit of hindsight, however, they should have been paying a lot more attention to Foo Foo.

On the status quo

In most countries – even Thailand – politics tends to be boring, and for good reason. In the late 1950s, the economist Anthony Downs demonstrated that, in principle, in democracies, the winning strategy for political parties is to pursue the voter with the most middle-of-the-road political views – that is, the 'median voter'. To understand why, imagine there are two political parties, and one of these parties is far to the right of that median voter. If the other party stakes out a position only slightly to the left of that party, it will win any election in a landslide. Why is that? Well, right-wing extremist voters will love the first, extreme right party, so it will pick up their votes. Voters on the moderate right will love the moderate right party. Everyone else (centrists, soft-leftists and left-wing extremists) will hate the far-right extremists even more than they dislike the moderate right, and so hold their noses and also vote for the moderate right. A landslide win.

So the first party tries again, moving a bit towards the centre. Its rival again sets up just to its left. That process continues until both parties are more or less dead centre, where neither can pick up more votes by moving. It is as if there is a gravitational pull towards the political centre, which is essentially the position that the greatest number of voters dislike the least. Hence government policy in democracies tends, in effect, to be dictated by that most unremarkable of citizens – the 'average Joe'. In the UK: Joe Bloggs; in Australia: Fred Nurk; in Germany: Otto Normalverbraucher; in a nod to social progress: the average Jo; in Thailand: the average Somchai.

Of course, only a few people – those who share the average Joe's views, or near enough – love the policy platforms of these centrist parties. Everyone else is unhappy, but would be even more unhappy with a party that moved even further towards the opposite side of the political spectrum; and so, parties cluster at the centre, the least offensive position for the greatest number of people. It is, it must be said, not much to get excited about. Has anyone ever complained that all major political parties and candidates look the same? Or that they are dull? They do, and they are, in order to win. Parties that ignore the median voter tend to lose repeatedly. Their best candidates desert them; their supporters go elsewhere; they either change their ways or go extinct. It is the iron law of milquetoast politics.

An important point: the average Jo, that middle-of-the-road voter, is technically a median rather than an average; hence she is not necessarily the average citizen. Consider the situation in the

United States. In the 2016 presidential election, for instance, only about 60 per cent of eligible Americans turned out to vote; and those who voted differed in important ways from those who did not. One of the most reliable differences is age. In that election, for instance, the turnout rate for eighteen to twenty-nine-year-olds was a bit more than 40 per cent; but for over-sixty-fives, more than 70 per cent. Similarly, in the 2015 UK general election, for eighteen to twenty-four-year-olds turnout was a bit more than 40 per cent; but for over-sixty-fives, nearly 80 per cent. In addition to being older, the average (voting) Joe tends to be richer, more educated, and – in the US and UK at least – whiter.

Over the years, Anthony Downs's theory regarding party strategy in democracies has been put to the test thousands of times across innumerable elections, countries and issues. It is at best a rough guide to reality. There are in practice lots of complications: parties' strategic and reputational concerns; the nature of the political system (which in the United States, for instance, over-weights votes in rural areas); the influence of money in politics; and so on. Still, politics in modern democracies tends to err on the side of the milquetoast. The political parties that win office tend to be centrist parties, and in countries with coalition governments, the average Joe's party usually ends up in the winning coalition. It is the politics of Blairism or of the Clinton Democrat. Is it left or right? Who knows? The point is, it wins elections.

But not always.

The populist

In 1997, Thailand suffered a punishing financial crisis. A few years later, there arose a dark horse political candidate – a billionaire and a populist; a man who claimed he was already so rich that the broken political system could not corrupt him; a man who pledged to restore the vitality of Thai businesses battered by foreign competition. Against all expectations, he won the 2001 general election, with overwhelming support from rural areas. Once in office, he quickly alienated the urban middle class; became the subject of multiple official investigations; attempted to fire or replace any public official who investigated him; lashed out at anyone who criticised him; promoted his own business interests; and appointed family members to high political positions.

Perhaps this sounds familiar?

Some of these coincidences are just coincidences. But there are often good reasons why history echoes so uncannily on opposite sides of the globe. This is a book about such patterns in history and why they occur. One element of these recurring patterns is the cast of characters. Indeed, many of the characters in this Thai drama will reappear throughout this book in various guises, so it makes sense to introduce them now.

Start with the populist. Thaksin Shinawatra was not initially a politician; he was, rather, a billionaire businessman with political problems. Thaksin had obtained a government licence to provide mobile phone services in Thailand. By the early 1990s, his company was the dominant player in the Thai mobile phone market; in 1992, its profits were 445 million baht (equivalent to about $30m today); by 1995, 3 billion baht ($200m today). It was a fabulously lucrative licence, but, because it was awarded by the government, it was also inherently political. In much of Southeast Asia, these licences went not to businessmen like Thaksin but directly to politicians or their relatives. A coveted mobile licence in Myanmar was awarded to the son of one of the country's top leaders; Cambodia's leading mobile phone company was owned by the prime minister. Soon, Thaksin's lucrative licence was attracting acquisitive glances from Thailand's political class.

In 1991, a group of Thai generals carried out a military coup, and it looked like Thaksin's goose was cooked. The generals pledged to root out corruption, and undertook investigations which quickly revealed that the government officials who had granted Thaksin's mobile phone licence were guilty of having received kickbacks of about 300 million baht (equivalent to about $21m in today's money), although not necessarily from Thaksin. After uncovering the corruption, the generals announced they would open the telecoms sector to competition. It soon turned out, however, that what they had in mind was not some far-reaching cleanup, but rather, handing out more mobile phone concessions so they could get kickbacks themselves.

That was still a big problem for Thaksin. More concessions would mean more competitors, and less profit. The country's military leaders were in the process of rushing out ten new concessions worth 5 billion baht ($337m today) when they themselves were deposed by a democratic uprising in 1992. Unfortunately for Thaksin, the new democratic government was also keen to feed at the telecommunications trough, and in short order, Thaksin's competitors were taking advantage of democracy's flowering by jumping into bed with Thai political parties. The conglomerate CP, owner of TelecomAsia, cosied up to the New Aspiration Party; Ucom forged intimate ties with the Democrat Party; while a smaller competitor, Loxley, flirted sometimes with the Democrats, at other times with Thai Nation.

Thaksin decided that he had to get into politics himself. His initial approach was rather surprising: he joined the Moral Force Party, the party of the Buddhist lay ascetic who had been one of the leaders of the 1992 democratic uprising. The followers of a Buddhist ascetic – whose religious views were, even to other Buddhists, somewhat extreme – were never going to mix well with Thaksin's money. When the party split and its leader retired, it caused the government to collapse and new elections to be held. The next government that took power was famously corrupt, but Thaksin led the remnants of the Moral Force Party, admittedly somewhat unwillingly, into the government coalition, and managed to secure the post of deputy prime minister for himself. His mobile phone concession was extended for five more years. Things were looking good. Thaksin diversified into cable television, satellite television and expressways – the common theme being businesses awarded by government licence.

But live by the sword, die by the sword. Many members of Moral Force did not like Thaksin, and the party soon collapsed around him. The next government was dominated by the New Aspiration Party – one of the parties supported by Thaksin's business rivals. New telecoms concessions were quickly awarded, which meant more competition. Thaksin was in serious trouble, so he doubled down, founding his own political party, the Thais Love Thais Party, on 14 July 1998. As the name suggests, it was nationalist. Initially, Thaksin pledged to pursue anti-globalisation policies and to make Thai businesses great again. 'This is an age of economic war,' he said, 'globalization and the international political system ... [are] increasingly ruthless.' At first, this platform did not get much traction, and many of the new party's founding members drifted away.

Then, in 1999 and 2000, there were major protests. Farmers' groups invaded Bangkok's northern suburbs. During an international conference in late 1999, the police blocked roads to prevent farm trucks from massing in the city. Intrigued by this raw display of people power, Thaksin's team met with rural leaders and the charities that had helped organise the protests. In March 2000, Thais Love Thais announced a new, rural platform. By August 2000, this platform had been fine-tuned to three simple (possibly focus-group-tested) points: a moratorium on agrarian debts for small farmers, a fund of 1 million baht (about $34,700 today) to encourage entrepreneurship in every village, and a 30 baht-per-visit ($1) scheme of public healthcare. It was a brilliant move, for the simple reason that rural areas were where the votes were. In roughly 80 per cent of all Thai electoral constituencies, rural voters constituted a majority.

Thaksin repackaged himself. His life story became a somewhat improbable rags-to-riches tale. 'As a rural kid, the son of a coffee shop owner, I helped my father with his orchards, newspaper delivery, and mobile cinema, until I began a computer business,' Thaksin wrote, in a manifesto published one month before the election (in fact, he had been born into a wealthy family of silk merchants; his father had decided to open a coffee shop on a whim). 'I married a police officer's daughter ... We started together from zero, facing troubles and triumphs together, helping one another to raise three children.' Thaksin played up the country boy angle: 'Brothers and sisters', he wrote, 'as someone born in the country-side, I'd like farmers to have a life that can be self-reliant, without debt, and with enough money to educate their children. I'd like them to get medical care when they are sick ... and have supplementary work if they are seasonally unemployed.'

The idea of a 'populist' was so novel that a word in the Thai language had to be invented for it. Thai academics wrote books and articles explaining populism's meaning and history. Thaksin seemed to master populist politics almost intuitively. Before long, he had ditched the business suits, picked up some earthy language, and was wearing unbuttoned shirts – sometimes unbuttoned all the way to his navel. It was a bit of an act, but it worked. With a vote-getting rural programme and a vast influx of Thaksin's money, Thais Love Thais won 248 out of 500 seats in parliament in the 2000 elections – only three seats away from an absolute majority. It was an unheard-of victory. Since 1979, no party had won more than a third of legislative seats. In the face of this stunning success, other parties fell over themselves to join Thaksin's coalition. Soon, his government controlled 364 out of 500 seats in parliament.

But why was Thaksin's populism so effective?

Populism is a term of political art, used by political movements to describe themselves. The first populists were Russian, the *narodniki*, founded in the 1870s. They attempted to convince the

Russian peasantry to rise up against the czar. To no avail: as one disgruntled *narodniki* put it, 'socialism bounced off the peasants like peas from a wall'. The next major populist movement was the American Populist Party, which drew its support from American farmers. It did better than the Russians, but still failed to gain national power.

All populists, by definition, claim to represent the people against a corrupt elite. Donald Trump provided a textbook example in April 2016 when he said: 'On every major issue affecting this country, the people are right and the governing elite are wrong.' Populists also usually claim that the reason corrupt elites have been able to subvert the popular will is because the political system is broken. Again quoting Trump: 'I have joined the political arena so that the powerful can no longer beat up on people that cannot defend themselves. Nobody knows the system better than me, which is why I alone can fix it.'

This focus on the broken system is extremely unusual in democratic politics – most political parties tend to take democracy as a given and compete on their policy proposals. In the oft-quoted words of the political scientist Cas Mudde, populism is a 'thin-centred ideology' because it is about the broken system and corrupt elites, rather than policy; without a firm policy platform, it does not really have a defined place on the left-right political spectrum. Some populists combine their populism with other, meatier ideologies – there are populist socialists, for instance, and parties of the populist right. The greatest of all populists (some of whom we shall meet in this book) enable their followers to fill in the blanks themselves. Argentina's Juan Perón, for instance, managed to attract support from both the radical right and radical left at the same time. That is quite a feat, but not as odd as it might first appear. As I have noted, populism is about the system. While people on the far right and far left would disagree vehemently on policy, they could plausibly agree that the system is broken. By dodging questions of policy, great populists can make an end-run around the average Jo's iron law of milquetoast politics.

Even populists who could not hold a candle to Perón tend to be adept at picking up support from unexpected places. The official Brexit campaign was led in part by Conservatives such as Boris Johnson and Michael Gove, yet it collected crucial votes from traditional Labour voters; Donald Trump campaigned as a Republican but picked up swing-state support from disgruntled Democrats. The 'thin-centred' nature of populism also enables populists to be flexible as circumstances change. Thaksin was a case in point: he started as an economic nationalist, added a rural platform, and eventually made an almost 180-degree turn from his initial position and began courting foreign direct investment. An impressive performance to be sure, but he could not have done it without unintended assistance from some of Thailand's more traditional politicians.

The old-school politico

There is another type of political character who is often on-stage when politics enters an unsteady state – even if it is the populists who seize the limelight. Let us call this character the 'old-school politico'. These are the politicians who have thrived under the old system, are indelibly associated with it and know how to make politics work better than anyone. If, prior to Thaksin, one had asked a resident of Bangkok to mention a politician who embodied everything that was wrong with Thai politics, there is a good chance they would have mentioned Banharn Silpa-archa. Like Thaksin, Banharn started out as a businessman. Also like Thaksin, his big break was a government decree – in this case, a ten-year monopoly on the construction of water pipes throughout Thailand. By the mid-1960s, Banharn was rich.

In January 1966, a mini-skirted Miss Thailand headed out to the backwater province of Suphan Buri (usually known as Suphan), adding a touch of glamour to the opening of a new ward at Chao-phraya Yommarat hospital. Who had given the money for the ward? Banharn. The governor of Suphan also turned out for the occasion, along with a large crowd, probably mostly there to see Miss Thailand. The hospital ward was named after Banharn, who was just getting started on a spending spree. In 1969, he donated 500,000 baht (equivalent to about $24,000 today) to build the first secondary school in the town of Don Chedi. Soon, four more schools in Suphan featured new buildings donated by him.

Banharn was also an avid booster of Suphan provincial pride. Not many people were; as a local civil servant put it: 'how many Americans know exactly where Kansas is? Not many. Suphan was like that.' One of Thailand's kleptocratic military dictators, General Sarit, had randomly stolen a priceless ceramic bowl from a Buddhist temple in Suphan. When Sarit died, the Thai government announced that rather than returning the bowl it was going to auction it for cash. Banharn showed up at the auction, casually outbid everyone, and brought the bowl back to the temple. There was a parade in Suphan with brass bands, but, modestly, Banharn declined to take part and instead returned the bowl privately. Well, not completely privately: the local newspaper ran a front-page photo of him and his wife kneeling humbly, returning the bowl to the temple's abbot. Soon, he was big news in Suphan. The king and queen of Thailand showed up at one of his school openings along with an estimated 5,000 people. Suphan residents were impressed by Banharn's donations. As a bank teller put it: 'I raise my thumb up for him. Who would have thought about sacrificing one's personal money in a place like Dan Chang?'

The donations paid off. In 1976, during a brief flourishing of democracy, Banharn ran for parliament, representing a district in Suphan. He crushed the opposition. Indeed, his vote total was the largest of any candidate in any district in the country. A promising start, but soon there would be compromises. In Thai politics at the time, politicians often paid voters to vote for them, although there was also some party loyalty: as one local party official put it, 'this is already a Democrat [Party] area, so we don't need to pay more than 100 baht [$2.50] per vote'. But even party loyalty tended to be bought, via the mechanism of party cards. A party membership card was a ticket to receiving government favours. As a local political activist explained: 'If you show someone a party card because you have no money, if you are lost or something, you will receive help and money. It is the same for all parties.'

Banharn participated in this money politics, of course. With his business fortune, he could certainly afford to. But he did something else as well. The sociologist Yoshinori Nishizaki, who had come to Suphan to conduct research on Banharn, got a taste of the difference on his first minibus ride into town. The driver said: 'Of course I like him! You don't have to ask that kind of question here. Anyone who was born in Suphan must like him.' The son of a rice farmer, interviewed later, was even more enthusiastic: 'Banharn doesn't actually have to use money,' he said, 'we fully support him, regardless of whether we are given money or how much we are given.'

What was Banharn's secret? In a small farming village, next to a new asphalt road, there is a large signboard that reads: 'the subdistrict administration Council of Bang Tathen and Khok Jet Luuk villagers would like to thank His Excellency Banharn Silpa-archa for helping channel the construction fund'. Nishizaki came across such signboards in many places. He was admiring one when a local farmer walked up and said: 'If you are interested in this kind of thing, there are some more around here. One is in the next village … Banharn built a bridge there.' It turned out that there were a lot of signboards about infrastructure built while Banharn was in office. In the most populous district of Suphan there were, by Nishizaki's count, more than 160 such signboards; approximately one signboard for every three square kilometres – well over 400 signboards in the province as a whole. Perhaps in a richer province, people would not have noticed, but out in Suphan, where many roads remained unpaved, residents remembered the schools, hospitals, roads and signboards. In many cases the new pieces of public infrastructure were opened with ceremonies featuring local dignitaries, Buddhist monks (Thailand is a Buddhist kingdom), fireworks and lunch. Between 1976 and 2002, Banharn attended an average of twenty-seven ceremonies in his honour every year, about 700 in total.

Suphan's people began to love Banharn. He won landslide victories in every election between 1976 and 2008, receiving between 63 and 94 per cent of the vote. Of course, he remained corrupt. Indeed, over time, Banharn gained a reputation across Thailand as a dark master of corrupt politics. Many middle-class Thais came to despise him. The national papers dubbed him a 'walking ATM' for handing out so much money. The king of Thailand eventually criticised him as 'unconcerned for the people'. But the people of Suphan tell a very different tale. 'Banharn eats [ie is corrupt],' says a security guard, 'but he gives a lot to us. Look at all the things he has built.' A primary school teacher defends him: 'at least he doesn't kill people, unlike politicians in Chonburi and Petchaburi. Corruption is better than killing.' Learning that the sociologist Nishizaki is American, another teacher chimes in: 'didn't Clinton use his power to sleep with women? To me, that is worse than taking a little bribe.' Indeed, many people seem to think that Banharn's corruption is a kind of asset. 'He had to rely on his bureaucratic clients,' explains a merchant. 'To return favors for their support, he had to give them a little money under the table occasionally ... So this is corruption for the sake of Suphan. That's okay.'

I call Banharn's politics 'share-the-wealth politics', because it involves delivering financial benefits to constituents – from roads and hospitals in Suphan to outright bribes to voters (scholars call it 'distributive politics'). When voters distrust politicians, share-the-wealth politics works wonders. The popularity of leaders like

Banharn is not impacted by corruption scandals, perhaps because voters never trusted them anyway. Banharn was judged on his ability to deliver the goods. Supporters of one of Brazil's most iconic politicians were fond of saying: 'He steals, but delivers!' The current mayor of Lima, Peru, campaigned on the unofficial slogan 'roba pero hace obra', which translates roughly as 'steals but does work!' In Louisiana (a place with its own problems of political corruption), bumper stickers in a 1991 governor's race read: 'Vote for the crook: it's important!' Of course, voters who distrust politicians are also more likely to vote for a populist; hence the old-school politico like Banharn and the rising populist like Thaksin are two fish often found in the same pond. They aggravate voters' distrust in politics and then thrive on it.

In 1995, Banharn became the nation's prime minister. And, as it turned out, it was the wrong time for a man of Banharn's peculiar talents to come to power.

The economic crisis

It would be odd to call a crisis a character, yet economic crises will be a recurring theme in this book. Economic crises tend to shake up politics. In the United States, when President George H.W. Bush was voted out after one term, the catchphrase of the year was: 'it's the economy, stupid'. And for good reason: studies of 'economic voting' indicate that the more an economy turns down, the more votes a serving government will tend to lose.

But not for the reasons one might expect. Generally, studies on economic voting have found that voters do *not* vote according to their wallet size. That is, they consider the question 'how is *the economy* doing these days?', rather than the question 'how am *I* doing these days?' In some studies, the wallet effect is weak; in many, it is non-existent. It seems that voters punish the government for being bad at economic management, rather than venting their anger about their poor personal circumstances. Readers might be suspicious. After all, do voters really know how the economy is doing? Perhaps voters think they are throwing out an inept government, but actually, their perception of how the economy is doing is largely based on their personal finances. In that case, might they be responding to personal hardship without realising it? Probably not. Overall, in most of the countries studied, voters – even those who do not regularly read the newspapers – appear to have a surprisingly accurate grasp of their country's economic performance. Voters' views on the health of the economy are tightly linked to macroeconomic indicators. Indeed, in most cases, voters' views of the economy's performance correlate more strongly with indicators such as the growth rate and the unemployment rate than with their own personal financial and employment status.

It is an extremely counterintuitive finding, and the media tends to get this point wrong. In the wake of the Brexit vote, commentators were quick to attribute the outcome to personal economic distress – as a howl of anguish from unemployed manufacturing workers or those with falling incomes. Similar comments were made in the wake of Donald Trump's presidential victory. Studies showed that life expectancy among white American men was declining, in part due to opioid and other substance abuse. Commentators linked this evidence of personal despair to the decision to vote for Trump. While it is quite possible that personal economic insecurity has led to an increase in opioid use, it is very unlikely that personal economic despair has produced the votes for Trump or Brexit. As the research on economic voting shows, voters punish governments for bad management, not for their personal distress.

Of course, even when voters throw out a poorly performing government, that may not change anything fundamentally. One milquetoast, middle-of-the-road politician is thrown out, only to be replaced by another. But at times, when the run-up to a crisis has been very long, and the economic downturn very deep, it appears that the entire political establishment can be discredited. One recent study found that after financial crises, vote shares of extremist parties rise dramatically – as much as 30 per cent. Perhaps people will even decide that the political system as a whole is failing them, and decide to throw the system out. Indeed, many of the 'original' failures of democracy (in Europe between the two world wars) took place during economic crises – most famously, the hyperinflation in Germany that accompanied the Nazi rise to power.

Happily, the link between economic crises and failures of democracy is not ironclad. That said, governments have it in their power to make the political impacts of an economic crisis much worse. Most notably, if a government responds to a crisis by cutting spending – via so-called 'austerity' measures – it is playing with fire. Recent research has found a strong link between austerity and political instability, including riots, demonstrations and political assassinations – in both Latin America and Western Europe. And of course, austerity is just what the Thai government introduced.

But let me backtrack a bit. When Banharn came to power, Thailand was at the tail end of a major economic boom. In the decade starting in 1985, the Thai economy expanded by more than 250 per cent. That boom had many causes. With its abundant labour force, Thailand was ideally placed to benefit from globalisation; with Japan's economy leading the world at that time, the country attracted a lot of Japanese investment in particular. But Thailand's boom was not egalitarian. Half the income gains between 1981 and 1994 went to only the top 10 per cent of the population (one reason why Thai history has echoed so uncannily in the United States was that the underlying conditions were surprisingly similar).

Between 1990 and 1992, Thailand deregulated its financial sector. Predictably, that poured fuel on the already hot economy. In one year, 1991, more international investment flowed into Thailand than over the whole decade of the 1980s. It seemed that everyone wanted to buy Thai stocks and lend to Thai companies. In turn,

Thai companies did what people inevitably do when times are (too) good: they ploughed this money into the property sector, and property values went up and up and up. Banharn's newly installed government then stoked the flames by increasing government expenditure by a whopping 10 per cent in its first days in office. Banharn had always found that spending more money was a sure way to win the people's hearts. Shortly after he took office, health funds allocated to Suphan jumped by 489 per cent, education funding by 534 per cent and funds for the construction of rural roads by 1,404 per cent.

Thailand's boom was soon raging out of control. Readers can probably guess how the story turns out. The 'Lehman moment' was the collapse of a company called Finance One, not a bank exactly, but it had lent more money than many actual banks. When the company collapsed, property values began to plummet and, as they fell, many of the nation's property loans went bad, all at the same time (again, this may sound familiar). As property was sold to cover the bad loans, prices fell further. By 1997, borrowers were failing to make payments on a fifth of all the loans Thai banks had made. No prizes for guessing what happened next: the bailout. Unlike Lehman Brothers, even Finance One got a bailout. The Thai government pumped 60 billion baht ($3bn) into the stock market and 50 billion into Finance One alone. A 430 billion-baht ($14bn) fund was set up for banks in trouble. Even as the financial sector was bailed out, ordinary Thais suffered. Huge numbers of Thai borrowers could not pay back their loans. Thailand's economic output declined by double digits. (By comparison, during the global financial crisis, the most severe decline recorded in the United States was about four per cent; for the UK it was about six per cent.)

And then came the austerity. The International Monetary Fund agreed to bail out Thailand, but in exchange it demanded budget cuts and tax increases. These demands led to the mother of all austerity programmes, including fiscal tightening worth about 3 per cent of Thailand's total economic output – roughly equivalent to the US government deciding to save money by wiping out the entire budget of the department of defense in a single year. Banharn could have told the Thai political establishment that such measures would cost them the love of the people. But by that point, he was no longer around: his government had collapsed, and been replaced by a 'technocratic' regime, which was eager to comply with the Fund's demands.

Of course, Thailand was not the only country to make that mistake. Indonesia, hit by the same crisis, imposed severe austerity, and its political system collapsed – a corrupt and dictatorial system to be sure, but the sudden rioting that followed killed more than 1,000 people. After the global financial crisis, of course, many governments, failing to learn from history, repeated these political errors. The most severe tighteners? According to calculations by Martin Wolf at the *Financial Times*, the country that tightened the most was the UK; second was Spain and third the United States. That is far from the only reason for the populist surge in those countries. But it did not help.

Or rather, it did help the populists, by discrediting the political establishment – just as Thailand's crisis and austerity undoubtedly helped Thaksin.

The educated middle class

But there is another character to be introduced, one that would soon take a starring role in the Thai political drama, and that is the educated, urban middle class.

The rich compulsively click the door-locking buttons on their limos when they roll past the slums, but ironically enough, those who tend to do more harm to the political status quo are those apparently harmless nine-to-fivers with well-kept lawns and practical cars (in Thailand, pickup trucks), proud of their above-average children and endearing pets. These people are educated and quietly competent. They are effective: they can organise (after all, they have been running the PTA for years); they understand enough about the workings of politics and the law to be dangerous; they have a bit of money. And they have the right personal qualities for political action: they are hard working, goal-focused and future-oriented.

On 17 May 1992, perhaps as many as half a million people joined the Buddhist ascetic's protests in Bangkok against the country's military government. A spot survey by the Thai Social Science Association indicated that the majority of participants were married, white-collar and reasonably well off. When the soldiers started shooting and arresting people, these upstanding citizens did not give up. They returned to the streets the next evening; again they were shot and arrested. After the third night of chaos, the Thai king staged a dramatic intervention. At 9.30pm, Thai television carried an unforgettable image: two men knelt before the king as he lectured them. One was the leader of the military junta; the other was the Buddhist ascetic who had been leading the protests. The violence ended quickly and Thailand returned to genuine democracy. The Thai middle classes had flexed their muscles. Not only the middle classes, of course – there were many other protestors in Bangkok that day, both rich and poor. But, as we shall see, the middle classes have tended to take a lead role in many of history's great uprisings.

When Thaksin took power following his populist campaign, many educated, urban, middle-class Thais were shocked, but probably did not see an immediate threat to democracy. Thaksin did what he said he would, rolling out agrarian debt relief and a 30-baht-a-visit public healthcare scheme enabling the poor to obtain primary care at a nominal charge. Soon he was presiding over a budding economic recovery; people began to use the term 'Thaksinomics' to describe his unorthodox but successful approach. 'I'm applying socialism in the lower economy, and capitalism in the upper economy,' he said, as only a populist could.

And then, a government anti-corruption office announced it was reviewing charges that Thaksin had concealed his assets. Certainly, he had made no attempt to hide being rich, but his approach to tax planning was aggressive, to put it mildly. During 1997 and 1998, when he first got into politics, he had been obliged to declare his assets. He had done so, but failed to mention the assets of his house-keeper, maid, driver, security guard, and so on – some of whom, for a time, had figured among the top ten holders of shares on the Thai national stock exchange. It insulted everyone's intelligence to pretend that those were not, in fact, Thaksin's assets.

Still, at the time, many voters wanted to give Thaksin the benefit of the doubt. So, apparently, did the constitutional court, which cleared him of the charges, albeit narrowly, on an eight to seven split. The judges, attempting to deliver a warning with their verdict, wrote that 'the heart of political reform is to nurture politicians who uphold sound moral principles and aspire to observe stricter dharma [Buddhist teachings] than other laymen'. It seems unlikely that Thaksin got the message. When the verdict was announced, officials ran into his office yelling their congratulations. Mobile phones rang constantly; cheering crowds gathered outside the building. 'The atmosphere was like a miniature epic,' one of Thaksin's supporters recalled.

Soon, Thaksin began using his political office to promote his own business interests, and those of his family. He saved his mobile phone empire from the risk of competition by changing the government's strategy for liberalisation of the telecoms network so frequently that no programme of liberalisation ever went forward. Eventually, foreign competitors, including Verizon and Orange, got tired of waiting and pulled out of the Thai market. By 2004, Thaksin's company was earning almost four-fifths of the total profit of Thailand's mobile phone industry. 'My motto is "you must be rich and don't stop becoming richer",' he said. 'The rich should not be envied.' He seemed keen that this motto also should apply to the next generation of Shinawatras. In 2004, he forced the firm that had won the concession to develop advertising on Bangkok's new subway system to share half the concession with a company newly established by his son, just out of university.

Soon, people began to fear that Thaksin had authoritarian leanings. Whenever he was criticised, he lashed out. 'Anything I do is wrong. Even my breathing is wrong,' he complained in a radio interview. When the media began to criticise him, he made veiled threats: 'If the press paid less attention to political issues,' he said, 'I guarantee the nation would progress impressively.' He made outrageous comments, and when questioned, doubled down on them. Police were accused of using excessive violence to carry out Thaksin's showcase campaign against drug traffickers. Thaksin's response: 'It is not an unusual fate for wicked people. The public should not be alarmed by their deaths.' In the wake of the anti-corruption investigation, Thaksin began to fire public officials who attempted to investigate him, and to stack key government bodies with his own supporters, including the constitutional court, the election monitoring commission and the anti-corruption commission.

But arguably the greatest danger posed by Thaksin was the sheer scale of his wealth; two months earlier he had made his debut on the Forbes list of billionaires with an estimated net worth of $1.2bn. The Thai middle classes had long despaired of the money politics practised by politicians like Banharn, but reforms to get the money out of Thai politics had been slow in coming. Thaksin showed just how dangerous money politics could be. He bought the support of political bosses who were willing to switch parties to join the highest bidder. One such, the marvellously named Snoh Thienthong, advertised his party-hopping services by saying: 'I am a man who can go anywhere.' By August 2000, about 100 sitting members of parliament had agreed to defect from other parties to become part of Thaksin's party.

Eventually, and too late, Thailand's urban, educated middle class began to turn against Thaksin. One hundred Thai academics signed a letter of protest against the regime's policies. A new newspaper was launched, taking a critical line on government policy, which rapidly surged to the third-largest readership in the nation. Thaksin appeared unconcerned. He said he had enough support to stay in power for the next twenty years. But he struck a tone of mock conciliation: 'If I'm still alive then I will appeal to the people to choose other parties out of sympathy with them for having waited so long, and out of sympathy with journalists for having no political news.'

True to his word, at elections held in October 2005, Thaksin's Thais Love Thais Party won an absolute majority in parliament – another historic first. Despite the landslide victory, the country was polarised: in the districts where the opposition had won, they won authoritatively. Thaksin was accused of vote-buying on a massive scale. Demonstrations against the government were planned. 'Our job is to decide what kind of signal we want to send,' explained an investment banker who had decided to get into politics. 'Do we want to give him carte blanche again? Or do we want to say, "The educated Bangkokians are watching"?'

Thaksin's rural base continued to cheer him loudly. He played up the populism, promising more village funds, land deeds for small farmers, new cheap loan schemes, free distribution of cows, training schemes, gift bags for every new mother, and so on. 'Four years ahead, there will be no poor people,' he said. 'Won't that be neat?'

The movement

As part of an escalating crackdown on the media, Thaksin forced the weekly commentary programme of a man named Sondhi Limthongkul off the air. Sondhi was yet another business tycoon turned political leader; he was also a former Thaksin supporter. As Pasuk Phongpaichit and Chris Baker, authors of a biography of Thaksin, put it, 'if you tried to clone Thaksin and made a slight mistake, you might well finish up with Sondhi'. But by that point many in the Thai middle class were looking for any opportunity to oppose the government, and Sondhi quickly became an opposition figurehead. When Sondhi took his show on the road, he was surprised to find more than 10,000 people turning up for each of his weekly programmes. By early December, some Bangkok protest marches had a turnout of 80,000 or more. One businesswoman-turned-demonstrator, who had initially supported Thaksin, complained: 'He is just too corrupt … He is changing the laws to protect his business and his family, and he is destroying our country.'

By February 2006 Thaksin was in trouble. The event that appeared to coalesce middle-class opposition began, ironically enough, with an effort at reconciliation. Hoping to forestall criticisms that he was using his political office to promote his business interests, Thaksin announced he would sell off his businesses to a Singaporean company. But the manner of the deal was characteristically outrageous. First, selling Thailand's dominant mobile phone network to a foreign company required tremendous chutzpah, given Thaksin's anti-globalisation rhetoric. Indeed, to skirt regulations designed to prevent such sales, he had to arrange some minor legal changes and use a complex pyramid structure. Even more strikingly, he structured the deal so that he paid a derisory amount of tax. It may have been done legally, apparently via some bespoke tweaking of tax regulations, but it was absolutely infuriating.

The result was the largest and most sustained series of political demonstrations in over thirty years. These were a tribute to middle-class professionalism: strikingly well-thought-out and executed with more than a little style; at times it was difficult to tell whether what took place was a protest or a music festival. There were stages, lights and amplification; the events were broadcast daily over Sondhi's media network. Stalls sold T-shirts, books, pins and other collectibles. Some of the swag was handed out free, including headbands, shirts and scarves, mainly in yellow – the colour of royalty in Thailand – emblazoned with slogans such as: 'save the nation', 'we fight for the king' or 'guardians of the land'. The organisers began to call themselves the People's Alliance for Democracy; eventually, they would be dubbed the 'yellowshirts'. On some days, as many as 50,000 people turned up. Thaksin, by this point looking increasingly authoritarian, attempted to declare a state of emergency, but the army refused to implement his orders.

He still had a trump card: money politics. Thaksin's party was using its unmatched funds to build an unprecedented base in province-level politics across much of Thailand. By 2004, his party had won control of forty-seven provinces. At the national level, Thaksin was rumoured to have raised the bounty he was paying to members of parliament from 50,000 to 200,000 baht per month (from about $1,600 today to about $6,400). A flood of smaller parties decided to merge with Thais Love Thais.

As the protests continued, Thai politics threatened to descend into chaos. Thaksin was in serious legal trouble; many Thaksin-appointed members of the electoral commission had been slapped with criminal charges. The middle-class protestors managed to spoil the April 2006 elections by calling on voters not to vote; in many anti-Thaksin districts, no candidate was returned, because fewer than 20 per cent of eligible voters – the minimum standard set by the Constitution – had taken part. After a second round of polling, fourteen seats in parliament remained vacant. As the situation deteriorated, two of Thaksin's cabinet members suddenly resigned. On 19 September 2006, tanks rolled on to the streets of Bangkok, and television stations abruptly cut to soothing slideshows of the royal family. The generals announced that they were restoring order, and that new elections would be held, without Thaksin. Thaksin fled into exile in London. 'I want to be a prominent businessman in the United Kingdom, if the British people will welcome me,' he said, before buying Manchester City, a Premier League football club.

It was an ugly end to Thaksin's government; but bringing down a billionaire from the nation's highest office was no mean feat. The soldiers signalled support for the protestors by wearing armbands in royal yellow, and tying yellow ribbons around tank barrels. Many of the protestors were obviously grateful. Some came out to have their pictures taken with tanks; for a time, among a certain Bangkok set, it was fashionable to wear military camouflage, especially with a yellow shirt underneath.

The countryside

There is one more character to introduce in this Thai tale, and that is Thaksin's rural supporters. A *Financial Times* reporter visiting the impoverished village of Al Samat found a growing anger: 'Thaksin has helped a lot of poor people very much, but people now want to steal his position,' said one old woman, waving a cooking knife to emphasise her point. 'When we watch TV, we really hate those protestors.'

Members of the middle class tend instinctively to expect the poor to be on their side in politics – after all, many in the middle class can recall a time when they, or their families, were poor themselves. Certainly, one would not expect the poor to have much sympathy for a corrupt billionaire who had been born rich. When poor voters do, against expectations, vote for a populist like Thaksin, members of the middle class tend to assume a trick has been played – that the poor are not clever enough to see through populist ruses; that their votes have been bought; or that their passions have run away with them.

Indeed, when the sociologist Nishizaki visited Suphan to investigate Banharn, that was what he expected to find – that poor people hated Banharn but were cowed into submission by his vote-buying; or that they had been fooled by him, and were unaware of his corruption. But neither assumption turned out to be true. Instead, many of the rural residents Nishizaki interviewed understood that Banharn was corrupt, but loved him anyway, for the tangible benefits he delivered. They were not fools, but were willing to overlook corruption in return for policies they liked – a very different view from most of the Bangkok middle class.

Thaksin appeared to produce a similar response. As a farmer interviewed in Al Samat put it: 'We know they accuse him of being corrupt but for us, the grassroots people, our life is better.' The depth of rural support for Thaksin became clear when the generals who had ousted the government held the promised elections on 23 December 2007. Soldiers were dispatched to the provinces with orders to stamp out vote-buying. Thaksin and about 100 other politicians were barred from running for office for five years. Otherwise, the elections were admirably free and fair. Thaksin's supporters took over a party called the People Power Party, changed its logo to mimic the old Thais Love Thais logo, moved its headquarters to the party's old headquarters, and installed a former Bangkok mayor named Samak Sundaravej as its head. At rallies, placards were held up bearing the message 'vote Samak, get Thaksin'. In case anyone still missed the point, one of the party's parliamentary candidates campaigned wearing a Thaksin mask.

For the Bangkok protestors who had brought Thaksin's regime to its knees, the election results were a bitter disappointment. Thaksin's People's Power Party won handily – not by as many seats as the original Thais Love Thais had, but only a few seats short of a majority. Pundits, most of whom had forecast he would lose, were completely wrong-footed. To their credit, the generals bowed to the people's verdict, and Samak (Thaksin's proxy) was allowed to form a coalition government. On 28 February 2008 Thaksin returned to Thailand, falling to his knees and touching his forehead to the sweet Thai ground as the press cameras clicked away. Still forbidden by the courts from re-entering politics, he went on a religious tour of ninety-nine Buddhist temples in the north and northeast. It looked a lot like a campaign tour.

Heroically but by this point somewhat quixotically, the Bangkok middle classes refused to give up. From May 2008, they returned to the streets. This time they were even better organised, making a permanent protest encampment at Makkhawan Bridge in Bangkok. This festival of resistance was on the scale of Glastonbury or Coachella – an elaborate central stage was covered by multiple camera teams, with large video screens on either side, and with more than a hundred large monitors dispersed throughout the crowd. This time around, the branding was even better: everything was done in royal yellow, including the stage decorations, the merchandise, and the clothes of the attendees. Society ladies began to attend, often by luxury automobile; servants carried mats and picnic supplies, and stood in the queue for the portable toilets on their employers' behalf. Mock degree certificates in 'saving the nation' sold like hotcakes. But behind the celebratory zeal, many yellowshirt protestors were aware of the awkwardness of their position. One lawyer took a break from assembling a street bunker made of concrete blast barriers, tyres and sandbags to talk to a reporter. He admitted that the election results had shown that the majority of Thais did not agree with what he was doing. And yet, he said: 'If the government does something unlawful, the people have the right to rise up.'

Absent an electoral majority, the protestors sought other sources of power. They recruited a militia, with training and leadership provided by ex-soldiers and policemen. By some estimates, there were eventually several thousand militia members; some were volunteers, but many, as the opposition leader Sondhi admitted in an interview, were paid. They were also well equipped for street fighting. In late August, the police captured an arms stash including 60 bottles of petrol, 1,558 golf clubs, 248 steel bars, 20 swords or spears, 27 arm shields made from PVC pipe, 56 plywood shields, 55 slingshots and 185 marbles. In the autumn, three guards were filmed operating from the back of a moving pickup truck in the manner of a medieval chariot: one repeatedly fired a pistol; another had a slingshot; the third held aloft a picture of the king. The ostensible purpose of the militia was to make the government think twice about any effort to clear the protest camps. But the militia was also used for darker purposes, including beating up pro-Thaksin protestors.

Eventually, the protestors began to realise that many in the military were on their side, and that as a result they could get away with very provocative actions. In August, the yellowshirts, led by their guards, invaded government buildings and forced the prime minister to evacuate. Efforts to remove them came to nothing; in one case, after repelling a police assault, the guards launched a cheeky counter-offensive on a police station (not the way it usually goes with police and protestors). Eventually, the Thai government gave up and relocated to the northern city of Chiang Mai, near Thaksin's birthplace. When the police finally attempted to remove the protestors using non-lethal force, they seriously injured at least twenty demonstrators and killed one. It is unclear exactly what went wrong. The police blamed poorly made teargas canisters that contained excessive amounts of explosive; it is also clear that the guards were armed and had fought back. Still, from the point of view of the press, it was police brutality. Expressing middle-class solidarity, some doctors refused to treat injured police. In a far more public statement of solidarity, the Thai queen attended the funeral of a protestor. The protestors invaded and occupied Thailand's international airport, leaving some 350,000 travellers temporarily stranded in Thailand.

As the protests escalated, public officials rediscovered their mojo. Indeed, they sometimes acted with undue haste; some court verdicts were rushed out before all the evidence had been heard. The courts forced Thaksin's proxy prime minister to resign; Thaksin was found guilty on charges of corruption and tax evasion and sentenced to two years in prison; he once again fled into exile. When another court ruled that the People Power Party had engaged in vote-buying, the party was disbanded and its leaders barred from politics.

This time, Thaksin's proxy regime had been ousted within the law, without military intervention – although admittedly the law had been stretched. The yellowshirt protestors at last abandoned their encampments in the airport and government buildings. On 17 December 2008, the Democrat Party leader Abhisit Vejjajiva became the 27th prime minister of Thailand. On the government's first working day, the foreign ministry, with evident satisfaction, voided Thaksin's diplomatic passport. (For a billionaire, this posed only a minor inconvenience; eventually, Thaksin gained passports from Nicaragua and Montenegro.)

The coup

But even this breakthrough was not the end of Thailand's populist nightmare; indeed, it was when things really started to go downhill. Thaksin's supporters would soon fight fire with fire, flooding into the capital from their homes in rural Thailand. Many of them wore red, and came to be known as 'redshirts'. By March and April 2009, the redshirts had set up an encampment outside the main government buildings in Bangkok, complete with an elaborate stage, sound system, food carts, and a video link by which Thaksin could address his supporters (phoning in from Dubai, he complained: 'there is only camel meat and camel milk here'). Many members of the shocked middle class continued to insist that even this turn of events was a product of Thaksin's money; they claimed it was a rent-a-mob, and certainly, Thaksin was funding much of the logistics himself. Participants were bused in from the poor rural areas of the north and northeast, as well as from the Bangkok suburbs where many low-wage workers lived. At times, Thaksin appeared mainly interested in using the redshirt protests to advance his own interests. At one point, he told the French news magazine *Le Figaro* that what he wanted was 'democracy, symbol of liberty, equality and fraternity, like you, the French! ... And then, it is also necessary that I manage to recover my frozen assets.'

Like Banharn's supporters, though, the redshirts were not simply stooges. They began to develop an ideology and political programme that was independent of their exiled leader. The demonstrators demanded that elections be held. They began to see the urban middle class as their enemy, and listened to lectures on how the middle class had supported fascism in Europe. Organisers set up schools that taught Thai history. The redshirts began to refer to themselves as *phrai* – roughly, peasants or commoners – a word borrowed from Thailand's feudal system, a word that had previously been used as an insult, now proudly repurposed. They described their middle-class opponents as *ammaat*, another feudal term, meaning high court officials or bureaucrats.

Many exhausted Thais just wanted peace. Perhaps partly for that reason, in April, much of the nation looked the other way as the military cleared out the redshirt encampments with more than a little brutality, on the pretext that protestors had disrupted an international summit meeting. Ten thousand troops were involved; it was the largest riot control action in Thai history. There were more than 100 injuries, and two corpses of demonstrators were found floating in a river. 'It looks like they don't consider us as humans,' said one redshirt organiser. Some members of the middle class began to express sympathy for the redshirts, at least in anonymous polls.

But the nightmare was not over. A year later, the redshirts tried again; this time the encampment held from March through May. The turnouts matched or perhaps even exceeded that of the yellowshirts. In April, the pro-Thaksin protestors expanded their activities, holding rallies in the heart of commercial Bangkok, and briefly occupying the parliament building (unlike the yellow-shirt protestors, they left later the same day of their own accord). The government attempted to repeat its clearance strategy of the previous year and sent in soldiers who used live ammunition. This time, the demonstrators fought back to a stalemate, at a cost of more than twenty deaths. The redshirts repeated their demand for elections to be held; the government rejected it. There was an attempt at negotiations. The government offered to hold elections, but ominously included the proviso that the rules of democracy needed to be discussed and re-examined.

This proviso reflected a debate that had been going on for some time among the leaders of the yellowshirt movement – at first sotto voce, and then increasingly openly. That debate was about whether Thailand ought to be a democracy. It was a bitter pill to swallow; middle-class protestors had given their lives to bring democracy to Thailand in 1992. But Thaksin had so much money, and in a system infected by money politics, there seemed to be no way to keep him out of power. Perhaps democracy had to be sacrificed, or at least restrained. 'Elections will work in certain countries, but not in Thailand,' one Bangkok restaurant owner explained. 'The government uses money to win elections – it's corruption.' Whether the claims about money politics were accurate or not, it was clear that another election was likely to result in a Thaksin victory. Proposals on the table included increasing the power of the king (in whom a great many Thais of all classes continued to put their faith), having a majority of parliament seats appointed rather than elected, and even requiring educational or professional quali-fications for voters.

When the Thai government mentioned its proviso about the rules of democracy, redshirt leaders, no doubt exhausted themselves, did not reject the offer outright; rather, they asked for clarification. But perhaps the idea of sitting down and talking about how democracy might be dismembered was, in the light of day, too awkward, and the government withdrew its offer. Thaksin said: 'I don't think that they [redshirts] are less educated; they are poor [but] I think they have a better understanding of democracy than many who have had a better education.' He had a point. The redshirts also seemed to understand that time was running out for them. Hoping for one of the king's miraculous interventions, in May 2010 they hung a banner on an overpass that read, plaintively, 'Where's Dad?' But the king had checked into a hospital and would not emerge for several years.

On 13 May, a Thai army general who had defected and joined the redshirts was shot in the head, allegedly by a government sniper, while conducting an interview with the *New York Times*. A few days later, the army attacked in force. The redshirts fought back, but eventually abandoned their positions, retreating to the commercial centre at Ratchaprasong. International sympathy began to turn towards the embattled rural protestors. For instance, Federico Ferrara, author of a book about the redshirt rebellion, explained the choice of their fallback redoubt thus: 'the redshirts understood that, in this day and age, Louis Vuitton bags and Hermes foulards make for better shields than human shields'.

As the military overran redshirt positions, the protestors fled, some of them burning buildings as they went. More than thirty buildings burned, including a major department store. In total, some eighty-nine people were killed and more than 1,500 injured in the second round of redshirt demonstrations. After the army had cleared the encampments, the redshirt movement was systematically dismantled; some 400 people were arrested; redshirt leaders were interrogated for acts of terrorism. A state of emergency was declared giving authorities the right to hold people without charge for thirty days and to forbid public gatherings. Eventually, charges of terrorism were filed against more than fifty redshirt leaders. The government began to impose aggressive censorship, blocking some 17,000 websites.

It was still not enough. In July 2011, when elections were held again, another of Thaksin's proxies, his younger sister, Yingluck Shinawatra, won handily. She took a page from Banharn's 'share-the-wealth' book, offering huge subsidies to rice farmers, a policy that delighted her rural base and quickly ratcheted up government debt. (Appropriately enough, the new party's slogan was 'populism for a happy life'.) Despite significant blowback from its high-spending policies, Yingluck's government managed to hang on to power until December 2013. Then, she called early elections; the elections were disrupted; the constitutional court invalidated the polls; and on 22 May 2014 a military junta took power. The army chief appeared on television and announced he was 'returning happiness to the people'. Over three years later, Thailand remained under effective military rule.

Hard choices

They had worn yellow; they had fought 'for the king' and, in the end, Thailand's middle classes got, if not what they wanted, at least what they could accept. Thaksin and his proxies were gone; the redshirts went back to the countryside and the suburbs. The generals were in power; but at least the king still ruled. A lot of middle-class protestors thought the generals had done the right thing. As one travel agency owner put it: 'Our country is for a long time in pain from separation [and] we really need reunion ... Forget democracy for the time being.'

But people had also forgotten about Foo Foo. Since appointing his poodle as Air Chief Marshal, Crown Prince Vajiralongkorn's behaviour had, if anything, become even more erratic. He was filmed wandering through a German shopping mall with a crop top that showed off his extensive tattoos; Bangkok gossips told tales of his playboy lifestyle. Perhaps he was just a relaxed, fun guy, but it did not seem like it. He divorced his wife from the birthday video and imprisoned her parents. Nobody likes their inlaws, but that seemed excessive.

In 2016, King Bhumibol died. There was brief speculation that Vajiralongkorn's more stable sister might somehow be placed on the throne; but soon, he was the heir apparent. I last visited Thailand in August 2017, and the new king's portrait was everywhere, from the airport baggage claim to government buildings to roadside billboards. It was a bit like visiting Cuba. I tried to get some man-on-the-street views on the new king, but people did not want to talk about it. Understandably so: the military regime aggressively prosecutes crimes of *lèse-majesté* (insulting the king). The prosecutions are partly a convenient tool of repression (one young activist who posted a link to a BBC biography of the new king on his Facebook page was sentenced to two and a half years in prison) and partly the hysteria of a regime deeply unsure of its legitimacy. An Australian writer who included a fictionalised passage about the royal lifestyle in a self-published novel (which had sold less than ten copies) was arrested at the airport and thrown in jail until the king pardoned him.

In the summer of 2017, I went to see the Public Theatre's production of Shakespeare in the Park in New York City. They had staged *Julius Caesar*, redone as a morality tale about the impossibility of saving democracy by non-democratic means. It was a great production, like much of the Public's work (the Public is the theatre responsible for *Hamilton*). But perhaps Thailand's story is even more apt as a morality tale for our times. As we shall see, contra Shakespeare in the Park, democracies do not necessarily die by accident, the victims of good intentions. In many cases they die by choice; by hard choices. One such hard choice is to prefer rule by the monarchy and military over rule by Thaksin and his cronies. Many of the educated, middle-class citizens of Bangkok I talked to in 2017 continued to think it was the right choice. Thais retain a great deal of personal freedom; the government appears to function; people are even unafraid to talk openly about politics (aside from royal politics). But it is a hard choice to make.

My tale of Thai politics has explained how the government fell, but not why. For that, we need to know the building blocks of instability. In the next chapter we will focus on the most fundamental: why, at times, do the people – the Thai middle class, the redshirts, those who voted for Brexit after years of staying away from the polls – suddenly rise up?

CHAPTER 2

Lenin was very surprised: why ordinary people get involved in politics

'Like Saturn, the Revolution devours its children.'

Pierre Vergniaud

The champagne socialists

When the outcome of a great struggle is all but assured, those about to win may be tempted to grandstand. Lenin's Bolshevik revolutionaries had taken the railway stations, power plants, telephone exchange, bridges and key ministries in St Petersburg. They could have all but walked into the Winter Palace, where the government was housed. The main defensive force consisted, somewhat incredibly, of an all-female unit known as the 'Women's Shock Battalion of Death', which existed largely for propaganda purposes (*à la* Mockingjay), and some students from the military academy. Trotsky, Lenin's right-hand man, thought they should not even bother with the palace, and get on with the business of running the country. But Lenin wanted a revolutionary climax for the history books: a coordinated naval, cannon and troop assault, launched via the raising of a lantern (a red lantern, naturally), with victory to be announced at the noon opening of the national congress of worker's councils. It did not go as planned.

First, the sailors turned up late, delaying proceedings by hours.

It was then discovered that the guns on the Peter and Paul Fortress were showpieces, useful only for firing blanks to mark the passing of the hours. Soldiers were dispatched to find working guns and drag them up to the fortress walls. Once the new guns were in place, there was no ammunition. Some shells were found and hauled up, so it was time to raise the red lantern; but no one had a lantern. A Bolshevik was sent to find a lantern, but became lost. When he got back with a lantern, the lantern was not red. Nor could anyone devise a means to attach it to the flagpole to raise it. During the delays, the government's chief minister escaped the Winter Palace in a Renault obtained from the US Embassy. By this point, it was well past noon. The Bolsheviks decided to postpone the opening of the national congress. At 3pm, Lenin announced to a local workers' council that the government had been overthrown. In fact, the assault still had not begun.

Once it finally started, the Winter Palace fell quickly; the defence forces offered only token resistance. After the Bolsheviks found the government ministers in the Malachite Room and forced the doors, the Minister of the Interior stepped forward. He handed a Bolshevik an official telegram from the government of Ukraine, saying: 'I received this yesterday, it's your problem now.'

But the Bolsheviks had, in a manner of speaking, walked into an elaborately laid trap. On forcing their way into the palace, they discovered that the floor was covered with 'empty bottles with expensive French labels' (as one of the first reporters on the scene put it). The Russian empire had stretched from modern-day Finland all the way to Siberia, and under the czar, much of this wealth had ended up in the hands of a tiny elite – estimated by the historian Richard Pipes at about 1,000 households. The Russian nobility quickly ran out of things to spend their money on and began to engage in ridiculous extravagance. One aristocrat, for instance, had a staff of some 800 household servants; twelve of them were assigned to the care of his illegitimate children. The czar, for his part, had assembled what might well have been the greatest wine cellar in history. Indeed, it was said that czarist Russia sometimes purchased more champagne in a year than France could produce. Famously, one of the czar's close relatives had paid about 20,000 gold francs for a barrel of the 1847 vintage of Château d'Yquem (the czar's favourite vintage). Perhaps it was worth it: the wine critic Michael Broadbent, tasting the wine in the 1980s, described it as having 'astonishing power and concentration', 'fabulous flavour, incredible finish', 'faultless bouquet' and 'glorious evolution in the glass'.

Once the Bolshevik troops discovered the cellar, Lenin's elaborately staged assault quickly devolved into an out-of-control victory party. Red Guards liberated bottles from the cellar and roamed the neighbourhood toasting each other and lynching people who looked rich (one Bolshevik leader, mistaken for bourgeoisie, narrowly escaped the mob, at the price of his fur coat). Bolshevik leaders assigned a man to guard the cellar. He was soon too drunk to function. Soldiers of the Preobrazhensky regiment were dispatched to restore order. They decided instead to restart the party. Soldiers of the Pavlovsky regiment were sent, and joined the celebration as well. A hand-picked group of troops was assembled from different regiments in the hope that they would keep an eye on each other. They discovered a common love of alcohol. Armoured cars were dispatched to disperse the crowds. The crews, inevitably, joined the party.

For weeks, whenever the leadership was not looking, the party would spring back to life. On the night of 4 November alone, a single St Petersburg police precinct not far from the Winter Palace reported that 182 people were arrested for drunkenness. Despairing, Bolshevik leaders sent troops to dump the wine into the street. They were forced to give up after drawing a crowd attempting to drink it from the gutter. They issued frightening if juvenile proclamations (the Bolsheviks were just getting started in the art of terror; they would get better). One such proclamation decreed that stocks of wine 'will be BLOWN UP WITH DYNAMITE two hours after this warning … REMEMBER, THERE WILL BE NO OTHER WARNING BEFORE THE EXPLOSIONS'. The revels continued. In the official Soviet history, the Bolsheviks imposed martial law in the area and sent in sailors from the Kronstadt naval base to gather up the wine barrels, remove them and destroy them. But eyewitness accounts suggest that the celebrations, in fact, carried on intermittently until some two months later, when the czar's vast supplies of alcohol had at last been consumed.

One should not read too much into the comic-opera climax of the Russian Revolution. After all, history has nearly forgotten about it. On the third anniversary of Lenin's seizure of power, a cast of 10,000 actors re-enacted the events – as planned, rather than as they occurred – on the site. This time, the sailors were punctual, the lantern was red, and all the guns fired on time. A crowd of 100,000 watched the great drama. A decade later, the legendary Soviet film director Sergei Eisenstein recreated the events (again, the planned version) in the film, *October*. It was so well done that decades later, US textbooks appeared with film stills mislabelled as photographs of the actual revolution. (Although more people were killed in accidents during production of the film than had died during the Bolshevik liberation of the palace.)

The anti-climactic final act notwithstanding, Russia's revolution was a remarkable achievement of political mobilisation. Just how remarkable becomes clear when one considers the challenges involved in convincing masses of ordinary people to get involved in politics.

On the weakness of crowds

If the status quo were a person, it would have a forgettable one-syllable name like Joe, Jane or Sam; it would wear sensible shoes, have 1.2 children, and drive a reliable car. In its youth it would have coloured inside the lines; in adulthood, it would insist on filling out all forms in triplicate, every duplication a protestation of love to current conditions. No one really likes the status quo, but it is so inoffensive that it is hard to get worked up enough to change it. No one ever dreamed boldly of bringing the status quo into being; at sometime in the past, it just happened and then refused to go away. To the best of my knowledge, no one has ever made a great political speech celebrating the status quo. The status quo is the worst possible option. Except for all the others.

Political change, by contrast, would be sexy; it would be unshaved (whether male or female), ride a motorcycle, and live in a charismatically decaying building with an amazing view. Your mother would warn you about it, but you would find yourself staring none the less. 'What are you rebelling against?' one might ask. 'What have you got?' would come its louche rejoinder. While the status quo struggles to get anyone to pay attention, political change, almost effortlessly, inspires passion. The idea of a better world appeals to everyone, although on close questioning not everyone has the same kinds of 'better' in mind. In its purest form – revolution – political change is downright dangerous. Yet even in this form, it has sex appeal: the iconic image of Che Guevara that has adorned student bedrooms for decades is said to be 'the most famous photograph in the world'.

Many years ago, the analysts at Political Risk Services, a political risk consultancy, looked back over their long track record of geopolitical forecasting, and found that they had achieved an extraordinary 90 per cent success ratio in forecasting which governments would be in power over the following six months. Although, they noted dryly, if they had simply forecast 'no change' their success ratio would have gone up to 95 per cent. Even in the modern day, the political status quo is uncannily persistent – more persistent even than seasoned political analysts would expect. But why?

In part, the status quo persists because it is very difficult to convince ordinary people to engage in political action – even against extremely unpopular governments. In the mid-1960s, the economist Mancur Olson provided an elegant explanation of this difficulty. Consider a mass of people with a common problem – say, for instance, Russia's workers. Let us assume they want to overthrow the czar, who has used a good portion of their nation's tax revenues to build up his personal wine cellar. With numbers on their side, one might think the workers could get what they want. But they face what has come to be known as a 'free rider' problem. Those workers who join political action against the czar will bear all the costs, in terms of time, effort and risk. Yet all workers will enjoy the benefits if the czar is overthrown. So the sensible choice is to avoid the costs and be a free rider. Knowing that, who will volunteer to charge into the Winter Palace? No one.

This free rider problem tends to doom popular rebellions before they start; essentially, everyone except a few nutcases decides to free ride and nothing happens. The problem is not that people are sheep (as I alleged in the introduction), rather, it is that they can think for themselves, and realise that any mass movement is likely to collapse before it starts. And so they do not join. Call it 'the weakness of crowds'. Ordinary people are rendered politically inert by their inability to act together. This problem plagues even day-to-day political activities such as demonstrations and labour strikes. In authoritarian regimes willing to use force against their citizens, overcoming the weakness of crowds is that much more difficult.

Of course, professional soldiers are paid to charge first into palaces. If that fails, they are usually threatened with penalties of mutiny or desertion. Indeed, some combination of payments and threats is the main way that the free rider problem is usually overcome. Companies coordinate mass action daily by paying their employees to follow orders. Labour unions offer benefits to members and favour 'closed shop' rules that make union membership mandatory. In a closed shop, the unions can deny work to anyone who wants to free ride. (Interestingly, Olson noted that surveys of union members generally indicate support for closed shop rules. It is rare that people want to be coerced; but in this case, union members appear to understand that the union will be more powerful if it can overcome free rider problems and force everyone to strike together. Corporations, also understanding this point, tend to lobby for laws that make closed shops illegal.)

Revolutionary movements usually have limited access to such blunt but effective tools. Although they try: during the Vietnam War, for instance, communist rebels attempted to compensate recruits by redistributing confiscated land to peasants – a triumph of practicality over ideology, as under communism, private property was supposed to be abolished. In Peru, the Shining Path guerrilla movement did something similar, paying its recruits a subsistence wage, cancelling debts and redistributing landowners' property to villagers. In countries rich in natural resources, opposition movements can often fund their operations by seizing and sharing oil, diamonds and the like (hence the term 'conflict diamonds'). And, as we saw in Thailand, political movements backed by billionaires tend to have certain financial advantages – which is one reason the rich tend to be so politically effective.

For political groups without such resources, the weakness of crowds means that smaller organisations, counterintuitively, tend to have significant political advantages. In a small group, everyone's action makes a noticeable difference. One member of a group of friends joining a revolutionary conspiracy might expect that if she does not make the effort, everyone else will notice and stop their own efforts. Hence small groups are more able to identify free riders and throw them out. As we shall see, much of Lenin's revolutionary activities took place in small groups. The weakness of crowds is why the main work of legislatures is done in smaller committees rather than the legislature as a whole; it is why farmers often have powerful lobbying groups, but the hundreds of millions of people who eat the farmers' food usually do not; it is one reason the political status quo is so rarely toppled – even when the government in question is extremely unpopular. In an authoritarian regime like Russia, the weakness of crowds makes mass uprisings almost impossible. Vladimir Lenin may have intuitively appreciated these challenges; his theories of revolution involved a small vanguard that would bring revolution to the people from without.

But what happened in Russia was not what Lenin had expected.

The frustrations of the Ulyanovs

Great leaders of anti-establishment movements tend to be odd ducks. Lenin was odder than most. His desk had to be in perfect order; each day before sitting down to write he took up a duster and cleaned. He sharpened his pencils until his lines 'came out like delicate threads'. He chastised family members if their buttons were not tightly sewn on. His handwriting was neat; his bookshelves were alphabetised. When he received letters that had blank spaces, he would cut off the unused parts to reuse the paper; he used some of these pieces of paper to keep detailed notes of his expenses. At night, Lenin would turn off lights his revolutionary co-conspirators had thoughtlessly left on. When he worked, he required absolute silence. He walked around his study on tiptoe because, his wife claimed, he was afraid of disrupting his thoughts with the sound of his own footsteps. He was, in short, the kind of man who sweats the details; he was also an intellectual straight out of central casting.

Lenin made nervous, schoolmasterly gestures when speaking, such as grasping the lapels of his jacket or tucking his thumbs under his armpits and rocking on his heels; early on, he sometimes wore a wig as a disguise and thus developed the habit of repeatedly touching his head to make sure it was still there; he, like his father, had trouble pronouncing his r's properly; and in his speeches and writing, he frequently sounded like the academic essayist that he was: 'in revolutionary measures taken by the revolutionary class, the proletarians and semi-proletarians [will] carry through victoriously!' He was unapologetically bookish, carting 500 pounds of his favourite volumes into exile. As violent political upheaval raged around him, he carried on writing polemics against rival European political theorists.

Lenin did not himself hail from, as a Marxist would say, 'the proletariat' (essentially, the working class). Lenin's family, the Ulyanovs – 'Lenin' was a pen name – had been elevated to the Russian gentry, on the grounds of Lenin's father's outstanding service in the Russian educational system. When Lenin was a child, the family had servants, including a cook and a nanny. The Ulyanov family members spoke fluent French, and would pretentiously mix languages in daily conversation. They also owned, jointly with relatives, a country estate, worked by some 40 peasants, which they used as a summer getaway. It was a Russian family moving on up.

Then, in 1886, the bottom fell out. Lenin's father was unexpectedly forced to retire from his prestigious civil service post; a few months later, he died. The Ulyanov family's grasp of success proved to be a fragile thing. Half the house was rented out to boarders. That summer, for the first time, there would be no holiday on the family's country estate. Vladimir began to act out, disobeying his mother. His elder brother Alexander, away from home at St Petersburg University, also acted out, and in a much more serious way. He abandoned his work for days, doing little but pacing his room. Soon, he had joined a conspiracy to assassinate the czar. The plan was discovered by the secret police. It was an enormous conspiracy, which had drawn in not just the distraught Alexander but a good portion of the student body – some seventy-two students were arrested. At the time, Russian universities were hotbeds of political agitation.

Lenin's mother, a slight but formidable woman, swung into action. She petitioned relentlessly for leniency for her son; her family (the source of the inherited estate) had some members in high positions, so she was not without avenues of appeal. Indeed, she was so persistent that the czar himself partly gave in to her demands, scribbling a note on the margin of her petition that she should be allowed to visit Alexander in prison. Unfortunately, it emerged that among the young conspirators Alexander had played a central role – he had made the bombs. With his mother's efforts, he might still have received a lenient sentence. But Alexander, bravely, delivered a political speech at his trial, rather than grovelling for forgiveness, which might have been wiser. On 8 May 1887, he was hanged together with four other members of the conspiracy.

That was only the beginning of the downfall. The Ulyanovs quickly became outcasts. Two days after the execution, a special issue of the *Provincial News* was put out, devoted largely to Alexander's crime. The government hung posters in public areas throughout Simbirsk province detailing his guilt. Unsurprisingly, few of Lenin's fellow students wanted anything to do with him (perhaps out of fear of the secret police, who had also arrested his entirely innocent elder sister). Vladimir returned the cold shoulder. 'I cannot but remark on his [Vladimir's] excessive reclusiveness,' wrote a teacher. Lenin then provided the first indication of his somewhat frightening determination, graduating secondary school with the maximum possible mark in all ten of the subjects he was tested on – even though his brother was hanged during the examination period.

The advancement of the Ulyanov family into the upper echelons of Russian society had been thwarted. Lenin was clearly angry at this fate. He later told a friend: 'I was 16 [the year of his father's death] when I gave up religion.' Lenin found it more difficult to be angry at his brother. One of Lenin's tutors remembered Vladimir commenting, 'it must mean that he [Alexander] had to act like this; he couldn't act in any other way'.

Lenin's mother decided that a strategic retreat was in order, and she took the family away to their country estate. As a result, in what must have been a dangerous frame of mind, Vladimir was left to his own devices with the collection of revolutionary socialist literature his brother had left behind. To that point, Lenin had shown no tendencies towards political radicalism that anyone can convincingly document. That was about to change. From his brother's collection, he picked up a banned book, *What is to be Done?* by Nikolay Chernyshevsky. 'It completely reshaped me,' Lenin later told a fellow revolutionary. 'This is a book that changes one for a lifetime.' He reread the book five times that summer.

What is to be Done? is, from a modern perspective, a bizarre book. Its reward, to the persistent reader, is that it is written in a sort of code. Chernyshevsky, a socialist agitator, wrote it while in prison, and therefore he knew not to write anything explicit; he would need to disguise his messages in the form of fiction. Hence the novel's central topic of socialist revolution is discussed entirely in allegory, including a series of dream sequences. The author, not without a sense of humour, sometimes leaves off the narrative to commiserate with the reader about how bad the resulting book is: 'yes, the first pages of my story reveal that I have a very poor opinion of the public ... I employed the conventional ruse of a novelist: I began my tale with some striking scenes taken from the middle or the end, and I shrouded them with mystery.' (An approach I have adopted for this chapter.) On the surface, the plot is a love story, albeit one that celebrates heroic sacrifice and bold defiance of social conventions. Hidden meanings appear via references to philosophy and literature. Along the way, Chernyshevsky explains that his characters are not really characters, but archetypes: 'I wanted to depict decent, ordinary people of the new generation, those I meet by the hundreds.'

When one cracks the code, as Lenin evidently did in those five readings, one realises that the archetypical characters are future revolutionaries, and their leader will be a man named Rakhmetov, who is charming, confident and intense. He has total control of his emotions; he abstains from sex, although women want him; he eats only steak, ideally raw steak; he reads nothing but great books; he does not drink; he exercises vigorously. At one point, presumably to show that he is truly hard, he sleeps on a bed of nails, with messy results. The reason for his discipline is that Rakhmetov is born into a noble family. Yet he must become a socialist revolutionary; a servant of the masses. Only those with a will of iron, Chernyshevsky implies, are capable of such assertions of personal destiny over caste identity.

Young Vladimir was transported. The story of a nobleman who, through force of will, turned himself into a great revolutionary seemed to have been specifically written for him. He sent Chernyshevsky a fan letter. From that point on, Lenin carried a portrait of Chernyshevsky in his wallet. He began to exercise, doing chin-ups on horizontal bars. History does not record if he attempted a diet of raw steak (perhaps so: throughout his adult life he would be plagued by stomach trouble). He sought out revolutionary agitators, including an infamous terrorist, and he had a go at translating Marx's *Communist Manifesto* into Russian.

Despite these dangerous flirtations, Lenin was still, at least officially, on the path to social advancement. But he was about to discover just how stacked against him the odds now were. After only three months at Kazan University, Lenin was expelled on the pretext that he had attended a meeting at which the Minister of Education had been criticised. His punishment could have been worse – czarist Russia was not kind to dissenters – but his mother pleaded the case, contending that if he joined his sister on the family estate, both could be easily monitored (his sister was at that point still under police surveillance). Lenin's mother then bought another country estate, hoping to set her son up as a gentleman farmer. Unfortunately, Lenin had no taste for it.

Next Lenin came up with the idea of undertaking legal studies via a correspondence course, but his application was rejected. His mother once again swung into action, appealing directly to the Minister of Education, writing: 'how painful it was to see my son wasting the best years of his life'. Lenin was allowed to sit the legal exams at the University of St Petersburg, and passed. After working briefly as a lawyer, he struck out on his own for St Petersburg, where he intended to become a full-time socialist agitator. Unfortunately, he was not much good at subterfuge, and was also – thanks to his brother – a high-profile target. In 1895, Lenin was arrested by the secret police for his role in fomenting workers' strikes. Oddly, jail put him in a jolly mood. Perhaps the fact that the die had now been cast – that he now stood no chance of social advancement, and could only become a rebel – took a weight from his shoulders. From prison, he informed his sister that he was now, in fact, 'in a better position than other citizens of the Russian Empire: I can't be arrested'. After about a year in jail, he was exiled without trial to Siberia for three years.

Lenin's Siberian exile was surprisingly civilised. Once again, he had his mother to thank; she had been sending letters to the government to the effect that her son was ill with tuberculosis and could only survive in a moderate climate. Hence Lenin (who was, in fact, in good health) was sent to temperate southern Siberia, a region known, admittedly somewhat optimistically, as the 'Siberian Italy'. At first, his mother attempted to accompany him into exile, although he was able to talk her out of it. Overprotective mothers can, at times, be a burden. By marrying his girlfriend, Nadezhda Krupskaya, who had also been sentenced to exile for revolutionary agitation, Lenin was able to obtain permission for his new wife to travel with him. For the first time since his summer holidays as a child, Lenin seemed relaxed. He hunted with a two-barrelled

Belgian rifle, walked in the woods, collected edible mushrooms, and polished his ice-skating skills (he was something of a showoff, performing 'Spanish leaps' and 'strutting like a chicken', according to his wife). He wrote to his mother that, as a result of his time spent outdoors, he had a tan and now looked 'completely like a Siberian'. He amused himself by creating a photo album of his heroes; the album included two pictures of Chernyshevsky. But mostly, Lenin wrote. In 1899 alone, he published five book reviews in St Petersburg journals, as well as his first book, *The Development of Capitalism in Russia*.

On returning from Siberia, Lenin once again threw himself into revolutionary agitation. He was promptly arrested; his mother, just as promptly, managed to get him out (by 'camping on the steps of the police station', according to Lenin's sister). Again risking the government's wrath, Lenin decided to go and visit his wife, who was still serving out her term in exile. The authorities, who had at this point apparently come to recognise Lenin's mother as an irresistible force of nature, agreed, on the condition that she accompany her son and keep him out of trouble. On returning, Lenin decided he had spent enough time in the czar's jails. He fled the country – first to Zurich, then Munich, and then London.

Lenin had been born as a member of a striving, self-improving, eagerly advancing class of Russians. Following the sudden death of his father and the reckless decision of his brother, the model pupil was fast becoming a dangerous radical. His anger appeared to be boundless, and it was increasingly finding a single target: the government. At a meeting in St Petersburg, Lenin contended, quoting another extremist, that 'the whole house of Romanovs' should be 'liquidated'.

And one day, the Bolsheviks would do just that.

The rise of the workers

Semyon Kanatchikov was born in a village called Gusevo, not far from Moscow, in 1879. Kanatchikov's father, a peasant, would work the fields in the summer and head to Moscow in the winter to work for a bit of extra money. Despite these efforts, the family had a hard time – of eighteen children, only three survived. Kanatchikov's father drank a lot, and when drunk would beat his wife and son. That maltreatment was apparently unexceptional by the standards of the time. The historian Orlando Figes has compiled numerous Russian peasant folk sayings, and a quite a few are not simply on the subject of beating one's family members, but contain *advice* on beating one's family: 'the more you beat the old woman, the tastier the soup will be'; 'beat your wife like a fur coat, then there'll be less noise' – that sort of thing. Still, by age sixteen, Kanatchikov had had enough of this existence, and he left for the city to become an industrial labourer. 'I wanted to rid myself of the monotony of village life,' he said, '[and] to free myself from my father's despotism.' Kanatchikov's father seemed to understand. He hitched up a grey horse to the family's cart and drove his son to the city.

One could hardly blame the czar for failing to realise that people like Kanatchikov would one day rise up against him. In 1900, Russia's industrial workforce was, at about two per cent of the population, roughly the same size as the nation's landed gentry – hardly a vast group, and considering their relative poverty, hardly threatening. Moreover, from the Russian government's perspective, these industrial workers were nothing more than peasants (indeed, in official statistics, they were still classified as peasants). The idea that they would overthrow a government would have seemed preposterous.

Russian workers, it must be said, did not live well. In St Petersburg, a wage of one ruble a day (very roughly equivalent to $10 today, or about $3,000 annually) would have been the approximate maximum an unskilled labourer might hope to earn. On that kind of wage, living conditions were as bad as one might expect: the average *room* in a St Petersburg apartment housed six people; the average apartment, sixteen. Kanatchikov, when he arrived in Moscow, was doing even worse than this average. He earned about two rubles a week, working 7am to 6pm at the painting shop in the Gustav List engineering works. He shared an apartment with fifteen other workers, which he described as 'dirty and stuffy, with many bed bugs and fleas, and the strong stench of humanity'. Even his small sleeping cot was shared with another man.

But these crowded-in workers did not necessarily see themselves as society's losers. Peasants continued to flock to these jobs: between 1897 and 1917, the population of St Petersburg nearly doubled. These urbanised peasants were, in a sense, an elite group. More than 50 per cent of the migrants to St Petersburg were drawn from nine provinces, most of which were, oddly enough, relatively far from the capital. What mattered was not distance, but education: the greater the level of literacy in a province, the more likely that province's peasants were to set out for the capital. Once they arrived in St Petersburg, these peasants, far from wallowing in self-pity, tended to grasp at further opportunities to better themselves. If they succeeded, they would be rewarded: records of the pay scale at a metals plant operated by the German company Siemens, for instance, indicate that workers could nearly quadruple their income by rising to the highest skill category. As a result, many workers were eager to obtain an education, and they did. By 1897, 75 per cent of male workers in St Petersburg and 41 per cent of female workers were literate – compared to a national literacy rate of about 20 per cent. By 1918, close to 90 per cent of male workers were literate.

Over time, these urbanised and literate workers began to see themselves not as peasants, but as a new and distinct social group. The migrant Kanatchikov, who learned to read and thus graduated from the painting shop to the skilled work of pattern-making (creating the wood patterns used for casting metal parts), saw his wage go up to nearly half a ruble a day, and then to nearly a ruble. He recalled his excitement at fitting in: 'in a word, I dressed in the manner of those young urban metalworkers who earned an independent living and didn't ruin themselves with vodka' (the height of urban fashion at the time were high glossy boots that, when pulled down, had lots of creases). In addition to new clothes, Kanatchikov acquired some new ideas. By age twenty-three he had devoured the first volume of Karl Marx's *Capital*.

The first contact of most Russian workers with Marxist ideas came through the work of some outgoing university students. Eager to spread socialist messages (I mentioned earlier that universities were hotbeds of political agitation), the students tried to recruit workers to the socialist cause. Given the catastrophic failure of the effort – a bit more than a decade earlier – to bring socialist ideas to the peasantry ('socialism bounced off the peasants like peas from a wall'), few probably had high hopes of success with the workers. But they were to be surprised. Because of the increase in wages that skilled labourers could enjoy, the workers desperately wanted an education; hence when students announced they were setting up 'study circles' they sometimes found themselves overwhelmed by the response. Soon, activists in the intelligentsia (including Vladimir Lenin), realising that the students had found a willing audience, started or joined workers' circles as well. As early as 1891, there were about fifty circles active in St Petersburg, with several hundred workers as members. The worker Kanatchikov, who had by then moved to St Petersburg from Moscow, joined one of these circles himself. The socialists were often astonished by the passion of their unconventional students. In most cases, workers were already working ten or eleven hours a day, six days a week, and yet they were willing to take whatever time the socialists could give. An 'underground university' was established to provide higher education to a few promising socialist leaders. It proved so popular that when socialist organisers later tried to shut it down to focus on propaganda, the workers objected.

In addition to literacy, arithmetic and history, the students taught socialist ideas. At first, many of the political messages the students were peddling were simply ignored. Workers' aspirations were, in a word, aspirational. Newly literate workers devoured daily newspapers like the *Petersburg Sheet* that offered self-help advice on fashion and etiquette coupled with stories about celebrities. The first book Kanatchikov bought was called *Self-Teacher of Dance and Good Manners*. The socialists' efforts were also hindered by culture clashes. Kanatchikov recalled clandestine meetings in homes of the intelligentsia: 'We were regaled with tea and all manner of strange snacks that we were afraid to touch, lest we make some embarrassing blunder … Some[one] would ask us if we read Marx. Any stupidity that we uttered in our confusion would be met with condescending approval.'

But the socialist organisers kept at it. They started with simple stories, songs and cartoons with Marxist messages. For instance, *The Four Brothers*, a socialist fairytale, told of four brothers who lived, as people inevitably do in fairytales, in a deep, dark wood. Each of the four then came to a tragic end at the hands of the status quo – one was done in by noble landlords; another by the military; another by factory owners; another by the church. In the *Tale of the Kopek*, a peasant lost a kopek and each time he tried to recover it he lost not only the original kopek but more and more of his possessions – for instance, after slaying a bear and presenting the skin to a merchant, it turned out it was a wolf skin that had been ordered so the peasant got the kopek but had to pay the difference by giving up his trousers. (Even today, the *Tale of the Kopek* remains a good description of the way one feels during the tax season.)

The czarist censor who was responsible for reviewing Karl Marx's *Capital* commented, 'It is possible to state with certainty that few people in Russia will read it, and even fewer will understand it', and approved the book for general sale. His logic was probably correct, but it was still a tremendous mistake: the first print-run of 3,000 copies sold out within a year of its 1872 publication (a rate of sale that exceeded the book's success in the author's native Germany by a factor of 15). Marx's writings did not, of course, envisage revolutions in feudal states such as Russia – countries of peasants and lords. Rather, Marx had expected that communist revolution would come first to industrialised, capitalist Britain. But, oddly, it was precisely the mismatch between Marx's views and Russia's economic situation that made the book's ideas so appealing. The attraction of Marx's *Capital* was that it *wasn't* about peasants: the victors in the coming revolution would be urban workers, which is precisely what self-improving migrants like Kanatchikov aspired to be. Marxist pamphlets of the late 1890s underlined the message: because of Russia's industrialisation, the workers would rise, and the peasantry would die out. Marxist literature was, in an odd sense, aspirational literature. Soon, ordinary Russian workers were starting to concern themselves with matters about which even their university-educated tutors might have had little knowledge. As one socialist organiser put it, the worker 'seeks one thing only: an answer to the questions that arise in his head; he seeks it passionately, tormentedly and in his search for a good and intelligent book will sometimes sacrifice his paltry wage'.

And miraculously, these ordinary Russians began to overcome the weakness of crowds. In January 1905, about 120,000 workers went on strike in St Petersburg. It was by no means a revolutionary movement, at least not at first. The marching workers carried banners painted with the czar's portrait and sang songs including 'God Save the Czar'. To be sure, the workers did have political demands; but these demands were touchingly obsequious in their phrasing ('we, the workers and inhabitants of St Petersburg ... come to THEE, OH SIRE to seek justice and protection'). As the unarmed demonstrators marched towards the Winter Palace, they faced off against cavalry, who sought to disperse the crowd with a mock charge. The demonstrators held their ground. Infantry then fired a volley into the crowd from close range. Forty people were killed. Astonishingly, the marchers did not give up, but again advanced on the Winter Palace. Soldiers took up positions. The unarmed demonstrators stopped and fell to their knees, adopting a symbolic position of supplication. A bugle sounded. The soldiers opened fire on the huge crowd, not only with rifles but with artillery. Some 200 people were killed.

The killing changed something, and it was not the change those who had ordered the massacre had intended. As one worker put it: 'I observed the faces around me, and I detected neither fear nor panic. No, the reverent and almost prayerful expressions were replaced by hostility and even hatred.' The day came to be known as 'Bloody Sunday'. Another worker who participated in the marches put it this way: 'I paid dearly for Bloody Sunday. On that day I was born again – no longer an all-forgiving and all-forgetting child but an embittered man ready to go into battle and win.'

Prior to Bloody Sunday, workers had been mobilised almost exclusively to industrial action targeting workplace conditions; after Bloody Sunday, their strikes targeted the government. The strikes spread – even, spectacularly, to a Russian battleship, the *Potemkin*, which mutinied against its commanders, eventually defecting to Romania. The czar's commitment to repression of these activities was unwavering. In one single, bloody, strike-breaking effort, in the port city of Odessa (where striking workers had been joined by sailors), some 2,000 people died. By this time, however, there was no stopping the workers. The unrest culminated in a general strike, which began in September 1905. Commercial activity in St Petersburg and Moscow came to a halt along with almost the entire national railway network. The workers became more and more organised over time. Ad hoc committees of workers were established to manage the general strikes. The workers called these committees Soviets – 'councils' in Russian – a word that would echo in history.

Czar Nicholas II, a gentleman of the old school, felt that a sufficiently bloody act of repression would resolve the situation, without the necessity of listening to any more demands from ordinary people. Many of his advisors disagreed. They worried that if force was used once again, the situation would escalate out of control. After all, the general strike was partly a response to an earlier act of repression. The czar's prime minister proposed an alternative: that the czar should agree to a programme of token reforms – a manifesto – designed to emulate the core demands of the striking workers. This manifesto would include the creation of an elected parliament, the Duma.

Following the announcement of the manifesto, the strikes soon dissipated. The window of calm gave the czar the opportunity to implement the repressive measures he had hoped for. Mass arrests followed – between 1906 and 1909, some 2,000 people were taken as political prisoners and sentenced to death. An outbreak of labour unrest in Moscow was put down by shelling the workers' living quarters with artillery. The czar was delighted by the restoration of order; he praised one army commander, whose unit had mostly killed unarmed civilians, as 'acting splendidly'.

On people power

What force enabled larger and larger groups of ordinary Russians to act together, despite the inherent weakness of crowds? The answer to that question is, it must be said, inherently political. Those sympathetic to mass uprisings have tended to argue that people rise up because they are suffering so intolerably that they cannot help but act. Those opposed to mass movements have tended to argue that people join uprisings because they are deluded or insane. This debate was already raging by the time of ancient Greece. Plato tended to think that people were easily fooled by charismatic leaders into joining mass movements (one reason for his famous distrust of democracy). Aristotle, although also somewhat ambivalent about democracy, contended that revolutions resulted from intolerable conditions of inequality.

In Lenin's day, one of the most influential theorists of popular rebellion was a French writer, Gustave Le Bon. Le Bon opposed the French Revolution and the Paris Commune, and he attributed these uprisings to the madness of crowds. Le Bon claimed that people in a crowd became, in effect, a collective person; but an unwieldy and demented person, with little capacity for logical reasoning and drunk on its own strength. Le Bon was not fond of crowds. 'By the mere fact that he forms part of an organized crowd, a man descends several rungs in the ladder of civilization,' he wrote. Of course, when Lenin read Le Bon, he had a different agenda: to discover how he might bewitch a crowd of his own – a bit like modern economics graduates who have reinterpreted Michael Lewis's *Liar's Poker* as a manual on how to succeed in investment banking.

Lenin was also an avid student of Marxism, and Marx had a different theory, contending that revolutions occur when a rising social class becomes powerful enough to overturn the existing political order. Bourgeois revolutions – like the French Revolution, for instance – occurred, in Marx's view, when the middle class became stronger than the aristocracy, given contradictions in late feudalism. Communist revolutions would, in turn, occur when the proletariat became large enough, and well organised enough, to overthrow the middle class. In the *Communist Manifesto*, the young Marx wrote: 'with the development of industry the proletariat not only increases in number; it becomes concentrated in greater masses, its strength grows, and it feels that strength more'. Obviously, Marx did not account for the weakness of crowds. Still, he had hit on an important point, as we shall see.

When waves of instability swept Europe in the first half of the twentieth century, including not only Lenin's revolution but the rise of fascist Germany and Italy, mass uprisings once again fell out of favour; explanations based on madness or delusion became popular once again. Some of these explanations had roots in the new field of psychoanalysis, others in sociology. Scholars claimed that people followed fascists in order to satisfy subconscious psychological needs; these people were, for example, narcissistic, anal-retentive, or perhaps acting on a 'latent tendency towards homosexuality'. A 1950s book called *The True Believer* became a bestseller in the United States, arguing that alienated loners joined radical movements in a desperate attempt to find a place to belong. Mass movements were, to use the term of art, pathologised – rebellion as a disease of the brain.

By the 1960s, however, another shift had taken place. Rebellion became cool. When idealistic, young, attractive students took to the streets to protest racism, sexism or the Vietnam War, it was hard not to empathise. Sitting out on college lawns, the students passed joints around and their professors took a drag, and eventually these professors began to realise that it was the *world* that was crazy, man, and the rioting students were, like, the only ones who were, like, really *sane*. In addition, survey-based research revealed that the people most prone to participate in mass political movements were not lonely perverts struggling to fill the holes in their hearts, but rather, unusually gregarious and sociable people. Which, if one thought about it for a moment, made a lot more sense.

There was a new crop of theories of rebellion. The political science masterwork of that era was Ted Gurr's 1970 book *Why Men Rebel* (even if the title is a little dated). In a sense, Gurr brought the theories of rebellion based on hardship and those based on psychology together. He argued that when people's personal conditions differed greatly from their expectations, they became frustrated, and therefore potentially angry – and thus, in some cases, violent. When a lot of people become frustrated at the same time, political violence can result. But even this theory proved to have holes. Gurr was asked to review a paper in which some brave researchers had managed to conduct a survey of participants in a riot. According to the survey, those joining the riot did not feel dissatisfied with their personal circumstances – rather, they thought political violence was a good way to get what they wanted, and that the government could not be trusted. Gurr said that if such results were corroborated, he would have to revise his own ideas. Soon, the results were indeed corroborated, at first by studies of race riots in the United States, and eventually by studies of political instability internationally. Repeatedly, scholars found that people joining in political unrest did not express any greater feelings of personal hardship than people sitting on the sidelines. The factors that did seem to motivate political action varied. In a study of America's largest race riots during the 1960s, for instance, the main common element that separated rioters from non-rioters, across ten different surveys, was that the rioters felt African-Americans had been mistreated by the police.

Eventually, these findings began to add up to a picture of how mass uprisings occur. It turns out that the theorists who believed rebels were out of their minds were mostly, although not entirely, wrong. The theorists who believed people were motivated by intolerable suffering were closer to the mark, but still had the wrong idea. One might argue that Karl Marx was the closest of all to getting it right.

It turns out there are two main factors that compel ordinary people to get involved in politics. The first was something that prior theorists had tended to downplay; a factor generally described as 'opportunity'. Essentially, people get involved in politics because they think they can make a difference. An example would be the Brexit referendum. Almost certainly, one major reason that millions of habitual non-voters turned out for the referendum was that they believed their vote would have a lot bigger impact on political outcomes than a vote in a general election. And frankly, they were right: at a stroke, the referendum result reshaped Britain's political and economic trajectory in a way that few general elections ever have. Between the 2015 general election and the 2016 Brexit referendum not much had changed: most people who were suffering were probably still suffering; most people who were crazy were probably still crazy. What did change was the opportunity to impact politics (it was, as UK Independence Party leader Nigel Farage put it, a 'once-in-a-lifetime opportunity to tell the establishment what you think'). Of course, opportunity is not the whole story behind the Brexit outcome. But, along with austerity, it is an important part.

The second factor that compels ordinary people to get involved in politics is the one that Marx was hinting at: namely 'people power' (scholars term this factor 'resources'). People power has lots of elements, but at its base are factors that empower the public. Particularly crucial are average levels of income and education. People who can draw on more financial resources tend to be more politically effective; people who are more educated tend to be more effective. Hence, as Marx said, a rising social class can produce profound political changes. Thailand is a textbook case: a rising middle class brought democracy to their country, and then, desperate to rid themselves of Thaksin, helped to bring that democracy down.

In Russia, it was the rising workers who began to mobilise politically. What made Russia's workers unusual was not their suffering – even though working conditions were bad, the lives of peasants (who made up the majority of Russia's population) tended to be worse. What made Russia's workers unusual was their upward mobility. Indeed, a detailed review of statistics on strikes occurring in Russia, by Leopold Haimson, found that workers who were more skilled, better paid and better educated were more likely to strike.

In a sense, those theories of crazy, suffering people joining rebellions had it almost backwards. It is competent, effective people who tend to be politically dangerous. Even today it is a point that is so counterintuitive it is often overlooked. For instance, much media coverage of the Arab Spring focused on people's suffering – factors such as youth employment or government corruption. The media generally neglected to mention that Tunisia, where the Arab Spring started, was exceptional because of its economic success; indeed, Tunisians had enjoyed a near doubling of average income in the fifteen years prior to the uprisings. That success is a large part of what made them able to topple their government.

Scholars studying the psychology of mass movements have repeatedly found that the people who choose to join protests or riots are those who believe political action will work. (Think back to the survey of rioters: those who joined the riots were those who believed that violent riots would be effective.) Essentially, people take a view of the goals desired, the opportunities to impact politics, the people power available, and estimate the chance of success. It might seem to be a blindingly obvious point. Then again, theorists spent years debating whether revolutions emerged from the insane, the easily fooled or the hopelessly oppressed. And such debates still recur: in the United States, for instance, *The True Believer* has enjoyed a resurgence of popularity since Trump's election. But the book's popularity may well say more about the psychology of those buying it than of Trump supporters; it can be comforting to hear that those who do not share one's own political views are lunatics.

Keeping the importance of people power in mind, it may come as no surprise that the first social movement to have a major impact on Russian politics was not the country's workers. The workers were rising, but were still far from the top of the people power pyramid. Instead, it was a group of disgruntled Russian gentry – people not unlike Lenin's mother – who were the first to launch a citizens' movement. During the 1800s, groups within the gentry began to agitate for reform, and they were rich and educated enough to be effective. In the 1860s, the czar, partly in response, created the zemstvos, local government bodies with responsibility for areas such as education, infrastructure and healthcare. In rural areas, the gentry accounted for close to three-quarters of zemstvo membership. They were not, in most cases, radicals; the epithet 'zemstvo men' came to refer to social reformers.

In 1896, the zemstvo men gave a name to their social movement, the All-Zemstvo Organisation, and made a request to Czar Nicholas II to create a national assembly. The czar responded by denouncing such 'senseless dreams', declared the organisation illegal, and began a programme of arbitrary dismissals of reformers from the zemstvos. In 1904, the zemstvo men, frustrated but undaunted, made another effort to organise at the national level, managing to convince Russia's mild-mannered Minister of the Interior to allow them to hold an unofficial meeting in the capital, St Petersburg (only 'for a cup of tea' said the minister). One hundred and three representatives of the reformist gentry assembled in private homes and restaurants. They elected leaders for a zemstvo movement. It was the first such national political gathering in Russian history; comparisons with France's Estates General – a prelude to the French Revolution – were made. More than 5,000 telegrams of congratulation arrived (demonstrating both the depth of support, and the financial resources of those doing the supporting). The zemstvo men presented the czar with further demands for political reform, including, once again, a national assembly. This time the czar did not reject all their demands, or expel them, but he still rejected the idea of an assembly. Perhaps he simply had no desire to share power; but they also made him nervous. The zemstvos employed about 70,000 professionals to carry out their work in local government (such as doctors, teachers, and so on). This group was seen as even more aggressively reformist than the zemstvo men themselves, and came to be known as the 'third element'. Perhaps the czar was reading his history, and thinking nervously of the French

Revolution and the mobilisation of the 'third estate' – the middle class – against the crown. Or perhaps he was worried that the nobility (who had in the past assassinated unpopular czars, and by 1911, had assassinated the czar's own prime minister) would turn against him.

If so, he was worrying about the wrong thing.

The February Revolution

On 4 April 1912, the 'Lena Goldfields massacre' took place. Workers at a large gold mine in Eastern Siberia went on strike because of spoiled meat in the company canteen, the same cause that had provoked the mutiny on the battleship *Potemkin* (with better cooking, Russia's monarchy might have survived). In addition to edible food, the workers demanded an eight-hour workday (instead of eleven to twelve hours) and a wage increase of 30 per cent. Perhaps because this was distant Siberia rather than the capital, the mine's management went for the military option. By the time the soldiers had cleaned up the strike, 170 workers were dead and nearly 400 injured. At first, mine management claimed the workers had attacked company headquarters. It soon emerged, however, that almost all the dead or injured workers had wounds in their back or sides; hence, when shot, they had either been lying on their stomachs or running away.

It took time for news to reach the cities. But, ten days after the massacre, workers in a St Petersburg metallurgical plant downed tools and walked off work in sympathy. Within two days, more than 100,000 workers in St Petersburg were on strike. Between 1912 and 1914, nearly three-quarters of the entire Russian factory labour force was on strike. Nothing like it had ever been seen in Western Europe or the United States, or indeed anywhere. The country was quickly coming to a point of no return. (As the climactic events of the Russian Revolution have been covered in so many excellent popular histories, I will here include only the highlights – look to the Notes section on further reading for stories of Rasputin; the intrigues of dual government; Kornilov's revolt; or the fate of the czar.)

On 23 February 1917, thousands of Russian female textile workers led a women's strike. That afternoon, they were joined by 100,000 other workers, mostly men (by that point, solidarity among Russian workers was such that sympathy strikes occurred almost as a matter of course). The next day, there were some 150,000 workers on the streets. The day after that, much of the St Petersburg workforce was on strike, and most major factories were shut down. The czar, panicking a bit, cabled his military commander, authorising all necessary force to 'put down the disorders by tomorrow'. By the next morning, the capital looked like a military encampment. There were checkpoints and mounted police patrols on the main streets.

On 26 February 1917, despite the militarisation of the capital, great crowds of workers (and by this point, the general public) assembled. Inevitably, one standoff between workers and soldiers led to bloodshed. A group of trainee soldiers, told to disperse a group of demonstrators, panicked and gunned down fifty people. In shock, they returned to their barracks. Their commander demanded that they march out again into the city for further action. Some of them refused, which was, technically, mutiny. The trainee soldiers, suddenly realising what they had done, panicked again, as did their commander. In the confusion, they shot him in the back. Terrified of retribution, the soldiers ran through the barracks of St Petersburg, seeking support. They found it: soon, much of the military garrison in St Petersburg was in outright mutiny. Many killed their officers, thus throwing in their lot irreversibly with the rebellion.

Soon, soldiers and workers had joined together to capture the city's military arsenal. They quickly found a new weapon to even the odds against the police and loyalist military units – the motorcar.

These were still a relative novelty in Russia, but nearly all the cars in St Petersburg were commandeered, mostly by people with a very limited understanding of how to drive. The writer Maxim Gorky said that small cars with soldiers' bayonets bristling from them looked like 'huge hedgehogs running amok'.

The workers and soldiers quickly took St Petersburg, routing the last police and royalist resistance. As in 1905, a 'Soviet of Workers' Deputies' was quickly established. Lenin's Bolsheviks took part, although they were a tiny minority, overwhelmed by other socialist parties, peasants' parties and soldiers' representatives. The leading reformists, mainly zemstvo men, banded together to create a temporary committee that would, in theory, hold the reins of power until national elections could be held. Quickly, an agreement was reached between the workers' leaders and the zemstvo men: the Soviet would be housed in the left wing of the Tauride Palace; the Duma in the right wing, and they would – somewhat awkwardly – run the Russian empire together. At first, the czar attempted to pass the throne to his son, but these plans were dropped. Two lawyers were found and charged with writing up the formal papers of abdication. They used the paper they had to hand, a child's school notebook. Thus did Russia's monarchy come to an ignominious end.

Lenin, still in exile, was taken entirely by surprise. In January 1917, he had given a speech to some Swiss socialists, including the now-famous line: 'We of the older generation may not live to see the decisive battles of this coming revolution.' Learning of the overthrow of the government one month later, he did not change his tune: 'It's staggering!' he exclaimed. 'It's so incredibly unexpected!'

On the struggle story

Lenin had good reason to be taken aback. Both he and Marx expected that there was strength in numbers – hence Marx's initial belief that communist revolutions would come first to advanced industrial societies where the manufacturing workforce was largest. Lenin desperately wanted Russia to be first, and much of his early writing consisted of implausible efforts to fit the square peg of Russian feudalism into the round hole of Marxist theory by reclassifying peasants as either capitalists or workers. Of course, neither of the social movements that were reshaping Russia – the reformist gentry and the rising workers – had numbers on their side. Rather, they had people power.

That said, not every social group that enjoys rising wealth celebrates with a rebellion. Something must convince the members of a rising group that they need to undertake political action; indeed, that something is another element of the resources groups use to overcome the weakness of crowds. Let us call it a 'struggle story' (for scholars, it is a 'collective action frame'). The struggle story is the element of mass uprisings that sometimes does relate to suffering. But the theorists who spoke of rebellions based in suffering had many of the key elements wrong.

A monumental study of the morale of US servicemen during the Second World War produced a few striking and seemingly inexplicable findings regarding the determinants of human happiness. For instance, black soldiers stationed in the South were happier than black soldiers in the North, which was the opposite of what one might have expected, given that segregation and racism were worse in the South. Members of the Military Police, who tended to be promoted slowly, were on average happier with their job status than members of the Air Force, who tended to be promoted quickly – again, counterintuitively. The answer to these puzzles, contended the study's author, was that relative hardship was most important.

What mattered to soldiers' happiness was not their absolute conditions, but their points of reference. In the segregated South, black soldiers compared themselves to black civilians – who were even worse off than the soldiers – and hence the soldiers felt that their conditions were not too bad. They did not compare themselves to black soldiers based in the North, with whom they had little contact. In a similar vein, soldiers in the Air Force, where promotions were rapid, tended to know a lot of people who had already been promoted, which made them more likely to feel relatively hard done by. Soldiers in the Military Police, by contrast, tended to see few promotions among their peers and therefore did not see anything amiss when they were not promoted themselves.

It turned out that feelings of relative hardship – hardship compared to one's peers – have a large impact on one's psychological state. These feelings also impact behaviour. Recent research has linked feelings of relative hardship to an increased likelihood of committing crimes, of illicit drug use, of alcohol use, of smoking, of bullying, and of skipping work or school. Effects of relative hardship have been identified not only in Europeans and Americans, but in Singaporeans, Mongols, both black and white South Africans, New Zealand Maoris, and numerous other national and cultural contexts. The most powerful type of relative hardship may be comparison with one's own past. People who feel that they have become worse off over time are particularly likely to take some sort of concrete action, whether coping or lashing out, in response. It is not absolute poverty that matters; it is one's expectations. Hence even people who are relatively well-off (like Lenin after his father's death) can experience intense psychological consequences if their expectations were even higher than their station.

Still, the above are examples of changes in personal behaviour in response to relative hardship. Study after study has shown that relative hardship, even though it has a big impact on personal well-being, has no apparent relationship to political action. That is where the struggle story comes in. Experiencing personal hardship triggers changes in personal attitudes and behaviours (like drug use or skipping school). Changes in political behaviours, however, come about only when one feels that a social group one identifies with is suffering collectively. Again, think back to the studies of US rioters. The African-Americans who joined the riots tended to believe not that they personally were treated unfairly, but that black people as a group were being treated unfairly by police. That is a struggle story; that kind of unfair treatment of groups inspires political action. Studies have shown that people who feel that their social group is poorly treated relative to others are more likely to participate in riots, to intentionally sabotage their job performance, or to support others who are rioting or striking. Think of it as a question of alignment. Someone who believes they are suffering *personally* compared to their peers will take *personal* action to remedy the situation – from filing for divorce to kicking the dog to taking up a gym membership. Someone who believes their social *group* is suffering will want to organise a *group* response; that is to say, almost by definition, a political response. More generally, convincing a group with people power to take political action is a matter of convincing them they have a political problem and that political action can solve that problem.

In Russia, the first workers to mobilise politically were those who saw their group's situation as having worsened over time. Marxist organisers were taken by surprise; Marx had thought that the first workers to form powerful unions would be factory workers. Instead, the first workers to unionise effectively were comparatively well-off skilled artisans in Moscow and St Petersburg (tailors, woodworkers, printers, bakers, joiners, jewellers, and so on). The unions these workers created were also the first to take on ambitious tasks such as printing union newspapers and creating benefits programmes for members. These artisans were particularly likely to be educated, and have high skill levels. But they were also losing their jobs, in large numbers, due to mechanisation and industrialisation. By the spring of 1905, for instance, one in six typesetters was unemployed, partly because of the introduction of mechanical printing presses. (These artisanal workers were also among the first to lend support to the small, extremist socialist faction known as the 'Bolsheviks', which openly advocated violence.)

Of course, implicit in the above is the question of identity. To buy into a struggle story, a person must first identify with the social group in question. For typesetters in Moscow, that was relatively easy; they were defined by their profession. For Russian workers as a class, that was more challenging. These workers worked in very different industries, and had emigrated to St Petersburg from different areas of the country – what did a typesetter in St Petersburg have in common with Kanatchikov at the engineering shop in Moscow, or well-paid metalworkers at the Siemens plant?

But a seed of a new identity had already been planted – as I mentioned, many of these workers desperately wanted to turn their backs on their peasant origins. The workers' movement made great use of a term peddled by socialist organisers, which was that workers were becoming 'conscious' (in Russian: *soznatel'nye*). In theory, 'consciousness' was the moment when workers woke up to the exploitative nature of capitalism. In practice, being conscious meant putting aside peasant habits such as drinking and fighting and ignorance. Many workers, who did not want to be peasants any more, eagerly adopted new conscious behaviours. 'We were of the opinion that no conscious socialist should ever drink vodka,' recalled one factory labourer. 'We even condemned smoking. We propagated morality in the strictest sense of the word.' (As a result, the czar's secret police, who by this time had realised the dangers posed by Marxism, sent confusing instructions to local police to increase surveillance of any Russian workers who drank only tea.)

The most effective struggle stories often describe some injustice for which mass action is the solution. The injustice in this case was the lack of dignity with which workers, as a group, were treated. 'Workers complain about being treated like machines, like things,' explained a worker in a printing shop. 'They [managers] don't count us as people.' Bakers in St Petersburg complained of being worked 'like horses' and fed 'like dogs'. The necessity of political action followed logically. 'We must force the bosses to see us as people, filled with the consciousness of their work,' said a cooper in Astrakhan. 'Most important, the time has come for the Russian worker to get out of his semi-animal state and to declare to capital that he is a man,' said another worker.

And that is just what the workers did. Strikers at the Baltic Works plant demanded evocatively, if ambiguously, that management should treat them 'as people and not as things'. Striking workers at one St Petersburg factory included an unusual demand amid the usual working conditions wish list (wage increases, shorter work days, free healthcare, a smoking room). This unusual demand was *vezhlivoe obrashchenie*, which translates, roughly, as 'polite address'. Broadly, *vezhlivoe obrashchenie* meant that supervisors would be polite to workers: not yell at them, not insult them, and not abuse them physically. Most concretely, this demand meant that management would address workers as *vyi*, the respectful form of the Russian word for 'you', instead of *tyi* – the informal form, used for children, peasants and animals. Eventually, this demand began to turn up on many of the lists presented by Russian strikers.

At the time, merely meeting with socialist activists – some of whom, like Lenin, were hapless magnets for the secret police – was dangerous. Striking workers were often arrested en masse. (One worker, perhaps a little naïvely, informed a police officer who was taking him into custody that he was 'fool' because he had never read Marx and therefore 'did not know what politics and economics [were]'.) Moreover, striking Russian workers, like striking workers anywhere, faced the usual challenges that sap the strength of crowds: for any single worker it made sense to return to work. After all, if the strike succeeded, all workers – including those who did not participate – would usually receive the benefits.

The story about the unjust treatment of conscious workers became a rallying point against free riding. 'Shame, comrades, for acting like lackeys in the face of brute force ... Shame on those workers who continue to believe that they can improve their situation by abasing themselves,' a worker in Elizavetgrad admonished. 'For workers who are conscious of their worth, all forms of abasement are impermissible,' declared a worker at a Langenzipen plant in St Petersburg. After a strike was broken at a cable manufacturing plant in St Petersburg, one worker said: 'when we resumed work, we were unable to look not only at the engineers, but also the foreman in the eyes, and the latter went about looking at us contemptuously, as if we were not people but a bunch of sheep'.

Of course, these quotes imply there was still a free rider problem; there were still workers who decided the rational thing to do was to go back to work. Still, the workers had enough people power to overcome this challenge. They had education, thanks in part to the study circles; the skilled workers had rising incomes, so they could survive a strike without pay; they had a new group identity as 'conscious' workers; they had a powerful struggle story that explained how they had a political problem and political action was necessary. Armed with those tools, ordinary workers created waves of strikes that eventually led to the February revolution that toppled the Russian czar.

A situation that Lenin, in exile, could take little credit for, but was keen to take advantage of.

The October Revolution

After the czar fell, Lenin raced back to Russia, arriving at the Finland Station in St Petersburg. He immediately set about trying to cultivate support for a Bolshevik takeover. It was an uphill battle. Many workers were socialists, supporting the public ownership of industry, but communism – the abolition of all private property – was for most, a bridge too far. At the time of the February revolution, estimates of Bolshevik Party membership ranged between 10,000 and 24,000. Either figure was a small fraction of the membership of the other parties that had opposed the czar.

Things were about to go Lenin's way. By 1917, the Russian economy was in freefall. Because of the First World War, goods were rationed; the average household was spending an estimated forty hours per week in shopping queues. As the economic crisis deepened, the more moderate parties who made up the government were increasingly discredited by their failed economic management. By April, the Bolsheviks had more than 100,000 members, matching the party of the reformist gentry. By July, they had 200,000 members.

In late August, there was an attempted coup – possibly, oddly enough, at the prime minister's behest. Whatever the origins of the coup attempt, eventually, the coalition government that controlled the Duma called on the Soviets for help. Lenin's Bolsheviks had been plotting armed takeover for months, so they had a group of semi-militarised workers on standby (in total, some 40,000 of them, led by the 'Red Guards'). This ragtag group, provided with government-issued weapons, played a key role in stopping the coup leaders and their army (after sympathetic railway workers halted the troop trains, stranding many of the reinforcements).

The Bolsheviks were redeemed. Those in prison were released. In St Petersburg local government elections, the Bolshevik share of the vote rose from 20 per cent in May to 33 per cent in late August. In Moscow elections, their share rose from 11 per cent in June to 51 per cent at the end of September. More importantly, in the Soviets, the Bolsheviks finally took charge. They gained a majority in the St Petersburg Soviet on 31 August and a majority in the Moscow

Soviet on 5 September. By October, party membership had risen to 350,000 people. The vast majority were workers. It was the moment Lenin had been waiting for. If the Bolsheviks had previously attempted to take power, giving 'All Power to the Soviets' as their slogan demanded, they would have had a revolution but not political control. Now, they controlled the key Soviets, and better yet, many of the workers involved in stopping the coup had held on to their government-issued weapons. Lenin wrote: 'History will not forgive us if we do not assume power now.' He returned to the capital on 10 October (he had to sneak into party headquarters because the guards did not recognise him; known mostly through his writing, Lenin had rarely been in the public eye). He persuaded reluctant Bolshevik leaders to attempt an armed insurrection. The insurrection was successful – thanks to some heroic interventions by sympathetic soldiers and sailors – and Lenin and the Bolsheviks eventually took the Winter Palace (although they then, of course, had to deal with that very large wine cellar).

There was even more to be done: Lenin had to consolidate power, including within his own party, a process that nearly caused the fledgling regime to collapse – one third of Lenin's Commissars resigned during the power struggle. The Bolsheviks also had to take Moscow, which required military force. The upwardly mobile gentry who made up the government ministries initially refused to cooperate with their new Bolshevik overlords (especially the country's first-ever female minister). It took months (and a few purges) to restore order in the civil service. Against the nobility who populated the officer corps of the Russian military, the Bolsheviks fared even worse. When the Bolsheviks initially took power, these nobles were distracted by the need to fight the First World War. Eventually, much of the czarist officer corps would launch a bloody civil war against Bolshevik rule.

One year into Lenin's government, on 30 August 1918, he went to the Mikhelson Factory in the suburbs of Moscow to deliver a speech on the need to defend the revolution. After he finished his speech, he was approached by two women who engaged him in conversation. One of them, a former anarchist, pulled a gun and shot three times. Two of the bullets struck Lenin, one in the base of his neck and the other in his shoulder. He was bleeding profusely and there was blood in his lung. Fearing a broader conspiracy, he was driven to the Kremlin rather than a hospital, walked upstairs to his apartment himself, and demanded that his doctors be Bolsheviks. He then passed out in a chair.

A few regrets

According to Marxist theory, the experience of factory labour would remake the workers of every nation into collectivists. This transformation would enable these workers to create an economic paradise. Communism was not explicitly described as a heaven on earth, but Marxist narratives certainly had such undertones. All previous political and economic systems would be undone by their internal contradictions. Communism would have no such contradictions and all people would live with their needs satisfied.

That was not, frustratingly, the world Lenin had brought about. He survived the assassination attempt and returned to work, if not to good health. But rather than a paradise, he found that he was governing a country beset by civil war, petty crime, peasant uprisings, worker strikes, burgeoning black markets and even famine. What had gone wrong? About a year after he had nearly been felled by an assassin's bullets, Lenin allegedly – the story cannot be reliably confirmed – paid a visit to the Nobel prize-winning Russian physiologist I. P. Pavlov (he of the bells and salivating dogs). Lenin had a question: could conditional reflexes be used to control human behaviour? 'Do you mean that you would like to standardise the population of Russia? Make them all behave the same way?' asked Pavlov. 'Exactly,' said Lenin, 'we must abolish individualism.' Presumably, Pavlov let Lenin down gently, but Lenin did not want to be let down. He persisted: 'man can be corrected. Man can be made what we want him to be.' (Lenin's hero, the socialist writer Chernyshevsky, had put it even more grandly, writing that 'man is God to man'.)

Perhaps one day science will be able to produce such a great – or, more likely, terrible – refashioning of the human psyche. But not in Lenin's day. In conjunction with civil war, Bolshevik policies (nationalising companies, replacing the monetary system with state rationing and creating a grain monopoly) turned a serious economic downturn into a full-fledged collapse. Lenin's government declared that all 'surplus' (that is, 'unneeded') grain produced by the peasants was state property, and dispatched armed brigades to requisition it. In a worker's paradise this measure might have worked as intended, but not in the real world. The peasants responded rationally by reducing production (because any extra grain they worked hard to produce would simply be taken). Predictably, the brigades also thought only of themselves: they often took all the grain they found, not just the 'surplus', so the next year the peasants had no seeds to plant. Production plummeted further and the cities were soon starving. As a result, a black market in grain sprung up. Huge numbers of so-called 'bagmen' travelled the rails bringing the peasants' remaining grain to desperate cities that would pay any price to have it. The Bolshevik solution to this problem was to attempt to arrest the bagmen. (Economists reading this chain of events will by this point be weeping.) One can understand Lenin's desire to abolish individualistic behaviour, under which circumstances the Bolshevik policies might, just possibly, have worked. But it was magical thinking.

Perhaps inevitably, as this catastrophe unfolded, even those who had supported the Bolshevik takeover most strongly began to have deep regrets. In the first half of 1918, an estimated 100,000 to 150,000 workers took part in strikes or other protests. By 1920, much of the nation's workforce was in outright revolt – during the first six months of that year, some three-quarters of Russian factories were hit by strikes, just as in the years leading up to the fall of the czar. On 23 February 1921, soldiers garrisoned in Moscow were ordered to fire on a group of striking workers, and refused. The Bolsheviks realised to their horror that history was in danger of repeating itself. They declared martial law in the city. In a bizarre but possibly brilliant strategy, Bolshevik generals, fearing that they were about to experience a widespread mutiny, announced a boot repair programme for the Moscow garrisons and took away the soldiers' footwear to stop them from leaving their barracks.

On 28 February, the Kronstadt sailors – who had played a central role in the Bolshevik seizure of power, and allegedly in cleaning up the czar's wine cellar – began to debate whether they should also join the revolt against Lenin's government. This defection of those who had been Lenin's strongest supporters would prove to be a tremendous propaganda embarrassment. It was the moment at which socialists worldwide, many of whom had supported Lenin's seizure of power, realised that something had gone very badly wrong. However, the sailors' timing was inconvenient not just for the Bolsheviks, but for their own efforts at rebellion: the Gulf of Finland was frozen, so troops could walk to the island. The Bolsheviks massed artillery and soldiers on the shore. Shelling continued for days, coupled with aerial bombardment. On 16 March, some 50,000 troops, hardened by years of civil war, advanced against the sailors; by midnight of the next day, the Kronstadt uprising had been quelled, at the cost of some 10,000 lives.

At the 10th Party Congress, ongoing at the same time, Lenin introduced major reforms that would become the so-called New Economic Policy (NEP). These measures were an almost immediate success: the workers' strikes quickly came to a halt. The programme began the (temporary) reintroduction of market economics into Russia. Most importantly, the peasants would be allowed to sell their surplus grain on to the open market. Eventually, more such reforms were introduced, including allowing small-scale private manufacturing. For Lenin, it was not a total retreat. Russia was very obviously a predominantly agricultural nation, and Marxists, including Lenin himself, had sometimes argued that a period of development of industrial capitalism might be necessary before communism could be introduced. It now appeared that the capitalist period would need to be a bit longer than initially expected. (Lenin would later claim that his original, extremist policies had not, in fact, been an effort to introduce communism, but a 'temporary measure' necessitated by the civil war.)

But there were more regrets to be had. Lenin had other problems – problems within the Communist Party he had created. And his health was failing rapidly. By 1921, when Lenin introduced the New Economic Policy, he was already finding it difficult to carry on working. He moved to a mansion in the countryside to convalesce. His misery was something of a mystery: Lenin was only fifty-two years old. Doctors could not agree on the cause. Some pointed to psychological illness; others felt that the bullet lodged in his neck since the assassination attempt was poisoning him (the bullet was removed, to no avail); others suspected hardening of the arteries; others concluded he had syphilis.

Shortly thereafter, Lenin realised he had another problem: he had to that point given little thought to the political future of his country, presumably not having imagined that he could die so young. He also realised that his young acolyte Stalin was not entirely loyal, as disputes over two pieces of legislation – one on foreign trade and the other on a new Constitution for the Soviet state – pitted them against each other. Lenin did not like any of the alternative leadership candidates to Stalin much better, and briefly hatched an implausible scheme where power would pass to a triumvirate of weak leaders; then he came up with another scheme involving the transfer of power from his generation to young Bolsheviks in their twenties.

Meanwhile, his health continued to fail. In June 1922, Lenin collapsed while walking in the park. In July, he collapsed again. Regardless, in October he moved from the country mansion back into his office in the Kremlin, in an effort to regain control over the government. Then, in late November, he suffered five fainting spells in a week. Realising his time was short, he decided to put his faith in Trotsky. He asked Trotsky to give a speech on his behalf to a meeting of the Soviet Central Committee. In mid-December, Lenin collapsed again and lost all mobility in his right arm and leg. Ominously, Stalin was put in charge of Lenin's medical regime. Stalin dictated that – ostensibly for health reasons – Lenin could no longer be involved in politics. 'Neither friends nor those around him are allowed to tell Vladimir Ilyich any political news, since this might cause him to reflect and get excited,' read the party's official order. But Lenin's wife secretly continued to inform him on politics and dictate his letters. Stalin found out and confronted her, unleashing a tirade of angry invective.

Lenin had one last political stand left in him. By this point, he was so weak that composing each sentence took several minutes. A scheme was contrived whereby a secretary would wait in the next room and Lenin would ring a bell when a sentence was ready. Through sheer force of will, he composed several articles to be read at the next Communist Party Congress. He dictated: 'Comrade Stalin, having become general secretary, has concentrated unlimited power in his hands, and I'm not convinced that he will always manage to use this power with sufficient care.' He followed up with an effort to dilute the leadership's power, proposing that a number of industrial workers should be added to the Central Committee. One of Lenin's secretaries leaked the contents to Stalin, who was therefore prepared for the onslaught. On 4 January 1923, Lenin made a further, even more direct, addition to these articles: 'Stalin is too crude … I therefore propose to comrades that they should devise a means of removing him.' Unfortunately, by the time of the 12th Party Congress, in April 1923, Lenin could hardly speak; the most he could manage were grunts and occasionally a barely-audible 'here, here, here'. One of his doctors described his condition: 'Vladimir Ilyich lay there with a look of dismay, a frightened expression, his eyes sad with an inquiring look, tears running down his face.' At the Congress, Stalin outmanoeuvred Trotsky, and Lenin's painstakingly-dictated words were read only in a private meeting, and not discussed or debated in the Congress.

From that point on, Lenin was partially paralysed, and could barely make himself understood. In July 1923 he made one last trip to the Kremlin. He managed to ask for a few favourite books to be taken from the library shelves. His wife kept him abreast of events; colleagues from the Communist Party came to visit. But Lenin could only watch the world around him. He could no longer hope to change it. In January 1924, at the 13th Party Congress, Trotsky and his allies made a stand against Stalin, which failed. It is unlikely that Lenin knew what had happened. His wife claimed she never told him. But a few days later, on 21 January, Lenin fell into a coma and died.

Russian lessons

One could argue that the Bolshevik victory was a people's victory – and a victory for those ordinary Russian workers who had achieved such miraculous feats of political mobilisation. After the revolution, former factory labourers were promoted to top positions in the Red Army, the secret police, state-owned industry and the bureaucracy. The Communist Party continued to recruit new members from among the factory labour force throughout the 1920s, and then promoted many members with working-class backgrounds to high positions. The day after taking the Winter Palace, Lenin signed a decree abolishing private land ownership. That decree was immediately applied to the church, the imperial family and the elite of the Russian aristocracy. That land was then handed out to the people: by 1919, almost 97 per cent of the country's arable land was in the possession of the Russian peasantry. Workers, for a time, remained a potent and mobilised political force. Their strikes helped to tame some of Lenin's excesses; for instance, pushing him into the New Economic Policy.

But the people's victory, if it was that, did not last. Peasant farms were forcibly collectivised by Stalin. By the 1930s, the programmes that promoted workers had been ended; after that point, the Communist Party tended to promote the children of its own members. After the revolution, the worker Kanatchikov rose to become director of the Communist University in St Petersburg in 1921, and then the Communist Party's Press Bureau. He also ran a newspaper and a department of historical research. In 1936, however, he was purged by Stalin and sent to hard labour in the Gulag. He died in a Siberian labour camp in 1940. If it was a people's victory, it was temporary and costly.

The political philosopher Hannah Arendt made a study of history's great revolutions; the lesson she took away was that no revolution should ever be about what she called 'the social question' – the distribution of wealth; the question of who gets what. She claimed that all revolutions that had attempted to address the social question (the French and Russian revolutions) had resulted in tyranny. 'Every attempt to solve the social question with political means leads into terror, and ... it is terror which sends revolutions to their doom,' she wrote. In Russia's case, the people's tragedy may have been unavoidable. As Arendt noted: 'it can hardly be denied that to avoid this fatal mistake is almost impossible when revolutions break out under conditions of mass poverty'.

With only slightly flawed timing, in 2016, ninety-nine years after the Russian Revolution, there was another workers' uprising of sorts. The political scientist Jack Goldstone delivered a lecture at Brown University's Watson Institute while I was working on this book. Goldstone, who spent much of his career studying revolutions, argued that the 2016 backlash fitted some classic patterns: 'threats to culture, threats to economic progress, concerns about terrorism ... have combined to create a global revolt against the elites that people feel have let them down,' he said. 'This is best understood as a revolutionary movement.'

Whether the events of 2016 were revolutionary or not, Goldstone's comment did make one thing clear: mobilisation politics tends to make people nervous. And for good reason. We have become accustomed to life in centrist democracies, where winning parties play to the milquetoast views of the average Joe. Mobilisation politics changes the equation.

In much of our lives, we act on our personal interests and concerns, or perhaps those of our immediate families. In our political lives, however, we act in groups. We do not stop thinking about what is good for us personally (which is why political action is so hard to organise). But our motivations to participate in politics are based in part on our social groups (the community where we live; our racial or ethnic background; our gender; our occupation). We think about whether we identify with that community, how it has fared in comparison with others, and whether it has been unjustly treated – in short, whether our community has a political problem.

One might expect that voting would be different. And, under ordinary circumstances, voting is different. If voting relied on political mobilisation, democracies would suffer from the weakness of crowds. People would free ride; they would let other supporters of a candidate do the hard work of voting; and indeed no one would bother to go to the polls and many popular candidates would lose. This slightly ridiculous scenario does not occur because some people just like to vote. Perhaps they vote to express themselves; perhaps they vote to applaud a candidate they approve of; or perhaps they feel it is their civic duty. Regardless, these people vote in just about every election, and they will vote whether or not anyone else does – and so the weakness of crowds does not apply. In ordinary times, political parties target these habitual voters, and focus on the preferences of the median voter among them.

But occasionally, winning elections becomes a question of mobilisation. The US Democratic Party recently has been accused of engaging in 'identity politics' – of trying to use the identities of various social groups to encourage those groups to mobilise. Arguably, the strategy has worked: for instance, in the 2008 and 2012 elections when Barack Obama ran, turnout among African-American voters was higher than that for white voters for the first time in US history. As I have mentioned, the Brexit referendum result also turned on the mobilisation of non-voters. That situation is unusual in modern democracies; it involves big changes to who is involved in politics; the kinds of changes that usually accompany a change in the political system. Hence today's politics can indeed feel like a revolution.

In both the US and UK, stories of a social group treated unfairly (compared to immigrants or elites) seemed to spark a strong response in voters in industrial and rural areas. These stories also told of a group in decline – as we have seen, a type of story that is particularly likely to motivate action. Only a few people appreciated the potency of these struggle stories before the surprising events of 2016. Nearly all pollsters (and betting markets) put Donald Trump's chances of victory at less than a third; Mark Blyth, a professor at Brown University, was predicting that Trump could win as early as the spring of 2015, and gave Trump a 60 per cent chance on the eve of the election, noting that his campaign had produced 'a powerful narrative'.

These surges of non-voters into politics were one reason the opinion polls failed to forecast the election results. In addition to models that assess how people will vote, pollsters rely on 'likely voter models' that attempt to predict whether people will show up on election day. Those models can fail when many people who do not habitually vote suddenly decide to do so. As Andrew Bridgen, a UK member of parliament for Leicestershire, put it, in explaining the Brexit outcome: 'When [pollsters] Ipsos MORI ring them they say "I've never voted in my life," so they … don't count them. But they came out to vote Leave.' (And the models failed again in the 2017 general election, when a lot of young people turned out to vote.)

I first visited Russia as a student in 1991. At the time, the Soviet Union's centrally planned economy had just collapsed. The ruble was so weak that one could ride the Moscow subway roughly 1,000 times on the proceeds of changing a single dollar bill. Despite the economic collapse, US–Russian relations were at a high point; almost certainly the highest point in modern history. Russians, especially young Russians, were eager to meet us. I recall roaming around St Petersburg with some black-market traders, drinking vodka and going to jazz clubs. One evening, one of those traders said something that I found profoundly surprising: 'Lenin was Russia's last honest politician.' As these Russians were experiencing their first heady days of freedom, just about the last thing I expected was for anyone, especially a young person, to say something positive about Lenin.

Still, Lenin was indeed honest. Once in power, he lived simply, and implemented, to the best of his ability, the communist utopia of which he had dreamed. Arguably, the resulting excesses opened a political space for extremists of an entirely different character – rebellions of the radical right.

CHAPTER 3

Reading poetry in Tehran: why regimes fall

'Where the breakdown of traditional authority set the poor of the earth upon the march, where they left the obscurity of their misfortunes and streamed upon the marketplace, their *furor* seemed as irresistible as the motion of the stars, a torrent rushing forth with elemental force and engulfing a whole world.'

Hannah Arendt

The dinner party

It is possible that the Shah's very greatness had gone to his head. He had rebranded himself *Shahanshah*, 'King of Kings'; and *Aryamehr*, 'Light of the Aryans'. He had claimed dominion over time itself, renumbering the Iranian calendar. Under the Shah, Iran spent more money buying foreign military equipment than any other nation on earth; by 1982, the Shah planned to have 760,000 men under arms, more than France and Britain combined. A government minister handed the Shah a copy of the *Daily Telegraph* – a favourable review of the Shah's latest book! 'What on Earth's "favourable" about it?' the Shah snarled. 'What do you suppose this word "megalomania" means?'

'Greatness,' said the minister.

'Greatness be damned,' said the Shah. 'Greatness to the point of madness.'

In 1971, the Shah decided to have a dinner party. The theme would be '2,500 years of monarchy in Iran'. Technically, 2,500 years marked the death of Cyrus, who was in any event the fourth king of the Achaemenid dynasty, but no one was going to tell the Shah 'no'. The Shah wanted to invite a few friends. The kings of Belgium, Denmark, Greece, Lesotho, Morocco and Norway all agreed to come. So did the US vice president and the president of the Soviet Union. Some of the Shah's friends were positively giddy. The Duke of Edinburgh raced his aircraft against Prince Bernhard of the Netherlands and King Hussein of Jordan to see who would make it to Iran first.

Prefabricated guest tents were shipped from France, requiring at least 100 flights by C-130 military transports. 'Tents' is perhaps not the right word; they were built by Jansen, a Paris interior design house, and had marble bathrooms (his and hers) with tile floors, maids' quarters, and the highest-quality Persian carpets. The Shah's tent, made from blue and gold canvas, was forty feet high and had scarlet velvet interior walls stamped with roses. To spruce up the grounds, 15,000 trees were flown in from Versailles along with 50,000 songbirds to roost in them. Unaccustomed to the desert, the birds died quickly. Haviland provided custom porcelain featuring the Shahanshah's coat of arms; the table linen was from D. Porthault; the glassware by Baccarat; Jardineries Truffaut did the roses; the cutlery was gold-plated. The Paris couture house of Lanvin created uniforms for thirty waiters and footmen. The guest rooms were stocked with Guerlain shaving preparations and a new line of makeup by Elizabeth Arden. The *New York Times*, difficult to please, complained the tents 'had all the charm of motel rooms everywhere'.

To amuse his friends, the Shah decided to put on a little pre-dinner show. The Shah's Court Minister gave his staff a pep talk: 'If the work is not finished [on time],' he said, 'I'll shoot every one of you. Then I'll shoot myself.'

The work was finished on time. The event would be held against the spectacular backdrop of Persepolis, the ruined capital of the Achaemenids; a palace complex for an empire which at its peak stretched from modern-day Pakistan to the Mediterranean Sea. Stone bulls more than twenty feet high with a king's head and eagle's wings flanked Xerxes' gateway. The ancient king of the Achaemenids was also evidently a great man, as he illustrated with many rock carvings of himself, heavily muscled, hoisting a lion by the mane while plunging a dagger in its belly.

The Shah decided that his party would last for three days; many of the friends the Shah had invited had lots of free time. Twenty-five thousand bottles of wine and champagne were flown in. The highlight was a 1945 Lafitte-Rothschild (which, admittedly, might have disappointed the Russian czar). Some 5,000 bottles of alcohol were consumed. Many of the Shah's friends had hangovers. Each day a car-sized ice block was flown in via helicopter to top up the ice buckets.

The show was perfect; there was a parade of some 2,000 soldiers, dressed as ancient Persian warriors, complete with life-size replicas of ancient ships. The Shah gave a nice speech. The highlight, though, was the banquet. Maxim's of Paris did the cooking. Maxim's had never prepared ninety peacocks simultaneously; they rose to the occasion. The meal lasted four and half hours, starting with quails' eggs stuffed with caviar, finishing with figs and sherbet. The Shah's friends ate more than a ton of caviar. They were very hungry.

The Shah's friends, seated at a seventy-metre table covered with a bespoke tablecloth, looked magnificent! The empress wore a Harry Winston tiara and her necklace had coloured diamonds larger than quarters. 'The Communists and the royals were perfection as often happens,' said Prince Michael of Greece, later. The Shah wanted to have a video to remember his special party. Orson Welles was the narrator.

Some people, it must be said, did not like the party: 'Islam came in order to destroy these palaces of tyranny,' said the Ayatollah Khomeini, who was not invited. 'It is the kings of Iran that have constantly ordered massacres of their own people and had pyramids built with their skulls.' The Iranian intellectual Ali Shariati lamented '5,000 years of deprivation, injustice, class discrimination and repression'. The Shah was somewhat hurt by criticism of the party's cost. 'What am I supposed to do,' he said, 'serve bread and radishes?' Privately, the Shah was rather proud of the extravagance. You see, his family had not always been kings. As he described it to a friend: 'the descendants of Charlemagne came to Persepolis to pay homage to the son of a corporal'.

The Americans seemed impressed; they certainly liked the Shah. On New Year's Eve of 1977, at yet another of the Shah's parties, the US president Jimmy Carter toasted him thus: 'Iran, because of the great leadership of the Shah, is an island of stability in one of the most troubled areas of the world.' One year later, the Shah's monarchy had collapsed; the Shah had fled into exile; an Islamic government would shortly thereafter assume power. To be fair, almost no one saw it coming. In September 1978, less than six months before the end, the US Defense Intelligence Agency had predicted that the Shah would remain in power for the next ten years. In May 1978, the British ambassador had cabled home: 'I do not believe there is a serious risk of an overthrow of the regime while the Shah is at the helm.' The CIA's station chief in Iran had allayed concerns raised by mass demonstrations, saying that Iran 'is not in a revolutionary or even prerevolutionary situation'. These errors were particularly remarkable because they were not made by ill-informed pundits. These were, rather, the assessments of elite analysts, backed by large intelligence-gathering organisations, with privileged access to the highest levels of the Iranian government. And they were completely wrong.

So why do apparently stable regimes fall?

A note before we begin. For words in Farsi (the primary language of modern Iran), I have tried to use the English transliterations that are most familiar to Western readers (Koran vs. Qur'an; fatwa vs. fitwa vs. fatva). Because these words sometimes entered Farsi from Arabic, that sometimes means, oddly enough, using English trans-literations of Arabic instead of Farsi.

On turning rebellion into revolution

Some regimes turn on themselves; some regimes collapse for no apparent reason. But let us start with the most exciting scenario, the mass uprising. Why do some popular uprisings topple entire political systems? How do popular rebellions become revolutions?

It took a long time for social science to come up with good answers to those questions, partly because – as we saw in the last chapter – many scholars were at first looking in the wrong direction, expecting to find the roots of rebellion in intolerable suffering or collective madness. The liberation of former colonies in Africa and Asia in the 1950s and 1960s, however, led to some rapid breakthroughs, thanks to the sudden abundance of data. Now there were many more countries to study, and a lot of them were seriously unstable. Instead of a few picked-over historical cases, scholars could examine new revolutions almost every year. They soon realised that rising social groups, like Russia's rising workers, were a big part of the cause of revolutions. Samuel Huntington, for instance, famously argued that modernisation empowered new segments of society (such as a rising middle class). Countries with flexible political systems could respond to the demands of these fast-rising social groups; those with inflexible systems could not; and in those inflexible but rapidly modernising places, to somewhat simplify the theory: revolution! Another prominent theorist, Charles Tilly, argued that one needed to look not only at the people power of the opposition (for instance, in Russia, the workers and mutinous soldiers) but also that of the groups

supporting the status quo (the czar and much of the nobility, especially the officer corps). According to Tilly, revolutions occurred
when the combined power of the opposition exceeded that of the
backers of the regime. The sociologist Theda Skocpol offered a
further useful corrective. She pointed out that rising social groups
could transform politics without revolution, and hence gradual
reform turned into sudden revolution only if someone pulled the
rug out from under the government. (As Plato observed more than
2,000 years ago: 'all political changes originate in divisions of the
actual governing power; a government which is united ... cannot be
moved'.) According to Skocpol, the main circumstance that caused
elite supporters to abandon their own government was war. Losing
a war, or indeed taxing too much during war, could cause sudden
government collapses (we already heard about the political dangers
of austerity in chapter 1). One common theme is that for a regime
to fall, it must be opposed by a fast-rising social group.

But that was not what happened in Iran, which was one reason
almost no one saw it coming.

An academic enterprise

The man known to most Westerners as the 'Ayatollah Khomeini'
and to most Iranians as the 'Imam Khomeini' was born simply
as Ruhollah, in 1902 (at the time, most Iranians did not have
surnames). Like Lenin, Ruhollah would be known to the world
by his revolutionary *nom de guerre* – 'Khomeini' was a reference to
his home village of Khomein. Khomeini's family had once been
well off, but by the time of his birth they were living on memories
of wealth; and then he lost his father, mother and aunt in quick
succession. There was a crucial consolation: the aunt had set aside
a small sum to finance his further education. He could attend an
Islamic college, a seminary, or *hawza*.

He would thus embark on a thoroughly academic enterprise.

The greatest Shia Islamic colleges, in the holy city of Najaf – in what is today southern Iraq – were established in the 11th century. These colleges managed, miraculously, to survive political turmoil, invasions, changes of official religion, and much else, with relatively little meddling in their curriculum; those clerics who teach and study there today believe they are continuing an unbroken line of teaching from almost 1,000 years ago – a claim that few other educational institutions in the world could match (possibly Oxford, which was also, in the 11th century, a collection of religious seminaries).

For students, *hawza* accommodation was spartan in the extreme. Each student lived in a small square room, furnished with a prayer mat, a small clay tablet (for putting on one's forehead during prayers), a rug, a blanket, a water jar and an oil lamp. And that, more or less, was it: one slept and studied on the floor. The food almost never stretched to meat – the staples were bread and cheese and possibly some grapes. Dates, raisins, pistachio nuts and the occasional watermelon broke up the monotony. In the desert, water was a constant problem. Because one needed to conduct a ritual washing several times a day, and bathe once a day, every drop was husbanded (Khomeini, even in adult life, reportedly never threw out a glass of water; he would save any leftovers he did not drink). Every day, the students would rise before dawn, drink some lukewarm water, say the morning prayers, and go back to sleep for about an hour until the sun rose. The morning would be taken up by discussions, lasting until noon. Then the master would lecture, the students would take notes and then later give their compiled and edited notes to the master for approval.

These methods and even the subjects of study borrowed heavily from ancient Greece, in part thanks to the Muslim scholar Abu Ali ibn Sina (Avicenna), who had preserved classical knowledge in the Eastern world. In each lesson, the teacher would set out an argument; the students would be invited to debate it.

It was a bit like the Socratic method of Western law schools, and probably just as punishing to those who were not articulate or quick-witted. Students immersed themselves in syllogisms, similes, and other techniques of rhetoric, which would have been familiar to lawyers arguing before the ancient Roman courts. An Iranian scholar, educated in a *hawza*, observing the educational system in the United States in the early 1900s, found American teaching methods to be startlingly practical in developing skills needed by industry; but also intellectually shallow. (The kids could do their multiplication tables, but had they pondered the relationship between things observed and the representation of those things in one's head?) A great many who passed through this educational system – even those Iranians who went on to further study in the West – would look back somewhat nostalgically, remembering the heated classroom discussions. One Iranian scholar, who went on to become a committed atheist, nonetheless said of his time in a *hawza*: 'I still remember those days with pleasure.'

Khomeini, unable to afford to study at the elite seminaries of Najaf, journeyed to a *hawza* in the nearby town of Arak. It was still a great opportunity. Khomeini was not only clever, but a commanding figure, and he shone in the personalised world of *hawza* education. He was five feet nine inches, tall by the standards of the day, and slim but athletic, excelling at the traditional Iranian sport of wrestling (although he later described his sporting career as 'brief and undistinguished'). He made an impression. Decades later, in front of television cameras, he would demonstrate the care he lavished on his clothing by rolling a turban that was about twenty feet long. He usually matched the colours of his socks and cloak; he was something of a connoisseur of eau de toilette. He had mesmerising deep black eyes, and took pains to maintain his beard, which he called, in one of his poems, 'the cherished friend of my face'.

Khomeini's fondness for poetry was somewhat unusual for a

religious scholar; the kind of extracurricular pursuit that could raise awkward questions. His poems, influenced by Sufi mysticism, can be quite surprising. For instance: 'I have become imprisoned, O beloved, by the mole on your lip! / I saw your ailing eyes and became ill through love ... / Open the door of the tavern and let us go there day and night / For I am sick and tired of the mosque and seminary ... / Putting on the cloak of the tavern-haunting shaykh and becoming aware / Leave me alone to remember the idol-temple, I who have been awakened by the hand of the tavern's idol.' The poem was supposed to promote contemplation, not, as it might first appear, apostasy. But it was not only Western readers who might have been confused. Years later, the Iranian government attempted to take all of Khomeini's poetry off the market, lest people take the wrong meaning.

Khomeini studied under the great Islamic scholar Haeri, and was soon a favourite student. He and Haeri shared a love of poetry, especially of Hafez, a great Persian poet of the 14th century. Soon, Khomeini wrote a number of poems dedicated to his instructor (to be on the safe side, he wrote his poetry under a pen name).

The crackdown

Khomeini had a superb teacher, but Arak was still a backwater. On that point, Khomeini's luck was about to change. Khomeini's teacher wanted to move their seminary to the holy city of Qom, to build a new centre of Islamic scholarship. Moving to Qom, to be sure, had its downsides. The summers were brutally hot, the drinking water tasted bitter because it was drawn up through a layer of salt, and until the 1950s, Qom was well-known for its pungent open sewers. But Qom was also home to the shrine of Fatima's tomb, a saint who was the youngest daughter of the Prophet Mohammed. Passing through the shrine gateway, one stepped into a vast courtyard, at the centre of which was a pool of clear greenish water. The tomb itself was topped by an enormous gold dome, and fronted by three great arches into which glittering mirrored glass was inlaid. Inside the tomb, a great box of sandalwood gave off a fragrant odour, and pilgrims circled the silver grating surrounding the sarcophagus, sometimes weeping as they did so. The site made Qom the second holiest city in Iran, after Mashhad.

By 1933, Khomeini was regularly teaching many of Haeri's classes in theology. He was still only thirty-one years old; it was an extraordinary honour. Unfortunately, a great problem in Iranian politics darkened these happy days. A few years before, the commander of the country's most powerful military regiment, the so-called Cossack Brigade (because of its Russian training), had seized power in Iran, eventually installing himself as the new shah, or king. He was a great bear of a man, six feet three inches in height, with a huge nose, close-trimmed hair and jutting jaw. Empowered by the tools of modern warfare, his was an increasingly dictatorial rule. Soon, he began to bring the clergy, the main competing centre of political power, to heel. The Islamic primary schools were replaced by secular education. The Shah removed powers from the courts run by the clergy, and then, in 1936, abolished religious courts entirely. For Shia legal scholars like Khomeini, it was a crisis. Had he not spent years studying Islamic law in part to provide justice for the people? Adding humiliation to injury, the Shah's military officers, when they came upon clerics in the streets, would sometimes forcibly shave their beards, or burn their turbans. The Shah outlawed the wearing of the traditional veil by women. On 8 January 1936, the princesses and the queen of Iran appeared unveiled in a public ceremony. The girls appeared untroubled; but the queen hid herself beneath a wide-brimmed hat and fox stole. After that, she would never again appear in public, not even at the coronation of her son. Even for the Shah's family, the forced pace of change was too much.

Khomeini was infuriated by the Shah's secularisation

programme. He spent a year refusing to venture more than a mile from the shrine at Qom, preferring isolation to the risk of humiliation. Soon, he began to contemplate radical political ideas.

On rebellions of the right

Rebellions of the far left have been around since very nearly the dawn of written history. A papyrus scroll describing the first recorded revolution, which occurred in Egypt a little over 4,100 years ago, includes a few soundbites of which Lenin would probably have approved: 'the poor man is full of joy'; 'the son of a man of rank is no longer distinguished from him who has no such father'; 'behold, the possessors of robes are in rags [while] he who begged for himself his dregs has bowls full to overflowing'; and 'the king has been taken away by poor men'.

Mass uprisings in support of the right, by contrast, are largely a 20th-century phenomenon (by left, I mean political movements that support change and wider distribution of power and wealth; by right, I mean political movements that support tradition and preserving the current distribution of power and wealth). Popular uprisings in support of the radical, anti-democratic right were particularly rare before the 20th century – although there were a few 19th-century prequels. For instance, the Ku Klux Klan in the United States of the late 1860s never came close to achieving political power on a national level; but it did have genuine popular support in the south. The Klan campaigned to deny African-Americans the vote – to turn back the policies imposed by the North on the South following the US Civil War. There were also (arguably) a handful of early radical right-wing rebellions in 19th-century Europe. In France in 1889, for instance, the handsome General Boulanger started out left, turned centrist, and then contemplated a military coup to restore the monarchy – for which he appeared to have substantial popular support – but, in dashing French style, instead fled the country and committed suicide on the grave of his lover.

In the main, though, public uprisings against democracy were extremely uncommon until the 20th century. Probably, two conditions were required, which did not occur until the 20th century in most places. First, the growth of a large middle class meant there could be large groups of people with something to lose from a government seeking to redistribute wealth and power. Second, universal male suffrage (which in practice meant extending the vote to poor people) meant that there was a risk that these poor people would vote for a left-leaning regime. In September 1899, for the first time in Europe's history, that happened, when a socialist politician took a position in government (in France, as a cabinet minister).

One might add a third condition: the Russian Revolution. The excesses of Lenin's revolution made it possible for most people – some would say, most sensible people – to imagine what a far-left government would look like in their country, and truly dislike it. Only two years after the Bolshevik takeover, the most infamous radical right-wing rebellion in history was launched, admittedly on a long fuse. It began in an otherwise unremarkable meeting room in Milan: Benito Mussolini presided; about 100 people attended. Mussolini launched a new political party he called 'Fraternities of Combat' – in Italian, 'Fasci di Combattimento' (many of the initial members were combat veterans). This movement would practise what Mussolini called 'fascismo', the solidarity of committed militants. The policy programme that he outlined was somewhat confusing, containing lots of socialist elements – an eight-hour workday, worker participation in management of industry, the confiscation of war profits. That said, Mussolini also declared that the purpose of the group was to 'declare war against socialism … because it has opposed nationalism'. Intent on demonstrating this purpose, a few weeks later, Mussolini and his supporters smashed up the offices of a socialist daily newspaper, killing several people in the process. (Even this move was a little confusing: Mussolini had himself been the editor of that socialist paper five years before.) Still, Mussolini clearly envisaged going around beating up leftists as a central purpose of his group, and just as clearly, he had many followers, recruited from the public at large, who were keen on this programme.

Marxists had no doubt at all as to what had caused the rise of fascism: it was a new trick of the bourgeoisie; a new form of false consciousness imposed by the rich on to the poor. Indeed, at the Third Communist International, with Joseph Stalin presiding, that line of argument became the official view: 'fascism is the open, terroristic dictatorship of the most reactionary, most chauvinistic, and most imperialist elements of finance capital'. The Marxists had good reason to think this way; they could draw on bitter experience. In an effort to see off socialist opposition, the Russian czar had secretly funded the Union of Russian People, an anti-Semitic political party. In addition, the czar's secret police had organised the Black Hundreds, violent gangs of toughs who would disrupt workers' gatherings. Although the term 'fascism' did not exist at the time, in retrospect, many historians – not only Marxists – have labelled the Black Hundreds 'fascist'. Still, these political 'movements' were not really fascist parties; without government money they would have had no independent existence.

So the Marxists were wrong: the most successful fascist movements have not been funded by the capitalists; rather, they have been funded by small contributions from passionate, committed members. The funding of the Nazi Party has been particularly closely studied. While a few German businesses did contribute to the Nazis – infamously, the steel magnate Fritz Thyssen, for instance – in most cases, the German businesses that contributed were hedging their bets by funding all non-socialist parties. Large German businesses contributed far more to the mainstream conservative parties, and particularly the Catholic aristocrat Franz von Papen. Quite a few major German firms contributed nothing to the Nazis prior to 1933. Instead, the Nazis relied on small contributions from the public, the sale of pamphlets and entry fees to mass rallies.

Of course, not all modern-day radical right movements are the heirs of Hitler. Take the uprising of the Thai middle class, for instance, which led to the overthrow of democracy in Thailand. Was that fascist? Speakers at the redshirt encampment claimed it was; and today, commentators are quick to call any right-leaning popular figure a fascist. But the label is often unfair.

Still, there are rules of thumb that apply to most anti-establishment movements on the left (even those with little sympathy for Lenin), and equally for movements on the right. On the left, successful mass uprisings that topple regimes tend to require the support of a rising social group (as in Russia). On the right, successful mass uprisings tend to require the support of traditional, establishment conservatives – not easily gained, as traditional conservatives usually have little love for the populist right (in fact, most populist right movements in authoritarian countries have been quickly crushed).

Italian fascism survived because it could make this uneasy alliance work. In his 1919 bid for parliament, Mussolini received about 5,000 votes out of more than 315,000 cast; it would have been hard to have done worse. It looked like fascism was doomed. But then he received an unexpected boost from the estate owners of the Po Valley. Unions of agricultural labourers had forced these landowners to pay better wages and hire workers year-round, rather than only for the growing season. When the landlords appealed to the socialist-dominated government for help against the unions, they received little sympathy. Somehow, the landlords came up with the idea of approaching Mussolini, who had his own militia, the Blackshirts. The Blackshirts, formed largely to beat up leftists, were happy to get involved. In just six months in 1921, the Blackshirts in the Po Valley destroyed 151 socialist clubs, 59 socialist headquarters, 119 socialist employment offices, 107 agricultural cooperatives, and much else besides. One hundred and two people died in the process – mostly socialists, but also twenty-five fascists and a few police and bystanders. The Blackshirts had been formed to oppose the left – if the landlords were going to fund them in exchange, so much the better.

The Italian fascists probably had not intended to become a tool of the landlords. Indeed, shortly thereafter, the party split, with one faction complaining Mussolini had become 'the bodyguard of the profiteers'. That said, Mussolini had gained a crucial insight: traditional conservative interests were willing to tolerate far-right populists because they were preferable to the left. In the case of both Italy and Germany, traditional conservatives invited fascist leaders to form governments – and passed over opportunities to suppress fascist movements – apparently because they believed that a radical right government was preferable to a populist left government. Indeed, the map of the fascist presence in Europe prior to the Second World War is a very close – although not precise – map of the countries threatened by socialist takeover (Italy, Germany, Hungary). In no case did fascists win electoral majorities on their own. The greatest electoral victory by the Italian fascists was 35 out of 535 parliamentary seats. Hitler did better, but even still, prior to being installed as chancellor and unleashing the forces of political intimidation, the best national vote total Hitler achieved was 37 per cent (the largest vote share of any party, but not a majority). Both Hitler and Mussolini were installed in power following the intervention of the traditional right.

All of which is to say that Khomeini, like any leader of a right-wing uprising, was going to need to appeal to both the people and the establishment – a difficult trick. And it looked like he would get little sympathy from the Iranian establishment. As the Shah explained: 'Every country has a certain type of regime. Ours is a one-person regime.'

Khomeini's movement

But there was another establishment to which Khomeini could appeal: the clerical establishment. Iran's Islamic clergy lacked the raw power of the Shah, but, in the past, had fulfilled many functions of government, and retained substantial political influence. Iran's clergy were educators; they were arbitrators in personal and business disputes; they had been judges in criminal cases. In effect, at one time, the clergy had run much of the country's educational and judicial systems. The clergy's relationship with another trad-itional establishment, the merchants of the *bazaar*, was particu-larly close, as the merchants relied heavily on Shia commercial law. There were intermarriages between the clergy, elite merchants and the landed gentry. For instance, Khomeini's grandfather, a cleric, had married the daughter of a local Khan.

Here is an excerpt from one of Khomeini's lectures, which, again, for Western readers, may be a little surprising. It relates to his authoritative five-volume work on the law of sale: '"The question arises whether there can be a condition in a contract of partner-ship to profit or suffer loss disproportionately to the proportions of the original capital invested in the partnership … [Absolutely not, because] from the inception of the partnership, the capital of the partners is assumed to be inexorably mixed … [After all,] the very meaning of partnership is the mixing of capital.' Khomeini was, in short, a superb legal scholar. Also, many of his lectures were very boring.

As an establishment man, Khomeini started to receive large religious donations from merchants and other supporters. He continued to live austerely; he poured the money into stipends for students, which helped to build further his reputation as a cleric.

He became known for an iron discipline; some said that during religious ceremonies his every movement was planned, down to where he placed his feet. He hectored his students that 'discipline and organisation' were crucial to their future success. By the late 1950s, he was arguably among the twelve highest-ranking ayatollahs in Iran.

But becoming a rising star was one thing; convincing his fellow clergy to turn against the Iranian state was quite another. Even more challenging would be to undertake such a turn while cultivating a substantial mass following. There was, of course, a popular preaching tradition in Shia Islam, but high-ranking Islamic scholars usually did not get involved. A type of street preacher, the *rowzeh-khan*, was sometimes hired to give recitals of the story of the suffering of the Prophet Hussein, a Shia martyr who died in 680 AD, when Hussein and seventy-two of his followers faced off against an army of several thousand. The *rowzeh-khan* was paid for each recitation; he might visit two or three religious gatherings in a single evening. A great *rowzeh-khan* was a performer, evoking, for a few minutes, all the drama and intensity of a passion play. The best left not a dry eye in the house.

When his teacher died in May 1961, Khomeini started to reach out to the public. According to Amir Taheri, author of a biography of Khomeini, he began to adopt the emotive cadence of the *rowzeh-khan* street preacher. His voice would crack with emotion; his language became blunt, even vulgar. In the 1960s, the Shah announced another modernisation push, including a programme of redistribution of land, a profit-sharing plan for workers, women's suffrage and a literacy corps. The explicit goal of this rather left-leaning programme was to erode popular support for socialism. Khomeini made the bold move of criticising the Shah in public; eventually, the four highest-ranking ayatollahs of Qom and the two main ayatollahs of Mashhad issued a joint statement that in effect supported Khomeini. Shortly thereafter, pro-Shah rioters – some of them possibly a hired mob – invaded the Faiziyeh religious seminary, ransacked the students' rooms, and killed at least one student. Khomeini thought the moment had come to unite a mass uprising and the clerics against the regime. Khomeini, a descendant of Mohammed and thus Hussein, announced that he would preach a traditional mourning ceremony for the student in the courtyard of the seminary. On the day, Khomeini journeyed to the seminary in the back seat of a light green Volkswagen Beetle convertible. In front of the car walked a group of students, shouting: 'Grand Ayatollah Khomeini, leader of the Muslims, the glory of the believers; may your head be safe – your ancestor [Hussein] was killed!' Behind the Volkswagen, another group responded: 'In mourning the religious students of Faiziyeh, killed for religion by the hand of the disbe-lievers, may your head be safe – your ancestor was killed!'

During the ceremony, Khomeini was in full *rowzeh-khan* flow. He started with a rhetorical question: if Hussein's killers wished to make war on Hussein, why did they kill women and children at Karbala? He answered his own question: 'It seems to me that [they] had a far more basic aim: they were opposed to the very existence of the family of the Prophet.' Ominously, he continued: 'A similar question occurs to me now.' If the Iranian regime wished to oppose the clergy, why did pro-Shah rioters attack and burn a seminary? 'We come to the conclusion,' Khomeini said, 'that this regime also has a more basic aim: they are fundamentally opposed to Islam itself.'

Famously, he continued, his voice shaking with emotion: 'Mr Shah, Your Excellency Mr Shah, you poor miserable man. I am giving you advice. Your Excellency, I am warning you; stop these acts and change your manners. I do not wish to see the day that, when you are kicked out by your masters, people are giving thanks. I don't want you to become like your father [who was deposed by the Allies during the Second World War] ... Listen to me, do not listen to Israel. Israel is no good for you. Poor, miserable creature, you are only 45 [actually 43] years old. Ponder a bit, have a bit of wisdom, think a little bit about the consequences of your acts.'

That public lecture was a risk; no one insulted His Excellency Mr Shah that directly and got away with it. On 5 June 1963, the military surrounded Khomeini's house. Khomeini's son stood on a rooftop, threatening to hurl himself to the ground if his father was taken away. Khomeini told him to stop it. The soldiers seized Khomeini, but then the mass uprising began in earnest. There were riots not only in Qom but several other cities, including Tehran. But the government suppressed the demonstrations ruthlessly, with live weapons. At least eighty-six people were killed; the opposition claimed several hundred. In total, tens of thousands had taken part in the rebellion. Nevertheless, the government had suppressed it easily.

Khomeini would survive. He did not have Lenin's mother to back him up, but something almost as good: the clerical establishment, which – although still not publicly opposed to the Shah – made subtle gestures of support. One of Qom's highest-ranking ayatollahs decamped to the Tehran suburbs, implicitly reminding the Shah of Khomeini's clerical position. The grand ayatollahs of Najaf, in Iraq, cabled their support. Perhaps as a result, the Shah was gentle. After a short stay in prison, or possibly an officer's club, Khomeini was lodged at a barracks, and released within a few months.

That same year, Khomeini tried again. In November 1964, he gave another speech, again as the *rowzeh-khan* fighting to hold back tears, broadcast through loudspeakers in Qom. His target was an agreement that would give American military advisors, their support staffs and their families diplomatic immunity. Under this agreement, if 'the servant of an American advisor should take any liberty with one of the greatest specialists in Shia law' that servant would have legal immunity, Khomeini said. He continued: 'The source of all our troubles is America. The source of all our troubles is Israel. And Israel also belongs to America. Our members of parliament belong to America … America has bought them all.'

There was one other thing one did not do in His Excellency Mr Shah's Iran, and that was insult America (the Shah's main foreign backer). Khomeini was arrested again; there were further riots, but no revolution. Eventually, Khomeini was sent into exile. He was sixty-three years old, suffering from chronic migraines and kidney trouble, and had little access to his supporters in Qom.

It looked like he had played his hand and lost.

On emotion and politics

I mentioned that the many theories attributing mass uprisings to collective insanity had been shown to be wrong. Survey research showed, for instance, that lonely, disturbed individuals were not the main support base for mass movements – which, considering that loners probably hate crowds, should in retrospect have been obvious. Perhaps partly because of such embarrassments, for many years theories of political action based on the subconscious were unpopular.

Recent years, however, have seen breakthroughs in research on human decision-making. Some of this research involves, in a manner of speaking, the subconscious mind; the person making the decision thinks they are being rational, not realising emotions are influencing their choice. Fans of the Nobel Prize winner Daniel Kahneman, for instance, will know that emotional states impact economic choices, making people 'systematically irrational'. Recently, methods ranging from laboratory tests to brain scans have shown that emotions also impact on political decisions. For instance, people with greater self-reported anger regarding political conditions will tend towards greater participation – they tend to be more likely to join campaign events, to donate to campaigns, to speak to friends about politics, and to turn out to vote. But when angry people do turn up at the voting booth, it appears that they tend to vote recklessly. Compared to other voters, they will tend to have spent less time seeking out information on the issues, to support riskier policies, be more likely to select policies that seek to punish others, will tend to make decisions based on prejudices and simple heuristics, and will tend to have given little consideration to the economic consequences of their decisions. (Of course, these are statistical tendencies: not everyone who is angry about politics will behave this way.)

We might well suppose that some of these findings are likely to transfer – that highly emotional people are likely to form the core of mass uprisings. Joining a mass uprising implies greater political participation, which is associated with strong emotion; joining a mass uprising (especially a mass uprising in Iran) is a bit reckless, and reckless political decisions are also associated with strong emotion. Emotions probably help overcome the weakness of crowds by making people a little less rational than they might otherwise be. As one recent study put it, 'anger is seen as the prototypical protest emotion'. A good struggle story probably works in part by triggering an emotional response – anger at the government or other social groups; hope and enthusiasm about the movement. (Indeed, some scholars contend that perceiving one's group as unfairly treated is not enough; to be compelled to act, one must also have an emotional response to that perception.) Probably, strong emotions helped to turn Russian workers' feelings of injustice into political action, and to turn non-voters into voters during the Brexit referendum. Probably, Khomeini's *rowzeh-khan* rhetoric was effective in inspiring an uprising partly because it was so emotive.

But that did not mean that Khomeini's supporters (or indeed Brexit voters) had lost their minds. As in behavioural economics, the research on political decision-making indicates that people generally do what is good for them, but make some systematic mistakes. Even if they sometimes get carried away, people still take a view on the likelihood of success before joining a mass movement. And with Khomeini in exile, the clergy still reluctant to take direct action, and the Shah willing to use force, most rational people would not have rated the opposition's chances very highly.

And then the Iranian middle class got involved.

Ali Shariati

Ali Shariati's father was a talented public speaker, and had begun a lecture series in which he presented the story of Hussein's ill-fated rebellion not as a sermon but as history. These lectures were popular enough that in 1947, they gained a permanent home, the Centre for the Propagation of Islamic Truths. Sometimes as many as 400 people attended.

Shariati was a shy child, afflicted with mange, which he tried to cover up with a felt hat. He buried himself in books (his father's library stretched to about 2,000 volumes). He had appalling dress sense and had to be reminded that socks ought to be matched or that one sock was not as good as two. But by the time he enrolled in teacher training college, he had begun to develop some of his father's articulate charisma. Shariati read Lenin and Lenin's hero Chernyshevsky. He read European philosophy and wrote maudlin essays: 'Let me die so that in the arms of eternity and in the desert of extinction I would be rescued from my agony and the pain which I dare not speak about.' It is very dangerous for teenagers to read European philosophy.

Rather precociously, just out of his two-year training college, he became something of a public intellectual. He translated an Arabic-language book about one of the first followers of the Prophet Mohammed into Farsi. His friends helped him gather enough money to publish it, and the book saw print in Iran in 1955, titled *Abu Zarr: The God-Worshipping Socialist*. According to the book, Abu Zarr's Islam was all about social justice. Abu Zarr had said: 'I am amazed that he who cannot find a morsel in his home does not rebel against the people with his bare sword' (evidently, Abu Zarr was not familiar with recent research on the causes of popular uprisings). Shariati claimed that Abu Zarr was one of those 'saviours of freedom who is sought by today's humanity'. Abu Zarr was an iconoclast, and therefore an outsider. After denouncing the leaders of the Muslim empire as corrupt, he had withdrawn to the desert to lead a simple existence, while continuing to speak out about the greed of the rich. The Prophet Mohammed had said of Abu Zarr: 'He lives alone, he dies alone and he shall be resurrected alone.' That loneliness no doubt appealed to Shariati's own existential angst.

Shariati fell in love with a woman after she denounced the Shah so loudly in her literature class that Shariati overheard her from outside the classroom. He proposed marriage; she turned him down. A year later, she finally accepted, and they were married in July 1958. He was late to his own wedding. Shariati won a government scholarship and studied in Paris. He walked the banks of the Seine, translated French philosophers, and may or may not have had a love affair with a French woman (he wrote a poem about it, but as with much poetry inspired by Sufi mysticism, perhaps it was really about something else entirely). By the late 1960s he had managed to land a teaching position at the University of Mashhad. He quickly became one of the school's most popular lecturers. Lean, tall and balding, he spoke hurriedly, chain-smoking cigarettes and never using notes. He claimed that the mechanism of consensus described in the Koran could be realised through democracy; he claimed that 'there is no compulsion in religion'. Most dramatically, Shariati reinterpreted the story of the martyrdom of Hussein at Karbala. He claimed that Hussein was a crusader for social justice, who had willingly abandoned a pilgrimage to the Haj to wage a holy war against corruption; and that he had done so because such holy war was necessary even when victory was impossible. 'Observing religious rites and rituals is useless when such rituals come to lose their meaning and spirit,' said Shariati. 'Turning around the Ka'ba is of no use to an enchained people.' The students loved it. By autumn 1968, one of his courses attracted over 250 students, filling the lecture hall past capacity. Shariati habitually showed up late, and sometimes talked past the closing bell, on occasion running three hours over time, and yet the students flocked to hear him. 'During his lectures, you would be so carried away with his performance that you wouldn't even feel the chair you are sitting on,' one recalled.

The secret police did not enjoy the lectures, and placed Shariati under constant surveillance. Briefly, Shariati was forbidden from lecturing. Initially distraught, after a few months he was allowed to resume his talks. By 1969, had begun a lecture series at a hall in Tehran called the *Hosseiniyeh Ershad*. With these lectures, Shariati became more than just an exceedingly popular professor; he began to appeal to the Iranian intelligentsia, drawing them to an Islamic vision of socialism. Even his initial lectures in Tehran were staggeringly popular, especially with young people – the hall, with a capacity of 1,700 people, was reportedly nearly full. 'It is not enough to say that we must return to Islam,' Shariati said. 'Such a statement has no meaning. We have to specify which Islam: that of Abu Zarr or that of Marwan the Ruler. Both are Islam, but there is a huge difference between the two. One is the Islam of the caliphate, of the palace, and of the rulers. The other is the Islam of the people, of the exploited, of the poor. Which Islam do you advocate?'

Understandably, many in the clergy turned against Shariati. They issued fatwas against him, directing pious Muslims not to read his works. They had good reason: Shariati's ideas reinterpreting Hussein's stand at Karbala had appeared in book form, and had started to attract some support even among the clergy; the resulting arguments were so divisive, in fact, that one cleric died in a brawl. Khomeini, in exile, was sent a set of Shariati's writings, together with detailed notes on which parts contained blasphemy. Khomeini replied: 'I studied the cases referred to, none of the reprobation or criticisms were valid.' Indeed, according to some scholars, Khomeini and his backers adopted many of Shariati's ideas.

Eventually, Shariati was once again allowed to take the lectern at *Hosseiniyeh Ershad*. As many as 3,500 people registered for a course of his lectures in 1971 alone. Shariati appealed especially to the young, and to women – he delivered a series of lectures on women in Islam. One pious student complained that some of the women attending the lectures were wearing miniskirts. 'If she's wearing a miniskirt, why the hell are you looking at her?' Shariati asked, sensibly. With his modernist, middle-class interpretation of Islam, Shariati was riding a broader social trend. With rising incomes and the spread of education, Iran's middle class had blossomed – to about 1.8 million people by 1977, including civil servants, teachers, engineers, managers, and their families. In an increasingly liberal environment, women joined the education boom. There were only 5,000 women in higher education in 1966; by 1977, more than 74,000. With numbers came confidence. At universities in Tehran, women would tease the bearded clerics in their classes with lines such as: 'I have a religious question I need to talk over with you, in private', or 'I'm ready to become one of your four wives.'

Shariati may or may not have been a sophisticated philosopher; his biographer, Ali Rahnema, had some doubts. But Shariati, in his lectures and writings, always wore his heart on his sleeve. 'Every month of the year is Moharram [the month when Hussein's death is remembered], every day of the year is Ashura [the day of the same], and every piece of land is Karbala,' he said. This rhetoric appealed to the young, and Iran at the time was a nation of young people; some 60 per cent of the population were less than twenty years old. 'Death in a righteous and just cause never leads to extinction,' Shariati said. 'An honest voice may be repressed but never extinguished.'

That last contention would be put to the test. By the early

1970s, a guerrilla movement was underway against the Shah's regime. There were numerous guerrilla groups, most of them tiny – partly because mobilisation is easier in small groups; partly because the secret police proved adept at infiltrating them if they got too large. The guerrillas were essentially terrorists, bombing government buildings and embassies, robbing banks, publishing underground newspapers, and assassinating policemen, industrialists and Americans. They were formed largely of the rising middle class. Of 306 guerrillas killed between 1971 and 1976, 139 were college students, 36 were engineers, 27 teachers, 20 office workers, and so on.

The *mujahedin* circulated Shariati's publications along with their own, and included Shariati's texts on their reading list for members. Female relatives of *mujahedin* members, seated in the second-floor balcony at the *Hosseiniyeh Ershad*, would drop recruitment literature on the men below. But Shariati, afraid of punishment, avoided direct association. For good reason. In the early 1970s, after thirty-five members of the *mujahedin* were arrested, the threat from Shariati's publications and lectures became clearer. The *Hosseiniyeh Ershad* was shut down. Shariati fled, but the secret police arrested his father and brother. Shariati gave himself up, and was thrown into prison.

On his release roughly two years later, Shariati said the worst torture was being forced to talk about philosophy with the warden. But Shariati genuinely seemed to have been broken. He published a few pieces recanting previous positions. He did, however, write a piece about another hero – an enemy commander who had defected to Hussein's camp during the hopeless last stand at Karbala. Shariati wrote that every individual was forced to make a choice between oppressor and oppressed, and hence that all of us, whether we liked it or not, were every day placed in that commander's position.

Unlike Lenin and Khomeini, Shariati did not have friends in high places to bail him out of political trouble. He was, like his hero

Abu Zarr, entirely alone. Shariati decided (again like Abu Zarr) that he would go into exile. Somewhat miraculously, in May 1977 the secret police let him leave the country for England. Some hope at last! Still, England did not delight him: 'How can I think and write about Abu Zarr and the desert, when I am confronted daily with my green and flowery surroundings?' he wrote. On 18 June, he was about to leave for Heathrow to pick up his family, when his wife called to say she had been prevented from leaving. Apparently, the regime was unwilling to give up its trump card over Shariati. That night, at the age of forty-four, he suffered a massive heart attack and died.

By the mid-1970s, the Shah's harsh repression of dissidents like Shariati had started to attract international attention. In 1976, the Shah's intolerance of dissent became a campaign issue for Jimmy Carter in the US presidential election. Amnesty International had called Iran one of the world's 'worst violators of human rights'. After Carter won the 1976 election, the Shah announced that political prisoners would no longer be tortured. Hundreds of dissidents were released. The Red Cross was permitted to inspect jails. The educated middle class was the first group to take advantage of the Tehran spring. In May 1977, fifty-three lawyers signed an open letter criticising the Shah. In the autumn, Iran's writers followed up with another open letter, signed by ninety-eight prominent intellectuals.

In October 1977, the director of Tehran's Goethe Institute, the German Cultural Centre, was somehow talked into hosting ten nights of poetry readings. On the first night, so many people turned up that loudspeakers had to be set up on neighbouring streets to broadcast the event. The crowds kept coming. An estimated 10,000 people attended – celebrating poetry, enjoying camaraderie, but most of all, enjoying a newfound freedom of expression. By the fifth evening, the event had turned political. One speaker asked for a minute of silence for writers who had suffered under the Shah; he mentioned Ali Shariati, who had died four months before. The

German director of the Institute, probably regretting his involvement and sure that he would be shut down by the secret police,
nervously drained a bottle of whisky while watching the proceedings. The crowds huddled in the garden; audio and video were
recorded and copies distributed throughout the country.

There was another set of readings held at a university in
Tehran, and someone in authority closed those proceedings down.
This action led to a turning point: up to that point, middle-class
opposition to the regime had been carried out by underground
guerrilla groups or in writing. When the reading was shut down,
the middle class, for the first time in decades, flowed out into the
streets. The angry crowd chanted slogans against the regime. The
police cracked down, hard. One student was killed. Regardless,
over the next week, the demonstrations got bigger. The authorities
temporarily closed all of Tehran's universities.

The Grand Ayatollah returns

That move appeared to sap the energy of the middle-class protestors. But the Shah had made another, grave error. In August 1975, he
had implemented a crackdown on so-called 'profiteering'. Inflation
had been rampant, a symptom of Iran's overheated economy, with
annual inflation rates hitting 25 to 35 per cent. The government
blamed the traditional merchant class – the shopkeepers who ran
the *bazaar* – for rising prices (a bit like Lenin's regime blaming the
bagmen). A 1975 decree imposed prison terms, exile or seizure of
property for shopkeepers who violated price controls. In the years
that followed, at least 8,000 merchants were tried in the courts;
some said as many as 17,000. These measures alienated a huge
number of relatively well-off Iranians. The traditional *bazaar* sector
still accounted for about two-thirds of retail trade in the country.

And a second, even more severe error: the Shah brought Khomeini
back into the fray. On 7 January 1978, the oldest newspaper in Iran

published an article denouncing Khomeini. It accused him of being a tool of the landlords; it accused him of writing erotic poetry. It is unclear why the regime arranged for the article to be printed. Possibly it was a belated response to the death of Khomeini's son in October; the crowd of some 3,000 people who had turned up to the memorial service had probably reminded the government that Khomeini was still popular. Although he was still in exile, some of Khomeini's lectures were taped and redistributed in Iran. Indeed, Iran's secret police estimated that there were some 100,000 of these tapes in circulation (along with tapes from Shariati and others). At times, they were sold in ordinary music stores, alongside the latest pop hits, simply marked 'religious sermon'. But these pop hits were advocating an uprising.

Khomeini began to promote the idea that ordinary Iranians were the '*mostaz'efin*', the dispossessed masses. Sounding a lot like Shariati, and very much the populist, he said: 'Hundreds of millions of Muslims are hungry and deprived of all form of health-care and education, while minorities comprised of all the wealthy and powerful live a life of indulgence, licentiousness and corruption.' He also said, more harshly: 'if the Shah is not destroyed you shall all become slaves of pagans. Foreigners shall take your womenfolk; they shall plunder all your natural wealth and put the Muslim community to eternal shame.'

There was an extreme popular reaction to the article attacking Khomeini. The *bazaar* at Qom, which had probably been looking for an excuse to lash out at the Shah's government, shut the next day. A huge crowd of religious students gathered in Qom and occupied the Faiziyeh seminary. The police fired into the crowd; possibly as many as twenty students died on the spot. The next day one of the highest-ranked ayatollahs criticised the regime on the BBC Persian service. The three grand ayatollahs of Qom put out a statement denouncing the violence and identifying Khomeini as a 'model for imitation', the highest rank for a scholar in Shia Islam.

This designation was somewhat miraculous. Ranks and titles in Shia Islam, ranging from 'capable of deduction' to 'model for imitation', are awarded by consensus and there is no formal procedure for making such a designation. It is perhaps unusual that a controversial figure like Khomeini would achieve the highest rank in Islamic scholarship. Western historians dispute how it happened. Some say he had earned it; others say he got it through deft political manoeuvring; others say the ayatollahs only awarded it to him to save his life – that they feared the Shah would kill him if he was anything less than a model for imitation. Regardless, that honour for Khomeini was a strong signal that the religious establishment was swinging against the regime.

Forty days later, marking the traditional mourning ceremonies for those killed in Qom, huge crowds gathered in the streets – the religious; the educated middle class; the traditional middle-class *bazaaris*; and the guerrillas, many of whom had by this point given up the gun and formed political organisations. In the city of Tabriz, there were thirty-six hours of almost continuous rioting. People attacked government offices, banks, cinemas and alcohol shops. At least one mourner was shot; several hundred demonstrators were wounded. At sunset, people gathered on the terraces of their homes and, hearing the call to prayer, shouted 'Allah Akbar!' (God is great!) in unison. Soon, millions would join this ritual.

The regime appeared to know that something had changed. It offered both the carrot and the stick. Members of the Writers' Association (which had arranged the poetry readings) were beaten up. The government abandoned the antiprofiteering campaign and jailed merchants were amnestied. As street demonstrations continued (albeit mostly at a lower level) throughout 1978, the regime made some remarkable concessions. It promised to reopen the Faiziyeh seminary in Qom. The Shah even promised free elections, to be held in June 1979. And then, Khomeini had what first appeared to be a stroke of bad luck. Iran–Iraq relations had thawed, so at Iran's request, the Iraqis booted him out of the country. After drifting for a time, he found himself wintering in an unremarkable suburb of Paris. He had never visited a country without a Muslim majority. Reportedly, he kept his head down on the taxi ride from the airport to avoid seeing anything that might distress him. He disliked the Western-style toilet; the house was quickly fitted with Eastern toilets.

The inconvenient conveniences were worth it. In France, Khomeini entered the modern world, with modern means of communication. The house was soon fitted with two telex and six telephone lines. Tapes of his sermons were produced in the thousands each hour. Reportedly, *bazaar* merchants contributed some $35m in cash to the operation (equivalent to about $116m today). Once Khomeini realised what a gift God had given him, his pace of work was tremendous. He was, by this point, in his late seventies, and suffering from a heart condition in addition to his other ailments. Nonetheless, during his four months in Paris, he gave 132 media interviews.

He made an impression. He gave interviews seated cross-legged under an apple tree, or on the floor of a tent set up in the garden. Khomeini described himself as 'a nobody', 'your servant', 'a minor religious student' and 'an old man in his last days'. He promised a revolution, but also that Iran's new government would be 'democratic' as well as Islamic. He pledged that women would be treated as equals to men (although he usually qualified this pledge with phrases such as 'in accordance with Islam' or 'on the basis of the Koran'). A BBC journalist described him as a 'tremendous presence from some remote century'. The CIA described him as 'a kind of philosopher king who means to end corruption and then withdraw to his school at the holy city of Qom'. The US ambassador to the United Nations called him 'a twentieth-century saint'. 'The *mostaz'efin* [the dispossessed masses] will inherit the earth,' Khomeini said. On the audiotapes he sent back to Iran, though, he sounded less saintly. He railed against 'Jews and cross worshippers' who were 'plotting to make Muslims accept the rule of the foreign enemies of Islam'.

By early December, the opposition had increasingly unified around Khomeini as a leader. The heads of the two main middle-class opposition parties, the secular National Front and Islamic Liberation Party, visited Khomeini in exile and issued statements of allegiance. A march on *Ashura*, the day Shia Muslims ritually remember Hussein's battle at Karbala, was spectacularly well organised – there was little of the rock-throwing chaos and violence that had plagued previous events. The poor, apparently responding to requests from their preachers, poured in from the slums and shantytowns. Foreign correspondents estimated the crowds at an eye-watering 2 million. The middle-class guerrillas marched too, but peacefully. The marchers put flowers in soldiers' gun barrels and chanted 'soldier, brother, why do you kill your brothers?' At the end of the march a seventeen-point declaration was presented. It called for the Shah to step down; for redistribution of the wealth; for emancipation of women; and for a government based on Islamic precepts. Like the marchers themselves, these points showed a remarkable unity of opposition from the left and the right. One study of the banners waved by the marching millions found that 50 per cent had anti-Shah slogans, 30 per cent were generally in favour of Islam, and 20 per cent pro-Khomeini.

Still, it came as a shock when, early in the new year of 1979, the Shah of Iran suddenly announced that he was abdicating the throne. He fled into exile and left the country's prime minister in charge. In February 1979, Khomeini returned to Iran aboard an Air France jet. Asked by reporters how he felt on returning home, he gave a mysterious and now-famous reply: 'nothing – I have no feelings'. He also said of his return: 'I am just a seminary student, do not overdo the ceremony.' That was a forlorn hope: the crowd awaiting him was estimated at between 1 and 4 million people. On arriving, he snubbed the opposition political leaders awaiting him at Tehran University – possibly because he could not reach them. Instead, he was taken to a cemetery, where he delivered a speech both celebratory and dark. (On the way, his Chevy Blazer was subjected to such enthusiastic jostling that it broke down; he was picked up and deposited in the cemetery by helicopter.) Khomeini promised free housing, electricity and water to the poor; he promised to bring down the interim government that the Shah had left in charge when he fled (specifically, he said, 'I shall kick their teeth in'). He then headed to the makeshift revolutionary headquarters which had been set up in a girls' school. (Oddly enough, the Bolshevik revolutionary headquarters was also in a girls' school.)

Although Khomeini was by this point firmly in charge of the opposition, it fell to the educated middle class to strike the final blow. When a large group of technicians at an Air Force base declared their loyalty to Khomeini, they were attacked by the so-called Immortals, the branch of the military most closely associated with the Shah. The guerrillas, still made up primarily of students and the intelligentsia, threw themselves into the fray; somehow, in a triumph of morale over armament, they carried the day. With that, the revolution was over. The next day, the armed forces declared their neutrality. The guerrillas seized thousands of weapons, liberated Tehran's main prison, and ransacked the headquarters of the secret police.

Power and compromises

Initially, it appeared that the middle classes were the victors in the Iranian revolution. Soviet historians certainly thought so: they labelled it a bourgeois revolution, like the French and American revolutions. Khomeini deposed the prime minister who had been picked by the Shah, and asked a member of the middle-class opposition – Mehdi Bazargan of the Liberation Movement, a party that followed some of Shariati's Islamic-left ideas – to form a provisional government.

A national referendum was held on Islamic government. The referendum was rigged, but subtly so. Rather than stuffing ballot boxes, the Revolutionary Council asked voters a clever question: 'do you favour an Islamic Republic or a monarchy?' ('Democracy' was not one of the options.) Nearly 98 per cent chose an Islamic Republic. This outcome was not entirely out of keeping with the idea of a bourgeois revolution. Many in the educated middle class, including supporters of Shariati and of Bazargan's Liberation Movement, had wanted an Islamic revolution. In the spring and summer of 1979, the so-called 'spring of freedom', people talked politics, enjoyed whatever poetry readings they wanted, and wore Che Guevara T-shirts in public.

Very soon, however, the clerics began to assert control. Members of the clergy won more than half of the seats in the first parliament. Real power rested with a Council of Guardians, a group of Islamic scholars charged with vetting the laws passed by the parliament, on which Khomeini would serve for life. And yet, during Iran's first presidential election, Abolhassan Banisadr, a left-leaning economist who had studied at the Sorbonne, won overwhelmingly. The candidate who received the second-largest number of votes was also secular. That said, when Banisadr appeared to be accumulating too much power and popularity for himself, Khomeini dismissed him.

Khomeini could throw his weight around in part because he had found another base of political support. This was the Hezbollah (Party of God), a vigilante group (not to be confused with the more famous Hezbollah Party in Lebanon). The Hezbollah was packed with the poor, especially new migrants to Tehran, who received a monthly allowance for joining. They set about terrorising their former revolutionary allies. They invaded university campuses, burned books and newspapers deemed to be un-Islamic, attacked offices and meetings of other political parties, sacked the offices of a popular independent paper, and engaged in street battles with activists from other parties, attacking their opponents with clubs, jackknives, chains and meat choppers.

The Hezbollah terrorised women. When Khomeini stated publicly that women should wear an 'Islamic form of modest dress', thousands of women joined protest demonstrations. Women had fought and died for Iran's revolution; many probably felt it was their revolution as well. Among 341 guerrillas who were killed during the revolution, for instance, 39 were women. In response, the Hezbollah attacked unveiled women, throwing acid on their faces. A female advertising executive, who had joined a protest march led by professional women, was interviewed by the *New York Times* shortly after having been clubbed by one of the Hezbollah. 'They fooled us,' she said, clutching an icepack to her swollen head. 'This is no revolution. This is a mullah's game. It's nothing more than a mullah's game.'

By the summer of 1980, the veil was made mandatory in public offices; by April 1983, it was mandatory for all women appearing in public, and the Hezbollah terrorised all those who did not comply. Some women did support this conservative turn. But before long, many middle-class Iranians began to object. In October 1979, the Writers' Association announced a new series of poetry readings. The readings never happened; the organisers wanted a guarantee that the Hezbollah would not assault the attendees, which the regime refused to give. In February 1981, thirty writers, lawyers, academics and journalists wrote an open letter to Khomeini protesting the government's autocratic behaviour. (It is another oft-remarked pattern of history: following many great revolutions, including France, Russia and Iran, moderate governments assumed power but were soon replaced by extremists.)

The objections from the middle-class guerrillas to the regime's new policies were less genteel. First the *fedayeen* and then the

mujahedin launched armed revolts against the new Islamic government, including a bomb attack that destroyed the headquarters
of the ruling party in Tehran, killing or maiming key figures in
the Islamic regime. Khomeini appeared on television, decrying
the tragedies in full *rowzeh-khan* flow. His government cracked
down without mercy. For three years universities and colleges
were closed. Hundreds of guerrillas were killed or fled into exile.
There were mass executions. Officials rode in armoured vehicles;
government buildings were barricaded and lit all night by halogen
lights. Before it was all done, some 6,000 people had been executed,
including the former head of the *mujahedin* during the revolution,
and three teenage girls. The mainstream Communist Party, which
had dutifully turned against its former guerrilla comrades, was
then outlawed, its members purged; some were executed.

The regime's economic policy oscillated wildly. At first, it
seemed that Khomeini's pledges to the dispossessed masses, the
mostaz'efin, might be realised. Slum dwellers were allowed to
occupy vacant flats in well-to-do areas. Clerics were given suitcases
full of banknotes and ordered to distribute the money in impoverished provinces. In the chaos after the revolution, peasants, who
still dreamed of having their own farms, seized almost one-tenth
of the farmland in Iran. The Council of Guardians seemed unsure
how to respond. The parliament passed land reform bills; the
Council of Guardians blocked them – the Islamic clergy, many of
them landowners through their charitable foundations, had always
opposed redistribution of the land. Finally, after peasants rose up in
protest, in April 1980 a land reform bill was passed. It was radical,
but suspended within eight months, and historians disagree about
how much was redistributed. Certainly, a lot of barren land, but
probably far less farmland. Landowners, backed by the armed
forces, then reclaimed at least some of the land that had been
redistributed.

Of course, some of the *mostaz'efin* did benefit: long after the revolution, the government continued to funnel the nation's oil money into the pockets of those who were the pillars of its support. One pillar was very clearly the urban poor who made up the core of the Hezbollah. The regime's cultivation of this support went well beyond the Hezbollah membership. In 1983, the government created a system of extensive subsidies, mostly directed at the poor. By the 1980s, these subsidies had grown to the point that they consumed almost 10 per cent of Iran's economic output; some 1.2 million people were beneficiaries. Basic necessities were subsidised, with demand controlled by rationing. Even certain luxury items – such as refrigerators or televisions – were subsidised for poor buyers; some of whom promptly and cleverly began to abuse the system, buying subsidised luxury goods and then reselling them to wealthier Iranians at markups of 400 to 600 per cent. Khomeini had said: 'the country belongs to the slum dwellers. The poor are the resources of this country.' In a sense, it was true. As in Thailand, the political loyalties of the poor proved to be more complex than expected; they did not side with the middle-class leftists who had imagined the poor as their natural allies.

At first, Khomeini seemed to think that in his new, Islamic Republic, everyone would become an Islamic scholar. A television series was announced in which Khomeini would provide a weekly two-hour commentary on the Koran. Only one episode was broadcast. The intellectuals were shocked; they had never seen this side of Khomeini, comfortably tossing out reasoning born of classical philosophical traditions. But the show was unpopular, and quickly cancelled. Khomeini reverted to his usual rhetoric, promising to attack 'satanic forces', pledging he would 'kick their teeth in'. Concerned about his image, he demanded that all portraits of him in Tehran that showed him either wearing glasses or smiling should be removed.

Eventually, Khomeini returned to Qom. Back in his modest brick and mud house where he had lived before being exiled, reportedly, he was happy. Qom was enjoying a renaissance; the seminary trade was booming; teachers in the nation's universities were required to decamp to Qom for summer courses taught by clerics. But Khomeini was also worried. Beset by internal conflict and the Iran–Iraq war, Khomeini wondered if his new Islamic republic would survive. 'I have the fear that, like Hitler, we may enter history as people who achieved quick victories followed by defeat,' he was alleged to have said, making an unfortunate comparison.

Despite the challenges, the regime did survive. But Khomeini was already an old man at the time of the revolution. The Constitution required that whoever replaced him be a 'source of imitation', the highest rank of Islamic scholar. Understandably so: the job requirement was, colloquially speaking, to interpret God's will on earth. In 1985, Khomeini's successor was announced, his favourite former student, one of the most learned of the grand ayatollahs. However, after that chosen successor criticised the regime's violations of human rights, an alternative had to be found. Casting about for another option, someone both loyal and learned, there was no obvious choice. Eventually, the Constitution was revised so that the country's supreme leader no longer had to be a 'source of imitation'. In the end, what mattered was loyalty.

Khomeini died of heart failure just before midnight on Saturday, 3 June 1989. The nervous government waited until 7.00pm the following day to announce his death. At the funeral, the urban poor swarmed to embrace their leader. He was to be buried in the cemetery where he gave his first speech in Iran upon returning from exile. Several million people gathered in the punishing heat of Tehran's summer; firemen sprayed water on the crowds; even still, people died as a result of the heat and the crush. Plans for a funeral procession were abandoned. Khomeini's body was flown directly to the cemetery by helicopter. Despite that precaution, once the helicopter touched down the wailing crowds burst towards the open coffin, trying to caress his head, to tear pieces from the shroud as sacred mementos. After his body was briefly exposed, the troops wrested away the open coffin and placed it on the roof of an ambulance to convey it to the gravesite fifty yards away, where Khomeini was at last laid to rest.

The Imam's teachings

The French tents flown in for the Shah's party were expensive, but well made. In 2001, some thirty years after the party, they were still standing. The Iranian government announced a plan to turn them into hotel rooms. An Iranian tourist who happened to be visiting Persepolis at the time commented ruefully: 'we haven't even been able to build a proper door in the past twenty years'. However, the plan went nowhere. By 2009, only the metal frames of most of the tents remained. Outside the Shah's family tent, the Iranian government had placed a sign decorated with a rose and a verse from the Koran: 'Examine what your predecessors did and learn a lesson.'

One lesson of the Iranian revolution was that scholars still had work to do in understanding why revolutions occur. Of course, Khomeini managed the crucial trick of simultaneously mobilising a mass movement and gaining support from traditional conservatives (in his case, the Shia Islamic clerics and the merchants of the *bazaar*). The support of the religious hierarchy was particularly crucial in helping Khomeini attain absolute power in the chaotic days following the Shah's departure; it was one of the few organisations in the country that had not been discredited. But still, the revolution's success is a puzzle. The Shah had, by the time he left, killed between 10,000 and 12,000 Iranian civilians over the course of fourteen months. The army was still behind him; so why walk away?

That question has given rise to speculation about the Shah's mental state. One of my mentors in political risk, Marvin Zonis, argued that the Shah's emotional stability rested on certain key supports, including the perceived admiration of his people, the belief that America would always bail him out, and a sense that he was divinely favoured. When angry demonstrations, American criticism of his human rights record, and ultimately, a cancer diagnosis, threatened all of these beliefs simultaneously, the Shah became listless and indecisive. As one of the prime ministers serving under the Shah put it, 'the country is lost because the king cannot make up his mind'.

Theories of revolution have come a long way since the 1970s. One of the most important refinements is in our understanding of the strength of political institutions – a concept generally referred to as the quality of governance. Some of the main elements of the quality of governance are the effectiveness of the government bureaucracy, the quality of regulation and economic policy, the rule of law, control of corruption and the maintenance of public order. Countries that do well in these areas tend to be far less likely to suffer violent revolution (or, indeed, any kind of serious political violence). For Europe and North America, where most countries have exceptionally strong governance, that is good news: regardless of how strong populist pressures become, violent political disorder is extremely unlikely. In Iran, by contrast, the Shah had nearly absolute power but governance was weak.

In recent years, scholars have been able to develop models that are successful in explaining many and perhaps even most outbreaks of political violence. Arguably the most famous such effort is the CIA's (unclassified) State Failure Project, which through various twists and turns gave rise to today's Integrated Crisis Early Warning System, maintained by Lockheed Martin. This effort employed a Who's Who of the greats of instability research, including Ted Gurr and Jack Goldstone. These new approaches combine statistical models with sophisticated artificial intelligence algorithms that parse news stories, social media, and the like, looking for early warnings of conflict. Of course, even these all-singing all-dancing models are not right every time. A few years ago, a US general took me aside and informed me, based on the model, that the next country to suffer a major political upheaval would be Jordan. Hearing this, I booked a holiday to Jordan, wanting to see it before the catastrophe. It was marvellous – Roman ruins, Crusader castles, excellent food, desert landscapes, and, of course, the incomparable Petra. And, several years later, there is still no sign of turmoil in Jordan. In politics, anything can happen.

That said, the rule of thumb that anti-establishment movements of the political right tend to require the support of traditional conservatives appears to continue to hold true even today. In 2016 and 2017, for instance, there were several votes held in countries where the populist right was strong – including not only the US and UK but also France and the Netherlands. The populists won only in the US and UK, in part because only in those countries did the populist right gain significant support from traditional conservatives. It is hard to imagine the Brexit campaign having succeeded if its leaders had not included mainstream conservatives such as Michael Gove and Boris Johnson; it is hard to imagine Donald Trump having won the US election if he had run as an independent rather than winning the nomination of the Republican Party. Donald Trump was no traditional Republican; but with the party's imprimatur, some 90 per cent of registered Republican voters voted for him.

I also mentioned a few theories on the causes of revolutions, and the importance of rising social groups in victories of the left. But generally, revolutions are special snowflakes – each requiring an essentially unrepeatable set of conditions. Jack Goldstone made a heroic effort to summarise conditions that apply to many revolutions and came up with four. Austerity or economic crisis was one; another was a strong resistance ideology and widespread sense of injustice (a sense of injustice is crucial to a good struggle story); another was internal divisions among elites (like Russia's reformist gentry or Khomeini's effort to turn the Shia clergy against the Shah); and lastly, favourable international relations (in Russia, for instance, not only was the czar's government losing a costly war, but the German government was funding Lenin's Bolsheviks in an effort to destabilise the Russian regime). Of course, not all of these conditions applied in Iran, which is why people have started speculating on a fifth condition, that the Shah might have lost his marbles.

That said, there are many other ways, besides violent revolution, for regimes to fall.

CHAPTER 4

It's OK to cry for Argentina: why rich democracies fail

'If I define, I exclude.'

Juan Perón

Rich as an Argentine

At the turn of the 20th century, Buenos Aires was rich – second only to New York as a port city on the eastern seaboard of the Americas, with an opera house second only to La Scala in Milan. Grand boulevards were constructed in imitation of Paris; the avenues lined with flowering jacaranda trees; the pavements redone in Swedish granite. Buenos Aires had gas, electricity and traffic jams. 'It is a great city in the sense in which Paris and London are great cities,' one visiting American wrote. 'It is a cosmopolitan, 20th-century metropolis with all the fixings, crowds, avenues, parks, subways, visiting pianists, confusion of tongues, screaming of brakes, shining of movie theaters …'

Parisians, for their part, knew about Argentina. 'Rich as an Argentine' was an expression the French used to describe obscene wealth. The phrase arose because of the opulence of visiting Argentine tourists, who not only brought an entourage of servants but engaged in various ridiculous extravagances; one brought along several cows on holiday because, he claimed, in Europe one could not get fresh milk. An Argentine became the president of the League of Nations; an Argentine won the Nobel Peace Prize. Europeans were envious of the rising nation's confidence. A Spanish philosopher said that Argentines 'would not know history without triumph'. An Argentine president claimed that his country was 'condemned to success'. The tango became a global phenomenon.

And then, something extraordinary happened. Over the next seventy years, Argentina underwent an almost continual economic decline, compared to other rich nations. In the early 1900s, Argentina was one of the ten richest nations on earth – richer than France, Italy or Switzerland; roughly on par with Germany or the Netherlands. Today it barely makes the top fifty; it is approximately on a par with Hungary or Turkey. Of course, everyone knows about the rise and fall of ancient Rome. But in modern times, there is only one country – Argentina – that has become rich, and then become poor (or more accurately, middle-income) again.

Economists debate the reasons for Argentina's decline. What did the most harm: was it an over-reliance on commodities; a failure to manage the budget; or an inability to advance the innovation frontier? But the interesting question, and one that is very relevant today, is not about economics. It is about politics: why did Argentina's leaders make such bad choices? One can understand a policy error or two; but for a rich country to undergo *decades* of decline is remarkable. After a few years, it became obvious that their choices were not working. So why did they continue to make these choices, year after year after year?

The putsch

The Spanish explorers who ventured up the River Plate in 1516 were hoping to find Native American empires to plunder. Instead, they found a vast, mostly-empty plain. At first a disappointment, that great plain became an engine of wealth. The *pampas*, more than 500 miles across, was said to have soil so rich one could drag a plough the length of it without encountering a stone. It fostered a boom in wool production in the 1860s and in cereal and wheat exports in the 1880s. But it was beef that made Argentina rich, following the development of refrigerated shipping. The British were so eager to get their mouths on beef directly off the *pampas* that between 1907 and 1914 they funded the laying of, on average, more than 1,000 miles of railway track a year, across the Argentine countryside.

Initially, Argentina's politics were dominated by those who had become rich off the agricultural boom – mainly, the landlord owners of great ranches known as *estancias*. By 1916, however, a rising middle class in Buenos Aires, employed in support sectors like retail, shipping and government, had started to throw its political weight around. A candidate backed by the middle class won the Argentine presidency; he was so reclusive he was nicknamed 'the armadillo' (Argentine armadillos live underground). He published rambling manifestos, was rarely seen in public and communicated with the outside world mostly through his advisors. A staffer at the American Embassy nonetheless affirmed his 'innate force and inherent greatness of character, which his peculiar physical charac-teristics – a pineapple-shaped head, a Mongolian [mustache] with straggling threads on either side of his mouth – could not dispel'.

By the 1920s, yet another social group was rising: industrial labour. The First World War had cut off international trade, which meant Argentina needed to produce consumer goods domestically rather than importing from Europe. But Argentina was rich, there was a lot of consumer demand, and soon, domestic industry was flourishing. With flourishing industry came strong labour unions. By about 1930, Argentine politics had evolved into an unsteady three-way contest: the middle-class Radical Party and the land-lord-backed conservative party were roughly deadlocked in the national legislature, while the socialists, supported by organised labour, had won control of the government of Buenos Aires.

That year, the landlords struck. They backed the overthrow of the democratic government via a military coup. Initially, the action also had a good deal of middle-class support, in part because many middle-class Argentines were worried about a Soviet-style workers' uprising. Indeed, the main violence associated with the coup was from supporters, who celebrated in the streets and then torched the armadillo's home. But the landlords who had backed the coup soon turned on their fellow coup supporters. When elections were held, the landlords banned the middle-class Radical Party from politics; the dead were resurrected in their multitudes to vote fraudulently in the landlords' favour; the police confiscated ballots from districts likely to support the opposition.

Today, Argentines refer to the years of landlord-dominated politics that followed as the 'infamous decade'. The landlords took a scorched-earth approach. Reasoning that socialists were dangerous, that the main support base of socialism was in organised labour, and that organised labour was strongest in large-scale enterprises, they decided that large-scale industry had to be repressed. Their policy programme was dubbed industrialisation 'without industrial revolution'; the idea was to keep enterprises small, by avoiding heavy industry. This repression of the unions did indeed keep the socialists down, but at a serious economic cost. Sometime during that decade, the expression 'Rich as an Argentine' vanished from European tongues.

Perón

Juan Perón was a man on the rise. He was solidly built, a military man, but his smile was so broad and constant that his opponents nicknamed him 'Colonel Kolynos' after a brand of toothpaste. Smiling that much was a bit daring for an Argentine man of that era, but Perón's hobbies were reassuringly masculine: motorcycles, horses, speedboats, racing cars. A report by the US Federal Bureau of Investigation said that he had a 'permanent sense of humor'. Even in civilian settings, he liked to wear a uniform, and he had a weakness for capes. In 1943, he joined a group of his fellow junior military officers in launching a coup against the landlord-backed regime. Through several reshuffles of the new government, he worked his way up to Minister of War.

And then, in August 1943, an event transpired that would define his political career – and Argentina's future. Perón was called upon to deal with a meatpackers' strike. Ever the charmer, he managed to negotiate a deal, getting the union's founder, a communist, released from jail and a pay rise of five cents per hour for the workers. Presumably, this approach was so unexpected – the landlords' usual response to strikes had been to send in the police – that the workers were effusive in their thanks. Perón, sensing an opportunity, asked to be made head of the national labour department. In October 1943 he got his wish. He then launched a charm offensive aimed at organised labour. He enforced laws regarding paid holidays, sick leave, pensions and minimum wages. He pressured factory owners to negotiate in response to strikes. He spoke to the unions at mass rallies. He was introduced to the rail workers' union as 'Argentina's number one worker'. His timing was excellent. The Second World War had once again disrupted world trade, leading to another boom in Argentine industry. The country's workers were rising. Between 1941 and 1945, the number of unions nearly tripled.

Perón's flirtation with the unions soon began to annoy the Argentine rich. Leading industrialists produced a manifesto demanding a reversal of his policies; the Rural Society, an association of landlords, signed on. The military regime, by this point riven by infighting, decided Perón's ambition was more trouble than it was worth. On 9 October 1945, Perón was seized from his apartment and imprisoned on an island off Buenos Aires. He wrote a letter to his lover, Eva: 'My adorable treasure … From the day I left you, with the greatest grief imaginable, I have not been able to calm my anguished heart.' He promised to marry her upon his release.

And then, on the morning of 17 October 1945, a miracle of political mobilisation occurred. Vast crowds poured into the city centre from the industrial suburbs of Buenos Aires; they came from as far away as the slaughterhouses of La Plata. To prevent the influx, somebody raised the bridges over the fetid river that separated the city from its suburbs. The people crossed it on makeshift rafts; some even swam it, until the bridges were lowered again. Many had probably never been to the upmarket centre of Buenos Aires before. Famously, they took off their shoes and bathed their feet in the grand fountains. The crowd was estimated at between 300,000 and 500,000 people; some said as high as 1 million. To this day, no one knows how the rally was organised. Union leaders had proposed a general strike; but the strike was not supposed to occur until a day later. Perón claimed that Eva had rallied the workers, but most modern historians give that claim little credence. The political risk analyst Jill Hedges, author of a history of Argentina, speculates that the trigger for the rally may have been that morning's announcement of a temporary cabinet, which did not include anyone sympathetic to Perón.

The crowd demanded Perón be released. A few hours later, when the vast crowd showed no sign of leaving, the government gave in; but Perón, perhaps savouring his freedom, let the suspense build. At 10.30pm he at last appeared. 'Workers!' he shouted, and a huge cheer went up, lasting several minutes. Perón said he would 'put on civilian clothes and mix with that suffering, sweating mass which with its labour makes the greatness of the country'. More cheers. He continued, warming to his theme: 'I want now, as a simple citizen, mixing with this sweating mass, to press everyone against my heart as I could with my mother.' 'Hurrah for Perón's old lady!' someone yelled. The speech evolved into an extraordinary dialogue. Perón would say something; people would cheer, comment or yell out questions; Perón answered (he had a little trouble with the question about where he had been for the past few hours). Eventually, he asked for the singing of the national anthem, urged the crowd to return home peacefully, and declared – on whose authority is unclear – that everyone could take a day off work.

The military and landlords were not quite sure how to respond. The middle class was horrified by the invasion of central Buenos Aires; they called Perón's supporters *descamisados*, the 'shirtless ones' (apparently a reference to Victor Hugo's *Les Misérables*). A member of the middle-class Radical Party had a more colourful term for those who backed Perón: a 'zoological deluge'. But soon, the derision had been turned into a badge of honour; the workers began to call themselves *'descamisados'* as they built a struggle story around their unfair treatment by the landlord governments during the 'infamous' years. When elections were held, Perón won handily, with 52 cent of the vote, even though almost every other political party in Argentina banded together to oppose him (in one of history's more surreal cases of political expediency, the landlords' conservative party joined an alliance with the communists). The US Embassy called the polls the 'fairest in Argentine history'. Perón, on entering the presidential mansion, raced up the stairs and slid down the banister.

But the force that would turn Juan Perón into a legend was not this improbable victory. It was a woman. Back in October, after being released from prison, Perón had quietly married his sweetheart, Eva, known affectionately as 'Evita', just as he had promised.

Why do populists suddenly appear?

After the Second World War, populists vanished from most of the world, but not from Latin America. In Latin America, they came in waves. The heyday was the 1940s through the 1960s when the likes of Perón governed, or were the main opposition, in many countries. There were hints of a populist return in the 1970s (in Jamaica, for instance), but they did not really come back until the 1980s and 90s. Some arrived in a new guise – campaigning against elites but then, once in power, implementing market-oriented reform policies. Alberto Fujimori in Peru was one example. In the 2000s, yet another wave of left-populists emerged, including Hugo Chávez in Venezuela and Evo Morales in Bolivia.

Why was Latin America so plagued by populists? At one time, scholars assumed, as a matter of course, that extreme inequality of income and wealth was the root of the problem. Latin American countries topped the global inequality charts. Indeed, they still do – as of today, nearly half of the fifteen most unequal countries on earth are in Latin America (most of the rest are in Africa). In the 1980s, however, it became clear that the presumed link between inequality and populism was not as strong as suspected. Parties of the populist right began to do well in Western Europe, in countries that were egalitarian and had well-developed social welfare states, including the Netherlands, Sweden and Finland. Scholars began to conduct statistical tests of the link between inequality and populism, and usually found no relationship. The upset votes of 2016 confirmed these findings: surveys of British voters, for instance, showed that those more concerned about inequality were more likely to vote Remain.

So why do populists appear? The answer to that question is still hotly debated, but there is broad agreement that both supply and demand are important. On the supply side are considerations such as the structure of the political system and the strength of populist parties. The key questions here are: how much opportunity does the system offer for populists to enter politics, and how effective are current populist parties? (Much like the 'opportunity' and 'people power' factors we looked at in chapter 2 as determinants of social movement success.) On the demand side is the question of how much voters want a populist leader or party. Here, factors such as economic crises that discredit establishment parties and a lack of trust in government play a role.

While there are lots of contradictory findings on populism, one point is fairly well accepted: like inequality, personal economic distress does not do much to increase populist support. In 2016, for instance, people who voted populist were, in most cases, voting on issues of policy, culture or values (especially immigration), rather than economic concerns. In a way, that is unsurprising: as we have seen, personal economic distress does not usually cause people to mobilise; nor does it seem to have a large impact on voting choices (when the economy turns down, voters punish the government's incompetence at managing the national economy rather than voting with their wallets).

That said, the economic distress of *communities* appears to have provided a large boost for populists. In recent years, studies have found that higher unemployment, lower income growth and greater exposure to globalisation in a voter's home county, province or region tend to correlate with voting populist (both right and left). US counties that suffered more 'deaths of despair' (premature deaths due to opioid use, for instance) tended to be more likely to vote populist. One particularly influential study showed that in US regions where more jobs had been lost to competition from Chinese imports, more voters supported populist Tea Party candidates. Similar results have been obtained for the Brexit vote, as well as votes for populist parties in Europe. Again, these findings match with what we have already seen: political actions tend to be *group* actions, and political reactions tend to be reactions to the treatment of groups. Some people in these communities were doing well; others were doing badly. Whatever their personal circumstances, it appears they were more likely to vote populist if the area where they lived (and thus, presumably, the community with which they identified) was suffering economically.

As a rule of thumb, populists tend to do brilliantly with such aggrieved communities, because they often rely on mobilisation politics; that is, they rely on surges in political participation to take them to power. In Perón's case, he relied on the *descamisados*, Argentina's workers, and a rapid expansion in union membership, which helped to transform these workers from a weak crowd into a powerful mass movement. Perón and Evita also campaigned to extend the right to vote to women, and then encouraged these women to come to the polls. Other Latin American populists reduced the voting age to sixteen, eliminated literacy requirements or made voting mandatory – in each case mobilising new segments of the public to participate in politics; relying on habitual non-voters to keep them in office – just as the Brexit campaign relied on former non-voters to sway the referendum outcome.

Juan Perón has been called the 'purest' populist of all time. As we saw in chapter 1, populism is unusual among political ideologies in that it is 'thin-centred': it does not say much about policy, but rather, campaigns for the people against the system. The purest populists, like Perón, deliver such a powerful critique of the system that they can all but ignore the left–right political spectrum. Perón once said: 'Peronism is not sectarian. Some say it is a centrist party: grave error. The centrist party, like that of the left or the right, is sectarian, and we are totally anti-sectarian.' It sounds like nonsense, but in Perón's case, it was true; he was able to pick up support not just from the unions but across the social classes, and eventually from both the far left and far right simultaneously. (The US ambassador to Argentina, profoundly confused, claimed that Perón was both a communist and fascist.)

Put like this, populism sounds great, at least as a winning strategy, so why doesn't every political leader become a populist, if it means gaining support from across the political spectrum? But populism

143

only works in certain circumstances (when many people distrust establishment politicians; when there are aggrieved communities to be mobilised). Moreover, there are costs. For instance, as a rule of thumb, populist administrations tend to be riven by infighting. Drawing support from groups with very different policy views has unfortunate consequences; essentially, one's own supporters may hate each other. Donald Trump's administration, for instance, combined pro-globalisation leaders with those bitterly opposed to free trade; it was never going to be an easy ride. Perón's government suffered from similar problems. He tried to put a brave face on things: 'I manage things best in a *quilombo* [whorehouse],' he said, a colloquial expression meaning a chaotic environment.

One last rule of thumb: populists tend to ignore established norms of political behaviour; for instance, they can be informal, direct and even obscene (or arrogant, like Thaksin). In a sense, their personal style becomes yet another critique of the political establishment they oppose. Perón's rhetoric was perhaps not as rude as Thaksin's, or as rule-breaking as Trump's tweets, but once in office, he did change the rules of Argentine politics: most notably, he began to live his personal life in public; and his extraordinary wife soon became a political power in her own right.

Evita

Evita was a fragile-looking beauty. Her skin was a porcelain white, perhaps partly because she suffered from anaemia. But she was no doll; she had struck out on her own at fifteen years of age, intending to make her way in Buenos Aires as an actress. She had the 'voice of a fishwife: raw and raspy, guttural, comfortable with slang and bad Spanish,' as one observer put it. She took an active interest in politics. During one heated discussion about a proposed government appointment, Evita surprised everyone by leaping in with her own opinion: 'he's a shit'. Later, her political opponents would publish a book denigrating her; but even the insults were tinged with awe. For instance: 'that strange woman was different than almost every other white woman. She was vehement, dominating, spectacular ... [with] a passion and courage unnatural in a woman.'

She was no great actress, but she did have presence. The United States strongly objected when she accepted an invitation from the Spanish dictator Franco to visit Spain. 'The gringos don't matter,' she said, and requested Franco join her in a publicity photograph: 'Won't gringo Truman be furious!' She turned the trip into the 'Rainbow Tour', a solo mission to Europe's great capitals, and became an international celebrity in the process. There was an awkward moment during a speech in Spain, in which she said: 'in Argentina we are trying to reduce the number of poor people and the number of rich people. You should do the same thing.' A noble thought, but not what Franco's Spain was about. On her return to Argentina, a huge crowd awaited her, as did Perón and his entire cabinet. As her ship docked, she struck a classic pose, leaning over the railing, tears streaming down her cheeks, waving a handkerchief.

Perón squeezed the landlords, redistributing wealth to industry. He established state monopolies over the purchase and export of grains and meat, and then grossly underpaid for the landlords' products. Rumours of coup plots swirled, but mobilisation of a rising social group kept him safe; the unions would bring huge crowds to the centre of Buenos Aires for rallies, reminding everyone of the October uprisings. The turnout was tremendous; the passion real. Perón was, after all, delivering the goods. Between 1943 and 1948, the real wages of Argentine industrial workers increased by almost 50 per cent; the wage share of national income rose by almost a quarter between 1946 and 1949. After the infamous decade, it was a remarkable transformation. The unions threw their support behind Perón, and he rewarded them. Between 1945 and 1951, labour union memberships increased by nearly a factor of six. Perón appointed union men to positions of power – to head the ministries of labour, of the interior, and the foreign ministry, for instance.

But it was perhaps Evita who did the most to deliver the nation to Perón. The Eva Perón foundation began operations in July 1948, and it was soon flush with cash. The country's trade union members were required to send contributions; the national lottery kicked in 20 per cent of its annual income. Soon, the foundation was building schools, public housing, hospitals and old age care homes. But when it built hospitals, it did not build charity hospitals, in the manner of, for instance, the Catholic Church. Rather, it built the kind of hospitals the rich of Buenos Aires might expect to enjoy, and then invited the poor to use them. It was, in a sense, wasteful, but Evita's point was that she was distributing dignity, not charity. Her slogan was: 'Perón fulfils, Evita dignifies'. In a stratified society, she empha-sised that everyone was born equal. One Peronist slogan, fanciful but lovely: 'In Argentina, the only privileged ones are the kids.'

While the landlord-backed governments of the infamous decade had generally been aloof, Perón and Evita lived their personal lives in public. The *New Yorker* magazine wrote: 'They are constantly, madly, passionately, nationally in love. They conduct their affairs with the people quite openly. They are the perfect lovers – generous, kind, and forever thoughtful in matters both great and small.' And indeed, no matter was too small for their consideration. Evita held court every day in the ministry of labour, receiving the poor who journeyed to Buenos Aires. They emerged telling stories of the things they had received: a sewing machine to start a home business; medicines; a house; a job; medical treatment; a football or bicycle for a child. Evita conducted these sessions well into the night. Having been raised poor, she was comfortable with the poor; she famously embraced and kissed a woman on the lips who had a syphilitic sore on her face. She said she wanted to be a 'bridge of love' between the *descamisados* and Perón.

The Argentine public returned that love, to an almost frightening degree. Juan Perón, in later years, seemed to struggle with her popularity. 'I took care of the nation,' he wrote, 'Eva, of the personal problems of its inhabitants. With her, with Eva, there was direct contact with the people. For that reason, maybe, some remember her more.' Evita, for her part, always backed Perón without hesitation. Her letters pledged devotion with almost uncomfortable intensity. In one, she wrote, 'I live in you, feel for you, think through you.'

In 1951, after some fiddling with the Constitution, Perón would be up for re-election. Somebody, probably not the Peróns, suggested that Evita should become the nation's vice president. The labour unions arranged an open forum for 22 August to promote the idea. Perón agreed to join, probably thinking it a wonderful lark and moreover good publicity. To his surprise, some 2 million people turned up, and it soon became clear that they genuinely wanted Evita to take office and that the situation was out of control. Perón had no intention of sharing power with his wife, and at first came on stage without her. But audience members insisted she appear. Soon, Evita walked out, to approving roars. She gave a speech, presumably off the cuff, passionate and violent. She decried the 'landed oligarchy', she called herself a 'humble woman'. Perón attempted to end the show. Someone called out that Evita must accept the vice-presidential nomination then and there; the crowd roared its approval. Evita, taken by surprise, struggled back to the microphone: 'Give me four days to think about it,' she said. 'No, no, no,' the crowd chanted. 'I do not renounce my place in the struggle. I renounce the honours,' she said. The chants again: 'No, no, no.' 'Comrades ... comrades ... I will do what people say.' With that, the crowd at last began to drift away. Many people clearly thought she had accepted the nomination. The next day at least one newspaper headline said so as well.

On 31 August, Evita appeared on the radio, announcing she

could not stand. She had no choice: she had discovered that she was gravely ill with cancer. Hence the potentially controversial question of her political role was put to rest. 'When they write the marvellous chapter that history will surely dedicate to Perón,' she said, she hoped it would note 'that there was at his side a woman who dedicated herself to bring to the president the hopes of the people, and that the people lovingly called that woman Evita.' In the election, Perón carried 64 per cent of the vote, a crushing victory. A lot of that victory was down to Evita: with her help, Perón's winning percentage was even higher among women, who had for the first time gained the right to vote. The Peronist party won complete control over both houses of the legislature.

Evita's speeches of October 1951 have entered Argentine national legend. 'My *descamisados* … take care of the general, be loyal to Perón as you are now,' she said. It soon became clear she was saying goodbye. People in the audience began to cry. 'I ask of you today comrades only one thing: that we will swear publicly to defend Perón and fight to the death. Our oath will be to shout for a minute … "my life for Perón!"' The people shouted the slogan. Evita broke down in tears; people in the crowd were openly sobbing. Even Perón lost his composure. Evita appeared for the last time in public on May Day of the following year. She was thirty-three years old; her weight had shrunk to about eighty-one pounds; Perón had to support her. Her speech was violent: 'the people will follow Perón against the pressure of traitors from within and without,' she said. 'Dead or alive I will go forth with the *descamisados* of the Fatherland, and we won't leave standing a single brick that is not Peronist … We will go out and take justice into our own hands.' Evita's anger was, in a sense, justified; there had been coup plots. Evita proposed arming the workers, taking a page from Lenin's book. Perón demurred.

In late July 1952, Evita fell into a coma and died. During the funeral procession, some 17,000 soldiers were required to hold back the crowds. More than 65,000 people visited every day that she lay in state; one or two had to be forcibly dissuaded from committing suicide next to her body. Perón stood next to the coffin for hours, his expression glazed. Heaps of flowers threatened to cover the entrance to the building, and still the people brought more.

In the year that followed, Perón attempted to keep the Evita phenomenon alive. Evita's autobiography was added to the school curriculum. At first, Perón tried to receive supplicants from the poor as Evita had. Despite the perennial smile, he was no good at it. When letters would arrive for Evita, the government would reply, as if from Evita herself: 'I'm in heaven with the angels. I tell them every day about the *descamisados.*' Even more surreally, Perón's desperation to keep Evita alive took physical form: he had her body embalmed, preserved with various chemicals, 'solidifying agents' and transparent plastic.

The resurrection

But without Evita, Perón lost some of his magic. The economy crashed; there were corruption scandals; the labour wing of the Peronist party battled against the political wing which in turn battled against the women's branch. Some of his rallies descended into violence. In one case, Peronist thugs attacked both the socialist party headquarters and the elite Jockey Club, hacking original paintings by Goya out of their frames and burning them, and plundering the wine cellar – fortunately not so well-stocked as that of the Russian czar. Soon, attendance at Perón's rallies began to dwindle. That made him vulnerable; his power had always depended, to some degree, on mobilisation. Perón began to develop unusual hobbies. An athletics camp for teenage girls was opened on a corner of his estate, and he took an unhealthy interest in the proceedings, attempting to teach the girls fencing. Some men might have been ashamed of such behaviour; Perón would ride through the nearby towns on his motorcycle with a gaggle of teenage girls following behind on their bicycles. (Perhaps he was trying to maintain the inexplicable link between great revolutionaries and girls' schools.)

In 1954, Perón's opponents struck. Naval warplanes bombed a Peronist rally held in front of the presidential palace. Their apparent goal was to assassinate Perón, and the first bombs came close, hitting the greenhouse on the palace roof. Mostly, though, the bombs hit the rally: some 355 people were killed and perhaps 600 wounded, but Perón was not among them. In response, right-wing ultranationalists who supported Perón led an attack on Catholic churches; roughly a dozen were burned. In September 1955, there was another coup attempt. Troops from the artillery school attacked and surrounded the loyalist infantry school in Córdoba; the navy took control of the southern ports. Perón quickly capitulated. Some said his forces could have carried the day, but, like the Iranian Shah, Perón seemed somehow distracted. At the time, he appeared tremendously upset about the risk that some newly built oil refineries would be shelled during the conflict. He fled into exile via a Paraguayan gunboat on the River Plate.

The coup architects inherited a number of problems. The most extraordinary of these was Evita's embalmed body. They put her in a crate marked 'radio equipment' and shipped the box around the country. Wherever it came to rest, flowers and candles would mysteriously appear. Presumably it was a harmless gesture by people in the army's rank-and-file; but gossips began to wonder if something more mystical was happening. Reportedly, a jumpy guard shot his own wife when she visited him unexpectedly in the middle of the night; he had mistaken her for a Peronist, or perhaps a ghost. The generals decided enough was enough, shipped the body to Italy, and buried it under a fake name.

By 1955, Argentina's new rulers had decided to erase Perón from the memory of the nation. Anything with his name on it – parks, buildings, monuments – was renamed or torn down. The

Eva Perón foundation was closed. Perón's name was crossed out of textbooks; later, new histories were written, and Perón and Evita were absent from them. It was made a crime to use Perón's name or likeness in public. Newspapers were reduced to calling him 'the fugitive tyrant'. Schools and hospitals Evita had built were destroyed, a pointlessly vindictive gesture. The presidential residence, one of the oldest stately homes in Buenos Aires, was also demolished.

In exile, the fugitive tyrant lived in a succession of Latin American and European countries while engaging in various hijinks. In Paraguay, he entertained a journalist by pulling out his dentures ('Everybody praises my smile, without imagining I can remove it with one hand'); in Panama, he picked up a nightclub dancer, twenty-four years old; in Spain, he took up yoga. The actress Ava Gardner, who lived in the same building in Madrid, sometimes stopped by for snacks (Perón's young girlfriend – by this time, wife – cooked a mean empanada). He also made unsuccessful attempts to sneak back into Argentina. Emerging from the boot of a Seat 1500, where he had been concealed during one of these attempts, his first words were: 'son of a bitch, what an uncomfortable way to travel!'

Eventually, the Argentine government tried to restart the policies of the infamous decade. The coup had strong landlord backing; their apparent objective was once again to suppress heavy industry and promote agriculture. By some calculations, the wage share of Argentina's national income fell by a quarter between the mid-1950s and 1960. The regime also suppressed public education. During the 1960s and 70s, only about half of Argentina's school-age population completed primary school – a return to the level of five decades before; national decline had set in in earnest. It was a brutal policy, but not an illogical policy – if one wished to control people power, suppressing education was one way to go about it. There were even some spurts of economic growth, especially in the city of Córdoba, which, because of plummeting workers' wages, became a cheap place to base foreign manufacturing operations. There can be upsides to decline.

By the end of the 1960s, the military ruled Argentina directly. Congress was closed and political parties were banned. Seeking to gain religious legitimacy, the regime embraced conservative Catholicism, forbidding miniskirts and long hair for men. Many Argentines had had enough, and wanted to bring Perón back. But the Perón whom they conjured in their imagination was not as he had been. For some Argentines, he was reimagined as hard left; essentially, a communist. A 'Peronist' guerrilla resistance movement sprang up. As in Iran, most of the guerrillas were members of the intelligentsia, and their initial efforts to start a guerrilla war failed badly, in part because the educated middle classes had no idea how to live off the land. Like the guerrillas in Iran, they turned to urban terror campaigns instead.

Meanwhile, in exile, Perón underwent a resurrection of his own, in a manner of speaking. On a trip to Argentina, Perón's new wife met a man by the name of Lopez Rega. Lopez Rega was an unearthly character – his skin a shade too pale, his eyes a bit too blue – with a long, thin nose and prominent cheekbones. He had authored several books on an occult religion called 'spiritism'. He followed Isabel, Perón's wife, back to Spain and somehow managed to worm his way into the inner circle. Lopez Rega believed that via a combination of ritual practices and an odd exercise regime, he could keep Perón alive. Perón, by this point, needed constant medical attention, and within a few months Lopez Rega had become, in essence, Perón's nurse. Eventually, to curry favour with Perón, the military regime owned up to where they had hidden Evita's body. Lopez Rega demanded that instead of reburying it, the embalmed corpse should be installed in Perón's house in Spain.

By this point, Argentina had slipped into serious unrest, especially the city of Córdoba (with its rising industrial labour force).

Guerrillas continued their attacks. The hardline dictatorship was overthrown by an internal coup in 1970. Desperate to restore stability, the new regime announced that presidential elections would be held in 1973, and that Peronists would be allowed to take part. A halfhearted effort was made to exclude Perón himself, still in exile, from the contest. But Isabel and Lopez Rega turned up in Argentina to lay the groundwork for the great man's comeback. Eventually, the Peronists decided to run a surrogate by the name of Campora. There was little doubt who was actually running: 'Campora to government, Perón to power' was the official campaign slogan.

Perón, from exile, achieved an extraordinary victory. In addition to majorities in both houses of the legislature, the Peronists took nearly every provincial governorship. On 20 June 1973 he finally returned to Argentina. As usual, it was a triumph of mobilisation; some 3 million people – perhaps ten per cent of the national population – made the pilgrimage to the airport. The fugitive tyrant was astonishingly vital, despite his age. It was almost as if Lopez Rega, the warlock, really had brought him back to life. But as is so often the case in such scenarios, the reanimated figure was not quite the person he had been. Many Argentines now imagined Perón as a figure of the far left; in reality, perhaps under Lopez Rega's influence, Perón was increasingly drifting to the right. Lopez Rega created a right-wing death squad known as the Argentine Anti-Communist Alliance to serve the Peronist administration. At the welcoming rally, members of the far-left Peronist Youth attempted to take up positions near Perón. Lopez Rega's death squad opened fire on them. More than ten people died, and hundreds were wounded. (A hazard of the populist strategy of drawing support from mobilised social groups with disparate views.)

New elections were called. Isabel was announced as Perón's vice-presidential candidate, fulfilling the role that should have been Evita's. Perón won the election with over 60 per cent of the vote.

He continued to gain support from both the far left and far right; even some members of the conservative establishment backed him, as the nation's only hope of achieving social peace. Asked by a journalist to name the various political forces in Argentina, Perón rattled off the main parties, but, mysteriously, left his own party off the list. When the journalist asked why, he said: 'but we are all Peronists!' Which had a grain of truth.

Miraculously, the inauguration went off smoothly. There was even an economic recovery, fuelled by high global commodity prices. Perón implemented some mildly redistributive policies. But Lopez Rega's right-wing death squad became increasingly active, targeting leftists and even leftist sympathisers. Perón was by this point almost never seen without Lopez Rega by his side. He passed draconian anti-subversion laws, which implied serious conse- quences for even non-violent dissent. When Perón addressed the crowds at the traditional Labour Day rally, the Peronists chanted: 'What's happening, general, why is the people's government full of gorillas?' Perón called them 'useful idiots'. To be fair, he had always been anti-communist; and in his absence, many of his supporters – especially those too young to remember him – had arguably become more communist than not.

And then, on 1 July 1974, Perón died of a heart attack. Lopez Rega rose to the occasion, making repeated attempts to force Perón's soul to return to his body. Apparently, he really did believe he had been keeping the president alive. As Perón lay dead, Lopez Rega gripped his ankles, and was heard to mumble: 'I can't do it … I can't … For ten years I did it, but now I can't …'

On populist economics

In 1990, two economists, Rudiger Dornbusch and Sebastian Edwards, made a remarkable appeal to the next wave of Latin American populists. Populist governments, they said, seemed to be stuck on the same bad economic script. They spent too much, which led to runaway inflation, which the populists tried to manage via price controls, which only, over time, made things worse. In the well-meaning but patronising manner that economists usually adopt when speaking to non-economists, they wrote: 'we do not doubt the sincerity of the policymakers who embark on these programs, and we share their conviction that income distribution is unacceptably unequal'. But 'populist policies do ultimately fail; and when they fail it is always at a frightening cost to the very groups who were supposed to be favored'. Juan Perón was a classic example. During his first term, he managed to share the wealth in Argentina, but his successes were short-lived. Soon, inflation spiralled out of control and, between 1948 and 1952, the purchasing power of workers' wages plummeted by some 20 per cent, hurting the very groups Perón had intended to help.

In truth, so-called 'populist policies' do not have much to do with populist ideology (railing against elites and the broken system). Nonetheless, the term fits often enough that it remains in common use. Indeed, some dictionary definitions of populism include 'disregard for future consequences of policies', or words to that effect. Since populists, by definition, campaign against elites, when there are policies the entire political establishment does not like, there is often a populist to be found behind those policies. As the political theorist Francis Fukuyama put it: '"populism" is the label that political elites attach to policies supported by ordinary citizens that they don't like'.

The economic policy choices that Dornbusch and Edwards labelled as 'populist' appear to correlate strongly with income and wealth inequality. Historically, countries with higher levels of income inequality have tended to do the following: run higher government budget deficits; end up with larger government debts; default on these debts more frequently; and, under certain circumstances, run higher rates of inflation. Economists have tried to puzzle out why these relationships between inequality and overspending exist. After all, Latin American voters have repeatedly elected populists, even though their policies did not deliver the promised benefits. At first, it was assumed that the poor were economically illiterate, and repeatedly fooled by charismatic, smooth-talking candidates. But really, this assumption did not fit the data very well. There was a new wave of theories, most notably a school of thought called the 'new political macroeconomics'. According to this school of thought, governments in unequal countries were making an effort to be responsible, but that effort was going awry.

Indeed, it turned out that countries such as Argentina were not, in fact, spending too much; rather, they were taxing too little. Consider a rather surprising comparison between modern-day Latin America and Western Europe. Today, Denmark, Finland, Ireland and Portugal are as unequal as Argentina – *before* taxes and government spending are considered. But these Western European governments spend so much public money on the poor (for instance, via public support for education and healthcare) that after-tax incomes in these countries end up being less unequal than in Argentina. So Argentina is not unusual in its level of spending. Indeed, compared to Europe, it is spending relatively little. Rather, what causes Argentina's policies to end up creating debt or inflation is the country's failure to match its increased spending with increased taxes. Again, consider the situation in the modern day: average personal tax rates in Latin America are around 29 per cent; in Western Europe, they are roughly 45 per cent.

It is not entirely clear why highly unequal Latin American countries fail to tax when they spend. One of the most influential explanations suggests that there is a political contest between the rich and poor; the rich, who have more political clout than the poor, elect to put up with inflation rather than being taxed. In essence, in highly unequal countries, leaders often attempt to share the wealth of the rich with the average Joe. But they only make it halfway:

they are able to spend more, but the poor have to put up with the burden of higher government debt and inflation.

Actually, although Dornbusch and Edwards were focused on populists, in unequal countries, many kinds of governments – populist, conservative, left or right – tend to follow these types of policies. The Shah of Iran did so in the 1960s and 70s, until his price controls alienated the *bazaar* merchants. The military regime that ousted Perón, ironically enough, doubled down on populist economics, increasing the budget deficit by 140 per cent in a single year. This approach was taken to even greater extremes during Perón's second coming (and his wife's brief government). By the mid-1970s, the Argentine government was printing money to finance the deficit. Inflation turned into 'hyperinflation' – reaching an annual rate of 500 per cent.

Following Perón's death, Lopez Rega was chased out of Argentina. Perón's wife briefly left the country as well, but then returned and managed to govern the country for about six months. In March 1976, the military launched yet another coup. The new military regime that took power turned heavily to repression as a means of social control; it turned the word 'disappear' into a verb. At least 8,900 people were 'disappeared'; some estimates ran as high as 30,000. At first, mostly leftists, guerrillas, trade union leaders and Peronist party members disappeared. After that, members of the Peronist youth (which was believed to have supported the guerrillas); followed by just about anyone who opposed the regime. For a time, the military government claimed that these people were imprisoned in secret facilities. Eventually, it became clear it had killed nearly all of them. Argentines call this era the 'tragic years'.

The military regime lasted until 1982, when it demonstrated its incompetence by bungling an effort to seize the Falkland Islands (in Argentina: Islas Malvinas) from Britain. When the military government fell, Argentines elected the middle-class Radical Party to power on a programme of peace and reconciliation. The country's new democratic government set about this programme with admirable vigour; the first item of business when democracy was restored was legislation to ban torture.

It's OK to cry for Argentina

'Don't cry for me Argentina,' Madonna sang, in the musical version of Evita's life story. Crying for Argentina, on the other hand, is perfectly acceptable. Even under democracy Argentina's by now extreme political polarisation lingered. The middle-class Radical government eventually pursued so-called populist economics with a passion Perón had never dreamed of. By 1985, annual rates of inflation exceeded 1,000 per cent; by 1989, 4,900 per cent. In restaurants, prices were written on blackboards instead of menus and altered hourly. In grocery stores, there were no prices at all; one just turned up at the till and discovered what things cost. At foreign-exchange counters, an employee would sit with a phone pressed to his ear, turning a crank that showed the current exchange rate on a display like a taxi meter. One could watch the value of the peso fall in real time. On utility bills, the amount due was shown on multiple dates, anticipating the inflation that would have occurred by the time the check went through the mail. It was ridiculous, but also painful. Argentines wrote angry letters to their president. 'You have forgotten about the workers and the pensioners! We are hungry!' one pensioner wrote (for people trying to live on their savings, hyperinflation was a nightmare). Other letters registered bewildered disappointment. 'Though I still think and believe that this [democracy] is the best system of government, we have reached a desperate situation, Mr President,' wrote a woman named Maria Luisa. 'How can you live if you cannot buy the necessities of life?'

At a loss to explain what had happened to their country, many Argentines began to blame themselves. 'The corruption is in our hearts,' a Buenos Aires psychoanalyst told the sociologist Sara Muir. 'In all our relationships we are corrupt ... We have the politicians we deserve.' A soup kitchen worker explained: 'We, the middle class, almost don't exist today.' And yet, she continued: 'But don't pity us. We're the corrupt ones ... We're not a moral people.' When the Argentine footballer Maradona confessed to his handball against England on television, it provoked a national debate. A small-business owner put it this way: 'Maradona's confession gave us the opportunity to talk about something we all know, but which we don't always want to say – the profound corruption of this nation, something we're both proud of and ashamed of.' Perhaps corruption had brought their nation to ruin. But maybe it was worth it to win the World Cup.

There is a word in Argentine Spanish, *chanta*, which means something like a charlatan or a confidence man. The *chanta* is despised, but also admired. Ever since Perón, Argentines have come to expect that their political leaders will be, in some respects, *chantas*. The populist president who took office in 1989, Carlos Menem, fitted the bill. He campaigned as a leftist, and then in office leapt to the other side of the ideological spectrum (in fine populist style). His government privatised; it followed orthodox economic policy; it adopted an economic approach to the United States Menem described as 'carnal relations'. For a time, these new policies seemed to work. But the Argentine government was still taxing too little to match its levels of spending; it was still pursuing populist economics. Instead of printing money, the government borrowed, and the debt doubled from \$62bn to \$127bn over a decade. In 2001, Argentina defaulted on these debts – the largest sovereign default in history (at that time), producing four years of recession; in essence, a great depression.

On the Argentine standoff

Of course, Argentina's fundamental problem was not corruption. Was Argentina more corrupt than Chile, which is now richer? Or Brazil? Rather, Argentina's problem was that its leaders had been faced with hard choices. One reason Argentina's leaders made the choices they did was that the country's politics had become so polarised. Political leaders, especially on the right, were willing to sacrifice economic progress to sap the strength of the opposition (particularly the unions). Probably, mobilisation politics and populism contributed to this polarisation, by undermining the centrist tendencies of democracy. Regardless of the cause, these hard choices were not stupid mistakes; they were, in many cases, deliberate choices, sometimes with catchy slogans attached ('industrialisation without industrial revolution'). Indeed, to this day, some Argentines might argue they were the right choices. Who is to say that if Perón had been allowed to govern unopposed, the country's situation might not have been even worse?

But it is possible that there is also something more fundamentally wrong with Argentina; something that goes deeper than Perón's politics. More than 2,000 years ago, Aristotle contended that democracy could not survive in societies that were highly unequal: 'Where some possess very many things and others nothing, either [rule of] the people in its extreme form must come into being, or unmixed oligarchy', or 'tyranny ... not of free persons but of slaves and masters, the former consumed by envy, the latter by contempt'. The classic modern works on democracy sound similar notes. For instance, Alexis de Tocqueville, the great nineteenth-century observer of American democracy: 'when the rich govern alone, the interest of the poor is always in peril; and when the poor make the law, that of the rich run great risks'. Or, more recently, Samuel Huntington, writing in the early 1990s: 'Democracy is premised, in some measure, on majority rule, and democracy is difficult in a situation of concentrated inequalities in which a large, impoverished majority confronts a small, wealthy oligarchy.'

Recently, the economist team of Daron Acemoglu and James Robinson, and the political scientist Carles Boix (working independently), have brought such insights into the world of statistics and formal models. One of the cases that Acemoglu and Robinson looked at is Argentina. Argentina's distribution of wealth was highly unequal – particularly the distribution of land. A series of accidents, some of them perhaps rather intentional, fostered the growth of enormous estates on the *pampas*. In 1826, for instance, an ill-conceived government policy resulted in 538 lucky individuals, most of them already wealthy, receiving more than 30,000 square miles in land, paying a modest 5,000 pesos in rent to the state for the privilege. Following a final push to force Native Americans on to reservations, those who financed the military campaign awarded themselves much of the spoils – again, about 30,000 square miles – by transferring that land to only 400 landowners. By 1914, 584 truly gargantuan landholdings accounted for almost *one-fifth* of the vast *pampas* plain.

Of course, winning political parties in democracies tend to pander to that dull but highly influential citizen, the median voter. The resulting centrist tendency usually helps to uphold the status quo. In a relatively egalitarian country, the average Joe would be middle class and arguably uninterested in inequality as a political issue. But in a highly unequal society, the average Joe will be poor, or at least feel poor, in comparison to the rich. Hence under democracy, it is possible that some political party will come along with the idea of redistributing that wealth to the average Joe – perhaps via more generous tax-funded pensions or unemployment benefits; perhaps more elaborate public services such as education, healthcare or infrastructure. Actually, when authoritarian regimes become democracies, that kind of wealth sharing tends to happen fairly reliably. Boix cites the case of Spain. Under Franco's dictatorship, Spain's tax revenues amounted to about 23 per cent of total economic output. When Spain became a democracy, tax revenues quickly climbed to 33 per cent of output. If the average Jo is poor but her country is rich, some politician is likely to hit on sharing the wealth as a vote-winning platform.

So far, so innocuous (although possibly distressing to readers of a conservative disposition). But the alarming implication of this line of reasoning is that in extremely unequal countries, the rich may feel they would be better off in the absence of democracy. Indeed, Acemoglu and Robinson point out that if one looks at history, countries tended to struggle quite openly with this problem. Initially, many countries provided democracy only to the rich; in the 1700s and 1800s, in many democratic countries, only men with property could vote. In the UK of the 1700s, for instance, membership of the House of Lords was confined to the clergy and aristocracy, and selection of candidates for the House of Commons was, in effect, controlled by either leading landowners or aristocrats.

The framers of the US Constitution had frank debates on this issue. As one delegate to the Constitutional Convention put it: the US Senate should 'consist of the most distinguished characters, distinguished for their rank in life and their weight of property' to 'establish a balance that will check the Democracy'. Otherwise, the poor might vote for a candidate who would share the wealth. Others pointed to a different problem: 'give the votes to the people who have no property, and they will sell them to the rich'. (As we have seen, a justifiable fear in unequal societies like Thailand.) Ultimately, though, these arguments failed to carry the day, because America – with no history of aristocracy – was relatively egalitarian. Property was 'pretty equally divided,' said Alexander Hamilton, so universal suffrage would not lead to class warfare. Noah Webster, famous as the author of the first American dictionary, noted that the United States had 'small inequalities of property'. They were right. One recent estimate suggests that in 1774, the top 1 per cent of Americans earned roughly 9 per cent of the nation's total income. In 2012, the figure was 19 per cent. In other words, *even when slaves are included*, the America of 1774 was far less unequal than it is today.

So the United States was at little risk (at least in the 1700s). But consider what happens if a highly unequal country does somehow become a fully-fledged democracy, where the poor can vote; or if a democratic country somehow becomes highly unequal. There is a possibility, admittedly a theoretical one, that the rich will turn against democracy. (And not only the super-rich: the educated, urban middle classes can turn against democracy, as we saw in Thailand.) Samuel Huntington reviewed ten coups and coup attempts that occurred in newly democratised countries in the 1970s and 1980s. He noted that successful coups were not simply the work of power-hungry generals; they almost always had outside support. As one former president of Argentina noted, successful coups in his country, like the coups that deposed the armadillo and Perón, 'have always been civilian-military in character'. Hence if there are a lot of wealthy people, sitting on the porches of their ranching estates, sipping *café con leche*, and thinking about how the infamous decade was not really all that infamous, it can be a dangerous thing.

It is far from certain that inequality will undermine democracy. The rich (and educated middle classes) might be strongly committed to democracy, or worry that an authoritarian regime could be badly run. The average Joe might believe that one day he will be rich himself, and prefer low taxes in anticipation of his future life of indolence and excess. Or he might have read his Russian history, and realise that communism does not always produce utopia. Or he might believe that lower taxes will deliver higher rates of economic growth.

And yet: in recent times, struggles over whether to share the wealth have been a key reason for democratic failures. Stephan Haggard and Robert Kaufman decided to dig through every case of a failure of democracy in the world between 1980 and 2008. As there are a bit more than a hundred such cases, the task is monumental but manageable. They found that in about 35–55 per cent of the cases (some were hard to classify), a conflict over redistribution of the country's wealth appeared to be at least partly to blame. In about 25–40 per cent of the cases, democracy was overthrown after some political movement threatened to tax the rich too aggressively, and the rich turned against democracy. In about 10–15 per cent of the cases, democracy was overthrown when a dictator took power on a pledge to seize money from the rich and give it to the poor.

It is a little ironic. The iron law of milquetoast politics can cause democracy to collapse, because the milquetoast thing to do is to soak the rich. The risk is probably a lot higher when people believe their country is very wealthy; it is probably higher still when people believe their country is very wealthy and their own incomes are unlikely to grow in the future. These conditions are probably a fair description of Argentina during its years of relative decline. Arguably, these conditions hold in the US and UK today.

One might call it the 'Argentine standoff', in honour of the so-called Mexican standoff, that scenario, beloved of Hollywood, in which the protagonists face each other at point blank range, pistols loaded. Hollywood cannot get enough of the standoff, because of the dramatic potential: there is no way to win, and no way to escape. In highly unequal democracies, something like this standoff can ensue. The rich and their money, and the average Joe with his vote, are stuck in the same country together. Ultimately, the rich know that some leader is likely to come along and pander to Joe's redistributionist interests; and Joe knows that eventually, at least some rich people may well throw their considerable influence behind an effort to roll back democracy.

The only question, really, is who shoots first.

Actually, there is one more question: when will they stop

shooting each other? In Argentina's case, they kept at it for some seventy years, by which time one of the world's richest democracies had become a middle-income country.

An American standoff?

Argentina has gifted the world an extraordinary cast of characters. Juan Perón, the purest of all populists; Lopez Rega, the Latin Rasputin; and of course Evita, whose life inspired a Broadway musical – and whose politics remains much-imitated to this day. (If you would like to imitate Evita yourself, the political risk analyst Hedges has recently published the first authoritative biography of her in English.) What was so remarkable about Evita? In effect, she made stone soup. She took money from ordinary people – workers' contributions and lottery tickets were among the main funding sources for the Eva Perón foundation – and gave that money to other ordinary people, and made everyone feel good in the process. From an economist's perspective, Evita's popularity was a little puzzling. From most people's perspective, however, economists are a little puzzling, and are also nerds.

But let me attempt an economist's explanation. Fans of Daniel Kahneman will know that people give drastically too much weight to events they can vividly imagine. The classic example is terrorism, which is so frequently and dramatically covered in the media that people tend to overestimate the risks. Evita, with her charisma and personal touch (reinforced by constant media coverage), infused sharing the wealth with human drama. Perhaps her charity was less impactful than, say, a modest increase in income tax. But to Argentines, who heard extraordinary stories of her generosity every day, it almost certainly felt like she was giving much, much more. 'I left my dreams by the wayside in order to watch over the dreams of others,' Evita said. 'I exhausted my physical forces … My soul knows it, my body has felt it.' Only the heartless could have disagreed.

Lots of politicians attempt this feat. Thaksin had a reality television programme that featured him wandering around a rural Thai village, ending poverty one villager at a time. Banharn, with his signboards and ceremonies, arguably did better at playing Evita, turning public spending into acts of personal generosity. Even Donald Trump had a little bit of Evita in him, with his tweets about saving jobs at individual factories. Job growth numbers would be more interesting, but probably only to economists.

What readers may most want to know, however, is the status of another of Argentina's gifts to world history: the standoff. After all, both the US and UK are highly unequal by international standards (and in comparison with their own recent history). In fact, by some measures, the United States today is slightly *more* unequal than Argentina when everything fell apart. Are we already in an Argentine standoff, with guns locked and loaded?

The good news first: the scholars who came up with the Argentine standoff theory do not think it applies. Acemoglu and Robinson claim, for instance, that globalisation has weakened the interest groups, such as labour unions, that once led campaigns for redistribution. And if no one is leading campaigns for redistribution, the rich have no reason to oppose democracy.

But I am not entirely sure we are out of the woods. If a few billionaires were staring at the gold leaf on their ceilings and thinking idly about how nice it would be if the poor did not vote quite so much, that might be a dangerous thing, might it not?

The next chapter is about a time in the United States when something very much like that happened.

CHAPTER 5

The American non-revolution: how the status quo is saved

'Comes the revolution, we'll all have strawberries and cream.'
'But I don't like strawberries and cream!'
'Comes the revolution, you *will* like strawberries and cream.'

Ballyhoo of 1932

The drinks party

The Louisiana politician Huey Long was known for getting into trouble. During an evening of drunken carousing he had gone into a restroom at the Sands Point country club and emerged with a large bruise on his face. His explanations were even more ridiculous than the injury: he said he had been attacked by gangsters lurking in the toilets; that he had been in a bathroom brawl with three or four men; that an assailant, hired by the House of Morgan, had attempted to dispatch him as he relieved himself. One witness claimed later that Long had stealthily approached a man from behind at a urinal and attempted to urinate between his legs. One can see the comedic potential and why Long left with a black eye.

The incident made national headlines. Long was telegrammed a public offer to appear in a ten-round rematch in Chicago's Soldier Field; allegedly, another telegram offered $1,000 per night (about $18,500 today) if he would appear in a Coney Island freak show.

A few of his political enemies had a medal made up, intended for whoever had punched him; it was shaped, appropriately, like a toilet seat. A Princeton professor provided the requisite Latin inscription, *publico consilio pro re in camera gesta*, translating roughly as: 'by public acclaim for a deed done in private'.

A few years later, in July 1935, Long made a surprise announcement: he was going to introduce the 'favourite drink of New Orleans' to New Yorkers. The nation's news media assembled quickly. For good reason: even if it was not precisely news, it was guaranteed to be a spectacle. Things started promisingly, from the point of view of those hoping for scandal. Huey Long had flown up the bartender from his favourite Louisiana hotel bar. The bartender started with gin, and then added a drop or two of orange-flower water, some vanilla extract, heavy cream, an egg white and powdered sugar. He shook the concoction with ice for about ten minutes, then poured it into a glass, added a bit of seltzer, and a lovely white froth rose over the top. Long eyed the process greedily. At the time, he had been on a health kick, and had not had in a drink in over a year. The bartender passed Long the cocktail. Long took a sip. Perhaps a bit more than a sip. 'I think that's all right,' he said. 'Better'd be sure about it,' he said, and downed it. He ordered another. 'I'm merely sampling this to make sure you gentlemen are getting the real thing,' he said, slurring slightly. He ordered another. Soon, he had his arm around a member of the audience. He mocked President Franklin D. Roosevelt. 'Why don't they hold the Democratic convention and the communist convention together and save money?' he said. One hour and five drinks later he somewhat unsteadily held up yet another glass: 'and this is, gentlemen, my gift to New York'.

Somehow, he managed to carry off his drunken press conference without incident. The fact that it took more than ten minutes to make each drink (the 'Ramos gin fizz') probably saved him. But it was a high-risk stunt. Indeed, so high-risk that historians have felt the need to come up with conspiracy theories to explain why he did it. Harry T. Williams, author of a sympathetic biography of Huey Long, suggested it was an effort to distract the US Treasury Department from interfering with a pending sale of Louisiana bonds. But Long was often unable to resist a good bit of clowning. In his regular Louisiana radio show he would sing songs of his own composition and perform impromptu one-act plays featuring his political enemies as the villains. The black and white footage of Long left to us by history does not do justice to his riotous style of dress. A few typical outfits: a white suit, purple shirt, red flowered tie and two-tone wingtip shoes; a charcoal suit, polka dot tie and gigantic flower in his lapel; a brown tweed suit, red silk necktie and pink handkerchief in his pocket; a white suit, pink necktie and an orange handkerchief; a plaid suit, pink necktie and orchid shirt (that last to visit the US president).

There was a good reason for Huey Long's clowning. Much of the American establishment – politicians, businesses and the media – despised him. Hence the best way for him to get media coverage was to turn himself into a story. When he first ran for governor of Louisiana, none of the state's daily newspapers endorsed him. When he ran for US senator, the same. But when he made a fool of himself, the media could not get enough of him. One of Long's first appearances on the national stage involved a dispute over the proper way to eat the southern dish of potlikker (leftover juice after vegetables are boiled, usually eaten with hard 'cornpone' patties made from cornmeal, hot water and salt). Long had on many occasions loudly proclaimed the importance of eating potlikker by dunking the cornpone in it. The editor of the *Atlanta Constitution* wrote an editorial that, as usual, denounced Long, but wrapped up with the lighthearted aside that true southern sophisticates crumbled their cornpone into their potlikker rather than dunking. Huey Long responded by telegram, ignored the substance of the editorial, and instead offered an elaborate, mock-serious denunciation of cornpone crumbling. The editor took the bait. He published

Long's telegram, and wrote a response claiming Long was in fact a closet cornpone crumbler. Long replied indignantly that any crumbling he may have done in private was merely an effort to demonstrate the inferiority of the technique. Soon, the eating of potlikker had become a national mock-debate. The *Constitution* received more than 600 letters to the editor on the subject. The manners columnist Emily Post was asked her views. Franklin D. Roosevelt weighed in, suggesting that the issue be referred to the party platform committee of the Democratic national convention. An eighty-five-year-old veteran of the civil war contended that the ideal technique was decided by dental issues: 'does it not depend in a great measure if the users have two sets, upper and lower teeth?'

Huey Long may have played the clown, but he was not joking around. 'When the time comes I'm going to knock this idea that I'm a clown or monster into a cocked hat,' he said. He planned to run in the 1936 presidential election, and allegedly, he said that when he was elected, 'I'm going to abolish the electoral college, have universal suffrage, and I defy any sonofabitch to get me out under four terms.' His political opponents were not joking, either. President Franklin D. Roosevelt called him 'one of the two most dangerous men' in America. Roosevelt blamed the unsettled economy for Long's success. 'These are not normal times. The people are jumpy and ready to run after strange gods,' he said.

Huey Long was indeed dangerous. He became something close to a dictator in Louisiana, and his political movement looked very much like a rebellion. The tale of his ferocious rise in American politics offers a good many lessons for the modern day.

A log cabin home

For a populist politician, Huey Long had the perfect backstory: when he was born, in 1893, his family lived in a log cabin. The Longs lived in Winnfield, a small Louisiana town with mud-path streets, no electricity and no running water. It was not quite as hardscrabble as Long liked to tell it. The family home was one of the largest in Winnfield. Apparently, Huey Long's father, also called Huey Long, just liked log cabins. Long's mother, however, did not – too draughty – and they soon moved into a more traditional home constructed on the same piece of land.

More than anyone else in this book, Huey Long was a natural revolutionary. He started his first uprising in high school. 'We had formed a secret society, a sort of circle that was to run things,' he later recalled, which operated by 'laying down certain rules the students would have to follow. If they followed the faculty instead of our rules, we kept them off the baseball team, or the debating team.' Long's effort to seize control of the student body from the high school's teachers and staff did not amuse the administration, and he was expelled in 1910. Seeking revenge, Long somehow managed to beguile enough of the town's residents into signing a petition demanding that the principal be ousted, and he was duly forced to resign. Call it a draw. Long's father attempted to defend his son's actions: 'the teachers had it in for him; he dictated to them. They were a sorry bunch of teachers ... Huey always had trouble with them.' It apparently never crossed Long Senior's mind that the teachers, not the pupils, were supposed to be in charge.

On leaving school, Long started work as a travelling salesman. He was gifted, or perhaps alarmingly persuasive: when he was nineteen, the Faultless Starch company hired him to head up its division office in Memphis. The man who hired him, possibly having second thoughts after recovering from a spell of bewitchment, said later: 'he is the damnedest character I ever met. I don't know whether he is crazy or a genius.' Long also seemed to be powerfully, if arbitrarily, empathetic. His legal partners recalled that sometimes, hearing a client recite their troubles, Long would cry. He was seen, on multiple occasions, to empty his pockets, handing over all the cash he had on his person to random beggars on the street. From his earliest days, Long was on a mission. When the legal cases started flooding in, he turned down nearly all the lucrative corporate work, and eagerly pursued individual lawsuits. He defended penniless widows against wealthy banks, and sometimes won. Huey Long was going to fight for the people.

Which, in Louisiana, was going to be a challenge.

The feudal state of Louisiana

The end of slavery in Louisiana had resulted in less of a social transformation than one might have expected. In the parishes where plantation agriculture dominated (in Louisiana, counties are called 'parishes'), African-American farm labourers vastly outnumbered whites, but the whites owned nearly all the land. In the richest parish, Madison parish, for instance, only one out of fifty black families owned land. Most of these families were stuck in poverty, with little hope of social mobility. As late as 1880, several Louisiana parishes did not have a single public school. Eighty per cent of Louisiana's blacks were illiterate, against an average across US states of 57 per cent. Conditions for poor whites were also bad: indeed, Louisiana achieved the unwelcome distinction of being the only state in the union where the illiteracy rate among whites increased during the 1800s.

Why was public education so abysmal? Partly because the plantation owners who controlled state politics had exempted themselves from property tax. But mostly, it was an exercise in the weakening of the people power of the Louisiana public. This point was demonstrated when the US Congress, taking notice of the catastrophe in Louisiana education, began debating a bill that would have bailed out Louisiana's schools. Free money? Thanks, but no thanks, said the plantation owners. As one Louisiana legislator put it, with admirable clarity, 'the two worst things that ever happened are universal suffrage and universal education'. The

Daily Advocate newspaper was even more direct: 'the education of a bad citizen will increase his power for evil and make him a worse citizen'. (If 'evil' included rising up against the state's plantation caste, then yes.)

Understandably, many poor white Louisianans were unhappy with the situation, and black Louisianans even more so. 'It is certainly no crime to be colored, but is fearfully inconvenient,' as one editorialist in a black Louisiana newspaper put it. In the 1880s, there was a movement called 'Kansas Fever', in which African-Americans attempted simply to flee the state, usually bound for Kansas. Some 50,000 tried, but most were turned back by lack of funds or the interference of plantation owners who did not want to lose their labour force. An estimated 10,000 people escaped. Unbeknownst to them, many of the 10,000 people who had left continued to vote in Louisiana elections for many years thereafter – their votes fraudulently controlled by plantation owners. Not without cause, Huey Long described Louisiana as 'the feudal state of America'.

Then, in the 1890s, a populist wave swept America. A Populist Party presidential candidate won four states in the 1892 election; in the 1896 election, a populist-backed candidate by the name of William Jennings Bryan won more than twenty states, and delivered some of the most brilliant political speeches in US history ('you shall not press down upon the brow of labor this crown of thorns, you shall not crucify mankind upon a cross of gold'). In Louisiana, the populist wave brought about a phenomenon that struck terror into the hearts of the plantation elite: poor blacks and poor whites began to discover their common interests. Between 1890 and 1900, about fifty populist weekly newspapers saw print, in more than twenty-five parishes. Between 1894 and 1896, the unthinkable happened: poor blacks and poor whites came together in Populist Party political meetings. The plantation owners reacted quickly. By 1896, they had arranged for the passage of new electoral laws, which gave registrars immediate power to disqualify voters on flimsy pretexts. An article in the *Daily Advocate* proclaimed the laws 'death on niggers and the kind of Pops [populists] who will be inclined to vote [with them]'. In 1898, a new state constitution was pushed through, including a requirement that voters pass literacy tests or show possession of property in excess of $300 (roughly $8,800 today). Together, the laws threw roughly 95 per cent of Louisiana's African-American voters off the electoral rolls, as well as disenfranchising tens of thousands of poor white voters.

It was, for the plantation owners, a Faustian bargain. They had solved their immediate problem, but also given up one of the main levers they had used to control state politics. To over-simplify a complex system: in Louisiana, only whites were allowed to select political candidates, but the relative power of the various parishes during the selection process was determined by the total number of voters (including both whites and blacks) in each parish. Hence the plantation owners could exploit the huge numbers of African-American voters living in their parishes (in six plantation parishes on the Mississippi floodplain, for instance, less than 15 per cent of the population was white). The problem was, the new laws were so maliciously effective that the exploited black voters all but vanished: by 1906, only about 1.4 per cent of the state's African-American population was still registered to vote. The plantation owners still had some tricks up their sleeves, including electoral fraud. But the legacy of the populist threat was that Louisiana politics became a much more open contest among the state's white population.

All that remained was for someone to come along and take up this opportunity.

On the plantation problem

By the turn of the century, America had been a democracy for more than 100 years. So why was Louisiana still so feudal?

Long before the theory of the Argentine standoff was

contemplated, social scientists had realised that agricultural landlords tended to have anti-democratic tendencies. Barrington Moore's 1966 classic, *Social Origins of Dictatorship and Democracy*, claimed that in Germany and Japan unreconstructed feudal landlords were among the traditional conservatives who aided fascists in overthrowing democracy in the years before the Second World War. Samuel Huntington claimed that landlords were often involved in coups against democracy: 'In rural societies and in poor societies, coup-prone military officers could often find active support and cooperation amongst ... landowners and primary resource extractors.'

Over the years, there have been innumerable attempts to explain why plantation owners seem to dislike democracy so much. One explanation is that landlords sometimes rely on systems of forced labour – like slavery in the US South or serfdom in Russia – that are incompatible with democracy. No one is going to vote to be enslaved. Another explanation is that land is less easily damaged than factories or offices, so plantation owners may have a higher tolerance for ugly politics. If there is an occasional rebellion, which needs to be repressed bloodily, so be it.

But perhaps the most influential explanation has to do with the Argentine standoff. Namely: wealth based in land, because it is immobile, is easily taxable. As Adam Smith wrote: 'money [is] a much less proper subject of taxation [than] land ... land is a subject which cannot be removed, whereas stock easily may'. Hence the Argentine standoff is probably a lot more likely to occur in plantation economies. In general, few people fear the average Joe, an unassuming character of reliably mild interests. Except, that is, for landlords in unequal societies, who live in terror of Joe's milque-toast preferences. And thus have a nasty habit of trying to repress democracy.

Of course, in the modern day, most countries have long since moved past the point where agricultural plantations dominate the economy. That is very likely one reason that the Argentine standoff, while still a concern, appears to be far less detrimental to democracy than it once was.

But Louisiana still had a plantation problem. And Huey Long was determined to solve it.

Commissioner Long

In 1918, Huey Long gained his first political office – Louisiana state Railroad Commissioner. It was not, admittedly, a spectacular start. But Long would be the *people's* Railroad Commissioner. He forced one railroad to build a new depot at Monroe; another to build shelters outside a station at Reston; another to raise boarding platforms at Bayou Sara and Plattenburg; another to repair a cistern at Bordelonville. When the public showed a lack of interest in his railroad heroics, he took a side job as a newspaper stringer, and, whenever he did something noteworthy, filed an article about it.

It seemed that someone campaigning on the failure of Louisiana's government to serve its people could hardly lose. In 1920, Louisiana's illiteracy rate was three times the US average; schooling was segregated and there were only three black high schools in the entire state. In addition to defunding education, Louisiana's elite had refused to allow public spending on infrastructure, probably to avoid the associated tax burden. In the 1920s, Louisiana had less than 350 miles of paved roads. Driving from New Orleans to Baton Rouge was a five-hour ordeal, mostly on gravel; today, it takes about eighty minutes. The problem for any candidate hoping to make political hay out of these failings was that ordinary Louisianans often did not participate in politics. The state's poll tax, at $1 (equivalent to about $12 today) was a serious disincentive to vote, especially given that, at the time, the average annual income for Louisianans was only about $1,270 (roughly $15,000 today). In a sense, that was an obstacle. But for populists like Long, who take habitual non-voters and turn them into voters, it was also an opportunity.

Long ran for governor in 1924, campaigning for the vote of the state's small farmers. He lost the race, but it was a noble defeat; in some areas, he managed great feats of mobilisation, and gained a majority in twenty-one rural parishes. The day he lost, he bought a new suit and began campaigning again. Louisiana's daily papers were almost universally against him. Under the headline 'Louisiana Must Not Let Bolshevism In', one editorialist contended that Long was a brilliant campaigner, but so was Vladimir Lenin. Perhaps the writer's grasp of Russian history was a little hazy; but the message was clear.

Soon, against the odds, Long began to terrify the state's political establishment. His charisma was so exaggerated it was almost a superpower. 'He fumbled for about fifteen minutes, trying out various appeals, feeling out the audience,' recalled a man who heard Long speak to a largely unfriendly crowd in Baton Rouge. 'Then he got one and he knew he had it and I never saw an audience change so.' A man who had been ordered to spy on Long's rallies, left the first rally midway through. Asked why, he said: 'I left because I was afraid. That guy was convincing me. I had to get out.' Watching Long give a speech, a state policeman put it simply: 'I couldn't believe people could be so spellbound by a man.'

Long also had endless reserves of energy – nervous energy in such proportion that it fuelled constant motion. He was always waving his hands, hunching his shoulders, or rocking on his heels. As one associate put it: 'he had a freewheeling body. Head, hair, arms, shoulders – everything would move in a different direction.' His pace of walking was more like a jog. This energy never flagged: 'he could never relax, even when eating ... he was too busy phoning or talking'. Reportedly, he slept only four hours a night. During the course of his second campaign for governor, he travelled some 15,000 miles, delivering about 600 speeches. In an effort to relax, he developed the habit of conducting meetings from his bed. Even there, he constantly tapped the headboard with his fingers or twisted from side to side. The phone would ring, he would leap up to answer it, and then race back and fling himself into the bed so that head and shoulders hit at the same moment, all the while carrying on a dialogue with whoever was in the room. He resembled a child on a permanent sugar high. A novelist characterised him as an 'overgrown small boy with very bad habits indeed'. In the words of a University of Chicago English professor he was 'an engagingly boyish figure, jovial and impudent, Tom Sawyer in a toga'.

He was also funny. His speech was peppered with overdone country aphorisms: 'as hungry as a seed tick'; 'as crooked as a boar shoat's tail'; 'as slick as polecat grease'; 'more trouble than a boat can haul'. He had a prodigious talent for political insults. He awarded nearly every opponent a nickname: 'bang tail Sullivan', 'chicken Jim', 'George J-J-Jackass Ginsburg', 'barrelhead Delahoussaye' – that last for a legislator who, Long said, demanded his bribes paid on the barrelhead. A good number of these nicknames stuck with their victims for life, including 'old feather duster Ransdell', poking fun at an aristocratic goatee; 'whistle-britches Rightor', which no one really understood, but was funny (flatulence? squeaky trousers?); and 'Shinola Phelps', for a rich man said to be so cheap he shined his own shoes with Shinola shoe polish. (Another pattern of history: populists tend to be masters of the political put-down. Donald Trump's insulting nicknames – 'crooked' Hillary Clinton; 'low energy' Jeb Bush – are only the most recent example.)

In his second gubernatorial campaign, Long's nicknames easily outmatched their victims. His main opponent, the former lieutenant governor, campaigned so weakly that eventually Democratic Party organisers asked him to stop and sent him back to his hometown so they could set about the serious business of rigging the vote. Long, by contrast, was on a mission. He adopted as his campaign slogan, 'every man a king, but no man wears a crown', from William Jennings Bryan. Though mostly folksy, Long could be eloquent when he wanted to. He claimed that his opponent, the former lieutenant governor, was 'candidate because he answered the call of the … convention, where assembled the lords, dukes, nabobs, satraps and rajas, who journeyed in special trains and were attended by bland masters'.

Long mobilised supporters with mass rallies throughout the state that held audiences spellbound. He won a crushing victory, polling 50 per cent more votes than his closest rival. He lost in the capital, Baton Rouge, where the state's political class maintained their homes, but that did not stop 15,000 of Long's supporters from piling into the city for an out-of-control victory party. 'You fellers stick by me,' he said, 'we're just getting started.' It was a joyous, but tense moment. The highlight of each year's Mardi Gras celebrations was a series of exclusive balls with grand orchestras where some of the nation's best cuisine was served. Traditionally, the landed families who hosted these balls would extend formal invitations to the governor. That year, Long received no invitations. One heiress later explained: 'Huey Long is not the first scoundrel to be elected governor of Louisiana. A good many of our governors have been scoundrels. But they have always been gentlemen.'

Invited to a celebratory dinner with Louisiana's business elite, Long seemed somehow chastened: 'I go into the governor's office as your servant,' he said. He had won an important battle; but the war was just beginning. When his first son was born, his wife proposed the name 'Huey P. Long III'. Long said he wanted to change it: 'it's better for the boy to have his own name so if things go bad for me, he can have his own name to make it on'.

On progressivism

Huey Long was not the only person campaigning, at least ostensibly, on behalf of America's poor. Long's uprising was made possible by another, grander social movement, which arose in the early 1900s:

the Progressive movement. Many of the tools that Long used to establish himself as the people's champion were Progressive innovations: the Workmen's Compensation laws that were the basis of his first legal cases; the position of Railroad Commissioner that served as his political springboard – these institutions had been created only a few years before by Progressive legislation. The Progressives had gone well beyond what the Populists were able to accomplish. The resources of the Populists had been limited – because of industrialisation and urbanisation, the relative clout of their small-farmer supporters had dwindled too rapidly. The social movement that would shake the foundations of American politics would be a rising social group. That group was the American middle class, and it would produce perhaps the most effective mass movement history had yet witnessed.

Being middle class is an empowering but desperately anxious predicament. Middle-class strivers have achieved something, but keep it only by their wits; their base of wealth is usually small enough that a serious miscalculation or indeed run of hard luck could send them back down to poverty. That awareness is stressful, but building for the future is perhaps even more stressful. Being middle class is all about deprivation, but of the cruellest kind – self-deprivation. The best middle-class children, when they take the marshmallow test, make the researcher eat the marshmallow. Being middle class is all about denial of today's pleasures in favour of future gains, or the gains of one's offspring. It is about making new friends and then trying to keep up with them. It is about denying what one wants if that thing is too proletarian. It is about worrying intensely about very small things. This is the world of the Tiger Mother. It is a world of discipline; of working too hard; of setting reach goals; of becoming slightly unhinged. And when such people are frustrated in achieving their goals, they become dangerous. There is nothing more deadly than a Tiger Mother in a cage.

Take Carrie Nation, for instance. Married to a lawyer turned minister, she had personal disappointments: her first husband had turned out to be an alcoholic; her second had 'deceived' her; her daughter was in poor health. Standing outside a saloon on Lower Kansas Avenue in Topeka, she roared: 'aren't you going to let your mother in, boys? She wants to talk to you.' The men cowering inside wanted none of it. Nation, by that point, had a reputation. She had smashed up several saloons in the town of Kiowa, Kansas, hurling bricks at liquor bottles. The next time she did it, in Wichita, destroying the fanciest bar in town using an iron rod, she was arrested. Eventually, she got out, and took a hatchet to several bars in Topeka, with the help of some followers. She was arrested several more times. Her minister husband divorced her; but Nation was happy. 'I have never had so light a heart nor felt so well satisfied,' she said, and taking time out from smashing up bars, went on the lecture circuit, railing against the drinking of alcohol and 'the idea that woman is a toy, pretty, doll … only a parrot, a parasite of man'.

In their politics, Progressives like Carrie Nation wielded the most middle-class of weapons: disapproval. She was a bit unusual in backing her disapproval with an iron rod; most Progressives were subtler although no less stern. It was becoming obvious that Americans at the top and bottom of the social scale were insufficiently concerned with matters of decorum. In 1894, a typical member of the new middle class, a physician from Kentucky, wrote: 'the rich become effeminate, weak and immoral, and the lower classes, taking advantage of this moral lassitude, and led on by their savage inclinations, undertake strikes, mobs, boycotts and riots'. The editor of the *Ladies Home Journal* decried 'unrest among the lower classes and rottenness among the upper classes'. The Kentucky physician sounded a call to arms: 'if it were not for the restraining influence of the sober, levelheaded middle classes – the true police of the world – civilization would be swept from the face of the globe, and men would become savages'.

Middle-class Americans could back their words with people power. They were among the biggest winners in the ongoing American industrial revolution. Back in 1870, only about 6 per cent of the US labour force had been white-collar workers. Thirty years later, with family members thrown in, the middle class made up 20 per cent of the nation, including 1.2 million professionals (like Huey Long, the lawyer), 1.7 million business managers, proprietors or government officials, 1.3 million salespeople and about 900,000 clerical workers. These people had disposable incomes and their houses were no longer utilitarian; they were constructed according to changing fashions – Queen Anne, Gothic Revival, Colonial Revival, Romanesque (or log cabin, in the case of Long's father). A Kansas newspaper editor described a gathering of Progressive agitators: 'here were the successful middle-class country-town citizens, the farmer whose barn was painted, the well-paid railroad engineer, and the country editor. It was a well-dressed crowd … proletarian and plutocrat were absent.'

A surprising number of leading Progressive activists were children of ministers (as were German chancellor Angela Merkel and EU competition commissioner Margrethe Vestager – two icons of modern progressivism). Yet the faith that defined the Progressive movement was not religious; it was a faith in the power of expertise. Experts were a 'natural aristocracy', explained one economist in the late 1800s. It was elitist, but not exclusive – anyone could join this empire of the nerds, they had only to be educated. It was, another economist claimed, an 'aristocracy of merit'. In a world of self-interested lobbies, experts would stand above it all. A sociologist of that era said: the 'moral capital of the expert, the divine spark that keeps him loyal and incorruptible' was the spirit of scientific inquiry. Another sociologist explained that what was needed was the 'comprehensive "scientific management" of mankind'.

'Scientific management' was a loaded term. It was coined by Frederick Taylor, who published *The Principles of Scientific*

Management in 1909. Taylor had come up with the time and motion study; the micromanaging of a labourer's every action to gain greater efficiency. 'In the past, the man has been first,' Taylor explained. 'In the future, the system must be first.' Taylor's educated, middle-class, white-collar middle manager would 'do the thinking for the men,' he explained, thus increasing a company's productivity. Soon, Progressive activists were applying this principle to society at large. As the famed economist Irving Fishing put it: 'the world consists of two classes – the educated and ignorant – and it is essential for progress that the former should be allowed to dominate the latter'.

The central mechanism of this dominance would be government. As a University of Wisconsin sociologist put it in a 1907 book that gained a wide audience, a government must 'establish righteousness' by regulating the public's behaviour. An economist opined that 'government should interfere in all instances where its interference will tell for better health, better education, better morals, greater comfort of the community'. The Progressive activist Jane Addams chimed in: 'if certain industrial conditions are forcing the workers below the standard of decency, it becomes possible to deduce the right of state regulation'. Which is to say, if the rich will not treat their workers right, the government should make them do it.

As one might have expected of such a nervous, hardworking, upwardly mobile class, Progressive activists were politically effective. They made alliances – with labour on some issues; with big business on many others. They found the ear of sympathetic political leaders (one Progressive activist giddily informed Jane Addams that his 'report was all grist to T.R.'s [Theodore Roosevelt's] mill ... I wrote some paragraphs which he more or less put into his keynote speech'). They conducted some classic social movement campaigns. But mostly, the Progressives were masters of political organisation. Other social movements in democracies would rely on rallies, public meetings, lobbying, pamphleteering, demonstrations, petition drives, and so on. The Progressives did some of these things too. (A few, like Nation, did a bit of old-school rioting.) But they became, in a sense, a movement of movements; the organisational tactics they deployed were subtle, innovative, and above all, effective. Like Lenin's mother, they knew enough about how politics worked to be dangerous – very dangerous.

One such organisational innovation was the 'expert commission'. Progressive activists would identify an issue, and then find elected officials sympathetic to their cause, if necessary after a pressure campaign. These officials would be induced to commission a group of experts to consider the issue; the experts would duly find that the issue required ongoing expert management, and recommend the creation of a new government department, to be staffed by experts. The first such commission was the US Industrial Commission, which met from 1898 to 1902. It recommended the creation of the government body that became today's Federal Trade Commission. The National Monetary Commission of 1908 to 1912 led to the creation of the US Federal Reserve in 1913. Through this method, in the early 1900s, innumerable new regulatory agencies were created: the Permanent Tariff Commission; the Department of Labor; the Department of Commerce; the Food and Drug Administration. Of course, both the expert commissions and the new departments that were created would be staffed, primarily, by educated, middle-class Americans. The Progressives were doing well by doing good.

Russia's workers could never have dreamed of such a thing. The Progressives did not overthrow the government. They had no need; their revolution was to reshape American law, policy, political structures and political leadership as they desired. For the working class, they supported Workmen's Compensation laws; new health and safety regulations; the eight hour workday; the minimum wage; tenement house reform; the abolition of child labour; and restrictions on immigration. To control, or at least moderate, the behaviour of the rich, the Progressives backed antitrust legislation; new standards for consumer protection; new taxes on income and wealth; and a raft of legislation governing the behaviour of industries, which created jobs like Huey Long's position overseeing Louisiana's railroads. In an effort to make the elected parts of government more effective, the Progressives backed direct election of US senators (previously, senators had been appointed by state legislatures) – another change Huey Long would exploit to great effect. Eventually, Progressives would help gain for women the right to vote, giving the average Joe, for the first time, a voice in the status quo.

In the years leading up to the First World War, the Progressives became so dominant it was a little frightening. In the 1912 presidential election, the Democratic presidential candidate was Woodrow Wilson, a quintessential Progressive; on the campaign trail, he said: 'if you are not a Progressive … you better look out.' His Republican opponent, William Howard Taft, was also a Progressive. But perhaps not Progressive enough – Theodore Roosevelt, unable to win the Republican Party leadership away from Taft, decided to create a third party called, perhaps inevitably, the Progressives. The Progressive activist Jane Addams delivered a speech at his nominating convention. There was only one possible result from that election: a Progressive victory.

And so, the Progressives won, in the person of Wilson, because Roosevelt's third party had split the Republican vote. Under Wilson, the Progressives quickly achieved a further increase in taxes (necessary for funding more government bureaucracies full of experts), and a wartime programme (during the First World War) that drastically increased government control of industry. Eventually, like anxious middle-class parents who find that disapproval is no longer enough to regulate the behaviour of their teenagers, the Progressives became a little obsessive. They imposed Prohibition on the drinking of alcohol, and began to campaign to limit the spread of movie theatres and place restrictions on divorce.

There was, inevitably, a backlash; following the First World War, the nation turned towards small-government conservatism. (The epigraph that started this chapter was actually a witty protest, from a Broadway revue, against the endless stream of new government programmes the Progressives put in place.) That said, even after the backlash, Progressives did not vanish from the political scene – far from it. By 1920, Huey Long was poised to shake up American politics, with an agenda that was both typically Progressive and unlike anything anyone had ever seen before.

Kingfish

In some respects, Long had perfect Progressive credentials. His first direct involvement in Louisiana politics was as an expert, testifying on the nuances of Workmen's Compensation law. Like the pioneering Progressive governor of Wisconsin, as Louisiana's governor Long would build up the state's land-grant university – although he seemed more interested in the football team than the economics department – and impose new taxes on the rich. Long's core supporters were usually more middle class than poor (in Louisiana, the poll tax had disenfranchised the poor). A case in point was A. L. Boley, a former government inspector living on a disability pension after serving in the army during the First World War. At first, Boley supported Roosevelt, but when spending cuts reduced his pension, he turned to Long (I mentioned earlier that austerity can be dangerous). Boley wrote to Long expressing his 'ever growing regard for your stand on matters concerning the common people as a whole'.

But in one area in particular, Long was no ordinary Progressive. Progressives almost always played down class warfare. 'We do not like to acknowledge that Americans are divided into two nations,' said the activist Jane Addams. 'Where wealth is growing at a rapid rate the multitude may be fed without breaking into the rich man's granary,' a progressive journalist contended. By contrast, class warfare was Huey Long's stock in trade. On the campaign trail, Long quoted an article from the *Saturday Evening Post* saying that 2 per cent of the American people owned 70 per cent of the nation's wealth (and it was true that inequality of both wealth and income had risen dramatically since the 1800s).

Upon his election in 1928, Long plunged into his legislative agenda with gusto. One of his campaign promises had been to distribute free textbooks to students. Predictably, Louisiana's *ancien régime* was uninterested in this programme, just as they had been uninterested in federal funding for the state's schools. Shreveport mayor Lee Thomas had this defence: 'this is a rich section of the state. We are not going to be humiliated or disgraced by having it advertised that our children had to be given the books free.' A legislator who opposed the programme would later put it more bluntly: 'I was elected with the support of powerful, wealthy people, and they were against it.'

But Long had a trick up his sleeve. In his first legislative session, he rushed all the bills being considered through the legislature, putting them to the vote with a minimum of debate – including not only his own bills but those of his opponents. Moved by this display, the legislature passed a good many of his bills along with their own, including the textbook law. Long then, with evident pleasure, vetoed every single one of his opponents' bills, letting only his own stand. At that point everyone understood Long was playing for keeps. Some 600,000 new textbooks were printed and distributed; partly as a result, school attendance increased by about 15,000 pupils. Long also began to build the roads he had promised. Initially, his map of improved highways looked bizarre – rather than paving a road at a time, he paved parts of roads for a few miles around each town; for the rest of the journey the driver had to use the original dirt or gravel. The idea was to give everyone a taste and leave them wanting more. 'When the people once knew the pleasure of traveling over paved highways their support for a program to connect up the links was certain,' he wrote.

In 1930, Long announced he was running for US senator; all eighteen of Louisiana's daily newspapers were opposed. He won by a landslide, carrying fifty-three of sixty-four Louisiana parishes. It was a triumph of mobilisation. In most Louisiana senate races, turnout was low; in Long's race, however, he garnered almost as many votes as he had when he ran for governor. After he won his senate seat, Long reached something of a tipping point. Parts of the Louisiana political elite began to acknowledge that he was now unstoppable. Soon, he had a majority backing him in the Louisiana House. He ratcheted up his spending on long-neglected public services. By 1931, Huey Long's highway programme, employing a thousand people, had expanded Louisiana's network of paved roads from not much more than 300 miles to more than 2,000. Eventually, his road construction effort would employ roughly 10 per cent of all people working on highway construction in the entirety of the United States.

Long was genuinely popular, but his uncanny dominance had a lot to do with share-the-wealth politics. In his single four-year term as Louisiana's governor, Louisiana had spent more than it had in the previous twelve years combined. He had also raised taxes on the rich, but not by much; it was populist economics. Eventually, the debt burden became so large that Louisiana's credit rating fell below the point where state bonds could be sold. Long also was a master of patronage. On reaching the governorship, he fired every member of a state board or commission that he could, replacing them with loyalists – applying this treatment to the highway commission, hospital board, state board of health, flood control board, and so on. To ensure loyalty, Long made each appointee sign undated letters of resignation, which he then kept on file. Together, these committees and boards controlled hiring decisions for thousands of state employees. Long gained control of the Louisiana legislature in part by putting members of the legislature on state boards, or using the boards to give legislators lucrative contracts or side postings (or withdraw the same). He also developed a political slush fund. State employees paid 5–10 per cent of their salary – estimated at about $1m per year in total (about $14m today) – to Long's organisation. Contractors doing business with the state had to kick back about 20 per cent of their bids. These funds were kept in what Long called the 'deduct box', and used for running the political machine. With his mass support coupled with machine politics, he was becoming an unstoppable force.

Huey Long began to refer to himself as the 'Kingfish', a nickname taken from the radio comedy *Amos 'n' Andy*. He said its 'homespun Majesty' appealed to him. When his phone rang in the governor's mansion, he would answer it with: 'This is the Kingfish.' Members of the plantation class were unimpressed. 'Common beyond words,' was how an ex-governor's wife described him. 'He has not only common ways, but a common, sordid, dirty soul.'

Mr Long goes to Washington

In the Senate, Huey Long quickly ran into trouble. He was, it must be said, not much of a team player. He was born to rule or die trying. He immediately provoked an irreparable break in relations with the leader of his own Democratic Party and ended up resigning all his committee appointments in a fit of pique. Possibly, his policies could have appealed to the average Joe in an increasingly unequal society. But his ideas were extreme. He introduced a bill that sought to limit family fortunes to $100m. It went nowhere. Long issued dire warnings. 'It is no campaign to soak the rich,' Long said. 'It is a campaign to save the rich. It is a campaign the success of which they wish for when it is too late.'

Soon, Huey Long was heading for confrontation with President Franklin D. Roosevelt – despite some points of agreement on Progressive issues and their Democratic Party kinship. The clash of cultures was intense. Roosevelt invited Long to his family's estate for dinner. At one point during the awkward conversation, Roosevelt's mother asked – within Long's earshot – 'who is that *awful* man?' During the presidential election, Long had offered to campaign on Roosevelt's behalf. Roosevelt's campaign chief turned him down, noting privately that Huey Long was 'somewhat of a freak' – an assessment that, frankly, is hard to dispute. Eventually, Long decided to campaign unofficially on Roosevelt's behalf in the Dakotas, Iowa, Kansas and Minnesota. He drew huge crowds. A Democratic state chairman sent Roosevelt a message: 'if you have any doubtful state, send Huey Long to it'. Later, Roosevelt's campaign manager admitted that 'we underrated Long's ability to grip the masses'. He continued: 'We never again underrated him.'

During the first year Roosevelt was in office, Long opposed about half of the administration's bills. Partly for good reason: Roosevelt initially appeared to have no interest in sharing the wealth. In fact, as the US economy continued to flounder, Roosevelt drastically cut the budget, imposing austerity in a downturn. '[He's] a phony,' Long eventually said of Roosevelt. 'He's living on inherited income.' By the spring of 1933, Long had broken openly with the president, and opposed just about everything his administration did – even progressive measures.

Increasingly, Long tilted at windmills, introducing radical bills in the Senate that had no hope of passing: to restrict incomes to a maximum of $1m ($19m today); to restrict inheritance to $5m ($95 million); and to allocate $1bn ($19bn) to college education for the poor. All failed. Long's rhetoric became more and more extreme. He attributed the Great Depression to inequality: 'In 1929, when the fortune holders of America grew powerful enough that 1 per cent of the people owned nearly everything, 99 per cent of the people owned practically nothing, not even enough to pay their debts, the collapse was at hand.'

Long began campaigning to raise his national profile. He incorporated a national Share our Wealth society, its copyrighted slogan: 'every man a king'. The society was launched with a speech broadcast nationwide, and by mid-1934, Long was beginning to gain support across the country. After a series of radio broadcasts in which he attacked Roosevelt directly, Long got more than 30,000 letters every day, for twenty-four days in a row. Soon, the Kingfish was receiving more mail than every other senator combined, more than the president himself. Long expanded his office in the Senate to house twenty-five clerks handling the mail in five rooms, along with a night shift of fourteen workers. By the end of 1934, his Share our Wealth society had over 3 million members, and by spring of 1935, somewhere between 4.5 and 8 million; soon, he was receiving an average of 60,000 letters a week.

On Labor Day in 1935, Long announced that he was running for president in the 1936 elections. It seemed unlikely that the Democratic Party would ever nominate him. That was fine, he told his friends: he would run as a third-party candidate, take enough votes from Roosevelt that a Republican would be elected, and then, in the 1940 election, the Democrats would nominate him to avoid having the same thing happen again. He was joking. Probably. But Long had time on his side. In August 1935, he was forty-two years old.

Roosevelt was worried. Huey Long was not the only unorthodox political figure loose on the national scene. The anti-Semitic radio priest, Father Charles Coughlin, was attracting a huge listenership; Francis Townsend, a retired California physician, had gained a large following with his idea of a programme of social security for the elderly. But Huey Long was the most dangerous. Roosevelt's campaign manager had conducted a poll, and found that Long might get between 3 million and 6 million popular votes – possibly enough to prevent Roosevelt from winning re-election. 'It's all very well for us to laugh over Huey,' Roosevelt told one of the experts in his brain trust, but 'we shall have to do something about him.' In October 1935, Long made the cover of *Time* magazine.

Meanwhile, Long himself appeared to be weighing the odds. He told a colleague in the Senate: 'a mob is coming to hang the other 95 of you damned scoundrels and I'm undecided whether to stick here with you or go out and lead them'.

Going too far

Back home in Louisiana, Huey Long had become something US politics had never seen before, and has not seen since. Long began to roam the chambers of the Louisiana legislature while bills were under discussion. Of course, as Long was not a member of the Louisiana legislature, he had no reason to be there, and on one occasion he was forcibly ejected by the Sergeant at Arms to loud applause. As early as 1932, however, he had turned the tables. He would sit in the back of the Louisiana House chamber, eating peanuts, and when voting started he would serve, in effect, as a de facto floor leader, moving from representative to representative and telling them how to vote. At other times, he would sit on the rostrum next to the Speaker of the House, or stand at the front of the Louisiana Senate chamber, watching the voting machine as each senator voted. When one representative dithered, an opposition legislator sarcastically observed: 'I wish [Mr Long] would make up his mind so Mr Wimberly will know what to do.' When a legislator was absent on a key vote, Long personally cast the absentee ballot, to no objections. He would race from room to room, barging in on committee meetings. The committee chairman would ask if someone had anything to say. 'No,' said Huey. The bill in question would be moved on. The transcripts of these committee meetings have the flavour of someone using a Jedi mind trick. For instance, on one occasion, a bill had just passed the Louisiana House by an overwhelming majority of eighty-four to six. The bill then went to a Senate committee, and Long barged in. 'I'm against that,' said Long to the committee chairman. One of the committee members spoke up: 'I'm against it too.' 'Senator Heywood moves an unfavorable report on the bill,' said Long. Senator Heywood said: 'I move an unfavorable report on the bill.' The chairman: 'The bill is reported unfavorably.' One of the attendees described the experience thus: 'when he explained them you couldn't see any bad angles, even though you knew they were there. I've often wondered how so many sensible men could sit there and listen and believe for the moment what he said. It was like we were mesmerized ... he carried you along with him.'

In 1934 and 1935, Long called seven special sessions of the Louisiana legislature, where the representatives passed 463 bills, the vast majority of which were of Huey Long's design and largely unread and undebated. At one of these sessions, each bill was considered in committee for an average of two minutes, and the Louisiana Senate passed an average of seven of Long's bills every twenty minutes. At another session, the clerk read only the first few words of the titles of each bill, enabling the Senate to get through thirty-three bills in thirty-five minutes. An irate senator asked when they would know the content of the bills they had just voted on. 'Tuesday, when they are passed,' said the Kingfish. At another session, the clerk was reading the bills so fast it was hard to tell where one word ended and the next began. Long felt this effort was insufficient. 'Tell him to hurry up,' he said. 'All they've got to do is vote.'

The laws Long was passing would eventually give him something approaching dictatorial power in Louisiana. There were laws to give the governor (one of Long's friends) permission to use the National Guard essentially as he saw fit; to give state (rather than local) officials the authority to hire and fire all policemen and firemen; to enable a state commission to set all tax assessments on property values; to award a fur trading monopoly to three families (presumably there was a nice kickback for the deduct box); and to demote a senator who had taken a patronage position from one of Long's opponents.

It must be said that throughout this time, Huey Long remained genuinely popular in Louisiana; indeed, spectacularly and somewhat terrifyingly popular. Many of the Kingfish's dictatorial measures required constitutional amendments, and therefore needed to be endorsed by Louisiana voters. On average, Long's amendments passed by seven to one majorities. 'A perfect democracy can come close to looking like a dictatorship,' Long explained, 'a democracy in which the people are so satisfied they have no complaint.'

Long's opponents had another word for him: demagogue. A former governor denounced his 'demagogical and Bolshevistic tendency'; one of Louisiana's daily newspapers branded him the 'little sniveling demagogue from Winn'; a US senator called him 'a demagogic screech owl from the swamps of Louisiana'. These accusations, while accurate, were levelled hastily. A Baton Rouge newspaper first labelled him 'demagogic' when, as Railroad Commissioner, he attempted to regulate oil pipelines. Long grew tired of these charges: 'Just say I'm *sui generis* and let it go at that.'

And indeed, he was. To claims that he resembled Hitler, the Kingfish responded: 'Don't compare me with that so and so. Anybody that lets his public policies be mixed up with religious prejudices is a plain goddam fool.' When he was compared to Mussolini, he said that unlike Mussolini 'I'll give them Tabasco, and then they'll like Louisiana' (Mussolini had forced political prisoners to drink castor oil). Long became famous for conducting meetings wearing green silk pyjamas and a robe, often while lounging in bed. Early in his governorship, he nearly caused an international incident by meeting the captain of a visiting German naval vessel while dressed in this manner; in his defence, it was during Mardi

Gras, and he probably had a hangover. Some said such behaviour was symptomatic of Long's lower-class nature. But frankly, no Louisianan of any class dressed in that manner. One perceptive reporter, after witnessing Long holding a meeting in the bedchamber of the governor's mansion, recalled depictions of a similar scene, perhaps in a history book or a painting; it called to mind an audience with France's Louis XIV; the Sun King. During one session of the Louisiana legislature, a representative put forward a resolution that every man in Louisiana should be awarded a castle, a queen, a set of green silk pyjamas, an annual income of $90,000 and the title of 'your Majesty'. It passed immediately, to laughter, some of it perhaps strained.

President Franklin D. Roosevelt would also go too far, although not in such a colourful fashion. Unlike Long and the Progressives, his excesses were not spurred by triumph; but rather, by fear; fear of Huey Long. Roosevelt's 'New Deal' programmes, such as the Civilian Conservation Corps, Public Works Administration, Civil Works Administration and Works Progress Administration, created huge numbers of jobs. With jobs came the potential for patronage: the right to appoint bureaucratic positions administering industrial recovery, agricultural adjustment and unemployment relief. By 1933, some 326,000 Louisianans either had federal jobs or received some kind of federal welfare cheque. By 1935, the Federal Emergency Relief Administration employed 70,000 people in Louisiana; the Civilian Conservation Corps about 42,000 people.

At first, Roosevelt resisted temptation. But then, recognising the threat posed by Long and his extraordinary control of Louisiana politics, Roosevelt began to act. Roosevelt's administration handed decisions over these jobs exclusively to Long's political opponents in Louisiana, consulting anti-Long leaders on whom they ought to employ. 'Don't put anybody in and don't help anybody that is working for Huey Long's crowd: that is 100 per cent!' said

Roosevelt. Eventually, Roosevelt began to cut off not only jobs, but also federal spending in the state. In February 1935, Roosevelt told his aides to go through the list of federal employees in Louisiana and fire any Long supporters. In April, Roosevelt suspended $2.5m in federal aid to the state – aid that would have employed some 2,000 Louisianans. That same month, he suspended $10m in Public Works Administration projects, along with their associated jobs. It was dirty politics, but better than the alternative: in 1934, Roosevelt had briefly debated a proposal to send federal troops to Louisiana to 'restore Republican government' in the state; a hard choice to be sure.

In the Senate, Long began to rage against Roosevelt 'with the fury of a firebreathing monster,' according to the *Los Angeles Times*. 'Our men of affairs and the powers that be are in a maze of confusion,' said Long. 'The hand of death has gripped the souls of our leaders, it has calloused their hearts and cankered their minds.' Long taunted Roosevelt as 'Prince Franklin' and the 'Knight of the Nouhrmal', referring to the Astor family yacht on which Roosevelt sometimes travelled.

Long could rage all he wanted. Roosevelt's programme of patronage support for Long's opponents had the intended effect. Emboldened, Long's enemies in Louisiana resumed their resistance. The Kingfish's Louisiana opposition launched a plan to impeach Long's friend from the governorship, backing up their plan with a force of 500 armed men who surrounded the state capitol building. Arguably, the show of force was a pre-emptive measure: in 1931, during a contentious political dispute, Long had sent national guardsmen, armed with machine guns, to surround the capitol. Long raced back to Louisiana and held mass rallies in districts where he controlled enough votes to potentially unseat opposition legislators. Quickly, vulnerable members of Congress switched sides, and Long's opposition folded, realising they did not command enough votes to make the impeachment measure stick.

Another Louisiana state election loomed. Just before the primaries were to be held, Long ordered the National Guard into New Orleans, and declared martial law. This time it was Long who was pre-empting: Long's opponents had invited a professional mercenary, returned from wars in Latin America, to take operational command of the city's police force. At the last minute, an agreement was reached to keep both the national guardsmen and the police away from polling stations; a minor military conflict was thus averted. In a reasonably fair but tense election, Long's candidates swept New Orleans. Outside New Orleans, Long's supporters did lose a few congressional races, where the opposition candidates had support from Roosevelt's patronage machine.

Through it all, Long was apparently having the time of his life. As he informed his wife, shortly after their marriage: 'I was born into politics, a wedded man with a storm for a bride.' Later in life, charging into the fray of yet another heated political battle, he paused long enough to confide in a startled bystander: 'this is the sport of kings'.

Limits to power

In June 1935, Roosevelt introduced a new tax bill, with the stated goal of achieving a 'wider distribution of wealth'. The bill included heavy inheritance taxes and new income taxes for those earning more than $30,000 a year (about $518,000 today). The House applauded the bill; the Senate was silent, aside from Huey Long, who, after the reading of the bill, said very loudly: 'I just wish to say "amen".' The columnist and comedian Will Rogers wrote: 'I would sure like to have seen Huey's face when he was woke up in the middle of the night by the president, who said "layover, Huey, I want to get in bed with you".' A couple of days later, the Kingfish announced in the Senate that he was indeed delighted to have Roosevelt's company.

But for Huey, it was not enough. He said: 'Billionaires are becoming bigger billionaires, the millionaires are becoming bigger millionaires, the poor are becoming poorer, and the middle class is disappearing.' Hearing that Roosevelt's tax bill would generate $340m a year (equivalent to an already-respectable $5.9bn today), Long said he would make a Share our Wealth tax bill that raised $165bn a year (almost $2.9 trillion). With that money, he promised to provide a basic minimum income and a 'homestead' for every family in America (a house, car and radio – the symbols of 1930s middle-class life). Long's national star was rising, and the 1936 elections loomed. Roosevelt's team feared the people power Long's movement represented. 'Father Coughlin, Reno, Townsend, et al., were all pygmies compared with Huey,' wrote one of Roosevelt's advisors.

On 8 September 1935, Long was walking through the state capitol building when a man fired one shot into his chest from four feet away. Long's bodyguards emptied their magazines into the would-be assassin, killing him instantly. Long, meanwhile, staggered backwards, and ran down a hallway and then down a flight of stairs. 'Jimmie my boy I've been shot,' he told an aide, who flagged down a passing motorist, who drove Long to the hospital. Long probably was not mortally wounded. Two of the state's top surgeons were summoned from New Orleans. Unfortunately, they crashed their car on the way to the hospital. The head of the state's charity hospital was on hand in the capitol and volunteered to step in. He had limited experience in surgery but managed to remove the bullet. However, he failed to check for internal bleeding. Thirty-one hours after being shot, Huey Long died. His last words, reportedly: 'God, don't let me die. I have so much left to do.'

Long's assassin, Carl Weiss, was thirty-three years old, a doctor from Baton Rouge. In one of his special sessions Long had passed a bill that would have ensured the end of one of his political enemies, a judge by the name of Benjamin Pavy; the judge was

Carl Weiss's father-in-law. Weiss's funeral was perhaps the most well attended of any political assassin in US history. Indeed, the calibre of the mourners who turned out was extraordinary, considering that Weiss had just murdered Long in cold blood. A great many members of the Louisiana plantation caste, including at least one former governor, could be found in the crowd, expressing their sympathy at Weiss's passing.

After Long's death, the deduct box, with its hidden millions, vanished and was never found.

On why sharing the wealth is so hard

In this book there has been a lot of 'share-the-wealth politics', but relatively little actual sharing of the wealth. Lenin got the job done, at substantial human and economic cost; Perón succeeded only temporarily. Even Roosevelt, who has gone down in history as a great redistributor – a 'traitor to his class,' as the biography by H. W. Brands has it – passed a tax bill that was nowhere near the measures Long had proposed, even though he evidently felt that the presidential race was at stake. Why is sharing the wealth so hard?

That question is at the heart of a lot of current research, because levels of inequality in many rich, democratic countries in the world have risen sharply. Between the end of the Second World War and the mid-1970s, levels of inequality in rich countries were relatively moderate – roughly on a par with countries like Norway or Finland today. Inequality in Norway and Finland has risen slightly since the 1990s; but inequality in the United States, for instance, has soared, and is roughly on a par with Mexico, Nigeria or Bolivia (by some measures). Inequality in the United Kingdom, Italy, Greece and Spain is on a par with Russia or India (again, by some measures). So, scholars want to know, what does it take to share the wealth?

It turns out that there are huge differences in how much

democracies tax and spend; and a few countries redistribute income, at least, fairly extensively. In Sweden, for instance, taxes and social welfare spending reduce the proportion of people living below the poverty line by 82 per cent, compared to the situation if there was no government spending. In the United States, the equivalent reduction is only 13 per cent. Because US pre-tax incomes are already more unequal than pre-tax incomes in Sweden, once one adds in the effect of Sweden's redistribution, the difference in income inequality between the United States and Sweden ends up being remarkably large.

In that case, why do Sweden and the United States take such different approaches? That question remains disputed, but there are some clear patterns that most scholars can agree on. First, within a particular country over time, left-leaning political parties tend to redistribute more, but not much more, than right-leaning parties. For most people, the idea that parties of the left tax and spend more would be so obvious that there would be no need to remark on it; however, trying to explain why parties follow through on their programmes is surprisingly difficult. Presumably an interest in the average Joe keeps major parties from going too far to extremes (as a matter of general tendencies). And yet, in practice, rather than going directly for the average Joe, parties of the left and right tend to pursue redistribution policies that are slightly, but measurably, different.

A second clear pattern is that countries that rely on electoral systems based on proportional representation (where the seats in the national legislature are allocated according to each party's share of the national vote – like Finland, Norway and Sweden) tend to redistribute, via taxation and public spending, far more than countries that use majoritarian electoral systems (where seats are allocated based on whether parties win in specific electoral districts – like the US and UK). There is an ongoing debate over why this difference exists. Some say unions are stronger in proportional representation countries. Others say proportional representation systems usually produce coalition governments, and in coalition governments the poor are likely to have more say. Others say underlying economic structures give rise to different types of electoral systems, which then in turn produce different types of policies.

Whichever is correct, we can draw one important conclusion: historically, the big differences among democracies in levels of taxing and spending have not, in most cases, depended on which party was in power; rather, these differences have related to the type of political system that was in place (for instance, the type of electoral system seems to have a big impact). This conclusion has an uncomfortable, although important, implication: it is probably very difficult to change the distribution of income in a country without making a fundamental change to the political system.

So how was Lenin able to share the wealth? By making a traumatic and violent change to the country's political system. How was Perón able to make some headway? First, by exploiting the shift from dictatorship to democracy (we have seen that democracies tend to tax and spend more than dictatorships), and second, by changing the rules of democracy to broaden the electorate (for instance, by giving women the right to vote). In terms of theory: these kinds of changes meant that the average (voting) Joe was poorer. Hence one could win elections with a platform of genuine redistribution. Without significant changes in a country's political system, history suggests that sharing the wealth may be all but impossible.

There is, however, one important exception.

Roosevelt in wartime

Even after Huey Long was assassinated, Franklin D. Roosevelt continued to shift to the left, perhaps because he realised it was good politics. Initially, he had not seemed to care much about the redistributive tax bill he had proposed. The head of the finance committee in the US House of Representatives had said 'if we don't get to it this session, the committee can spend some time on it in the fall'. Roosevelt did not seem too bothered by that response, and had almost immediately left Washington for several days. Perhaps the tax bill had been intended purely as a symbolic gesture. But in the end, it did pass, and it was popular.

So Roosevelt continued to ratchet up his leftist rhetoric. In January 1936, kicking off his campaign for re-election, he said: 'In the hands of the people's government ... power is wholesome and proper. But in the hands of political puppets of an economic autocracy such power would provide shackles for the liberties of the people.' Americans evidently loved this kind of stuff, even when it came from a rich man; they also appeared to love Roosevelt's social programmes. In the 1936 presidential election, Roosevelt was re-elected with 61 per cent of the popular vote, the largest vote share in American history.

When America slipped back into recession in 1938, Roosevelt blamed 'private monopolies and financial oligarchies'. He said: 'Misuse of the powers of capital must be ended, or the capitalistic system will destroy itself through its own abuses.' In April 1938, he finally consented to a huge increase in public spending; the kind of thing that Long had done to such effect in Louisiana. He told his secretary of the treasury to include a line in his speech referencing the programme's 'purpose to protect the weak, to give human security, and to seek a wider distribution of our national wealth'. The secretary of the treasury did not like it, saying: 'If you want to sound like Huey Long, I don't.' But Roosevelt insisted.

And what of the tax bills? In the summer of 1938, Congress passed legislation dialling them back. At first, Roosevelt threatened the presidential veto, but ultimately, he let the rollback stand. It is, as I have noted, hard to change a nation's levels of taxation; and Roosevelt was no ideologue. He was always reading the tea leaves of public opinion. Roosevelt was elected to a third term in 1940, although not by such a wide margin as before.

During his third term, he changed course yet again, and at this point, at last, struck a revolutionary blow. The costs of the Second World War threatened to swamp the federal budget. Roosevelt proposed a major tax increase. Initially, he asked his brain trust of Progressive experts to come up with a measure that sounded like a posthumous tribute to Huey Long: 'in the higher income brackets, the tax rate should be such as to give the practical equivalent of a top limit on an individual's income after taxes, approximating $25,000,' he said (about $364,000 today). Roosevelt did not, in the end, take such an extreme approach, but the Revenue Act of 1942 was nonetheless draconian: it put the highest rate of personal income taxes up to 88 per cent, and reduced exemptions. A further 'victory tax' took 5 per cent of all incomes over $624 ($9,200 today), to be partly repaid after the war ended. Eventually, Roosevelt would also raise taxes on inheritance to more than 70 per cent.

Even if his purpose was to raise revenues for the war, Roosevelt's wartime taxation programmes ended up being more revolutionary than anything Huey Long had accomplished. These extreme rates of taxation, far higher than anything imposed in continental Europe during that era (the economist Thomas Piketty has called them 'confiscatory') lopped off the top end of the American income and wealth distribution, putting a decisive end to the era of extreme inequality in the United States. Inequality fell sharply, to a level on a par with that of Europe's most egalitarian countries, and would not begin to rise again until the late 1970s. As *Fortune* magazine put it, there had been a revolution in the American distribution of wealth, 'though not a head has been raised aloft on a pike staff, nor a railway station seized'. Roosevelt, more modestly, stated that 'such provisions will give assurance that the sacrifices required by war are being equitably shared'.

Roosevelt was not alone in such rhetoric. Research by the

team of Kenneth Scheve and David Stasavage and Walter Schiedel (working independently) has made it clear that, outside of changes in the political system, there is one major reason countries raise taxes: war. For instance, the highest income tax rates imposed by rich countries in the 19th century were imposed in the UK during the Napoleonic Wars and the United States during the Civil War. Once these wars ended, income taxes were eliminated in both countries. During the First World War, top rates rose dramatically worldwide (in the UK, from about 8 per cent to 60 per cent; in the United States, from 7 per cent to 77 per cent). Only Germany somehow managed to avoid raising income taxes; but then, perhaps that is not so surprising, as Germany was not a democracy.

Such tax policies are risky: as we have seen, austerity can cause governments to fall, which is probably one reason why outside of the pressures of wartime, countries rarely take the risk of imposing large increases in taxes. But the Second World War was both ruinously expensive and posed an existential threat. Hence most governments were willing to take the risk. And thus, the Second World War inadvertently resolved the problem of income inequality in most of the Western world (and Japan, which was catapulted from a quasi-feudal society to become one of the more egalitarian nations on earth).

At least, until very recently, when inequality in many of these countries has risen again, to levels last seen in the 1930s.

Why did Huey have to die?

In the 1980s, the documentary filmmaker Ken Burns made a biography of Huey Long. It is worth watching, not only for Burns's art, but because many of the people he interviewed, having reached old age, spoke freely. 'I don't care who the people were that I associated with, every time there was a gathering of two or three people somebody would say, that sonofabitch ought to be shot,' said Cecil

Morgan, who as a young man served as a Louisiana legislator facing off against Long. 'And the tension was extremely high, and the feeling was so strong, that there was hardly any other conversation, throughout the state.' A journalist, the wife of the editor of one of those anti-Long daily newspapers, said: 'I can't remember any Saturday night that I went anywhere that we didn't talk about killing Huey Long – it was just the normal conversation.'

Listening to these comments is more than a little chilling. These are intelligent, civilised Americans. But in a polarised political situation, they were willing to contemplate hard choices. When Huey Long gained power, the plantation caste did not think of coming up with some more appealing political platform of their own, probably because there was none – it is unlikely that there was a political platform that was acceptable to both Louisiana's people and the state's landlords. Hence they started to think about killing him. The journalist again: 'I think we were living through revolution. I think what Long was doing was a revolution. We were fighting [against] that revolution ... We were ready to fight to stop this man.'

In reality, Huey Long did not make all that much progress in seizing the wealth of the plantation owners. But that was probably about to change. In 1935, Long managed to get the state's poll tax abolished. Hundreds of thousands of Louisianans, a good many of them poor, registered to vote for the first time – the size of the state's electorate increased by more than three-quarters. But before the first election under this new system could be held, Huey Long was dead.

Which brings up one lesson Huey Long has left us for the modern day: for those interested in reducing inequality, focus on the politics. There are a great many Progressive proposals on tackling inequality, from enhancing public education to raising taxes, but none of these proposals are likely to go anywhere without a change in the political system – reducing the influence of money in politics, making it easier for the poor to vote (as Long did), or perhaps even instituting (as in Argentina) mandatory voting, which tends to bring more poor people to the polls. Without a change in the political system, changing the distribution of wealth is very difficult – even for a man like Huey Long.

Another lesson: if you want to put an end to mobilisation politics, one way to do it is to give the people what they want. Historians have looked into Roosevelt's tax bill and concluded that it was very likely a response to Huey Long's Share our Wealth movement. Roosevelt conducted a secret nationwide poll regarding Huey Long's prospects in the 1936 presidential race (the first scientific opinion poll ever conducted during a US presidential contest). Following the poll, the Roosevelt administration began directing a disproportionate share of New Deal money to states that were leaning towards Long; indeed, Long's projected impact on the outcome of the race explains a majority of the differences in New Deal spending among states. Evidently, Roosevelt was both worried and willing to act. And then, shortly after Long declared his interest in running for president, Roosevelt introduced a tax bill that mimicked Long's proposals. Especially after Long's death, Roosevelt also began to adopt some of Long's populist rhetoric.

When populists claim the system is broken, a well-functioning democracy should be able to prove them wrong. In the 1970s, the great champion of free markets Milton Friedman complained that the US Socialist Party – which had received less than 1 per cent of the vote in the 1928 election – was nonetheless the most influential political party of its era, because 'almost every economic plank in its 1928 presidential platform has … [subsequently] been enacted into law' (including unemployment insurance, a public pension system, limits on working hours, abolishment of child labour, and higher taxes). That was distressing to Friedman, but also a sign of democratic vitality. One reason radical movements have rarely made much progress in the United States is because mainstream parties have been flexible enough to copy the popular parts of their platforms. Which may at times be unappealing, but is surely better than the alternatives. When democracies are not responsive in this way, it is sometimes called a 'representation gap'. The existence of such gaps appears to correlate with greater electoral success for populist candidates and parties.

What about today? Will people stay mobilised, or will responsive democracies lead to a rapid return to politics as usual? That is a topic for the next chapter.

CHAPTER 6

Is your nation doomed?
A handy guide

The golden opportunity

Rod Blagojevich, the governor of Illinois, was a happy man. A senator from Illinois, Barack Obama, had just become president of the United States. It fell to Blagojevich to appoint a replacement to finish out Obama's senatorial term. He could, in essence, pick anyone he wanted. As Blagojevich explained over his wiretapped phone: 'I've got this thing and it's fucking – *golden*. And I, I'm not giving it up for fucking nothing.' Blagojevich talked about handing the office to his son, but really, what he wanted was money. He solicited bids. Illinois congressman Jesse Jackson Jr's team offered $1.5m. But before Blagojevich could hand over Obama's seat to the highest bidder, he was arrested. Congressman Jackson was also arrested, for stealing campaign funds to buy fur coats and Rolex watches.

Jackson's crime was, in a sense, unremarkable; former Illinois congressman Dan Rostenkowski had stolen much more in the 1990s. But Blagojevich's offence was new: he was the first governor in Illinois history to be impeached and convicted for corruption while in office. And yet, even Blagojevich had not accomplished anything all that impressive. Since 1973, four Illinois governors had been sent to federal prison, including Blagojevich's immediate predecessor. Blagojevich was unusual only in getting nabbed while still in office. Moreover, by Illinois standards, Blagojevich was in the amateur leagues. Between 1991 and 2012, Rita Crundwell, the comptroller of the small town of Dixon, Illinois, stole more than $50m, even though the town's annual budget was only about $8m. In one of her peak years, she stole nearly two-thirds of the town's budget, forcing Dixon into layoffs of municipal employees. Proportionally, Blagojevich should have aimed to steal about $20bn. Blagojevich got fourteen years in prison. Crundwell, in tacit recognition of her greater achievements, was sentenced to nineteen and a half years.

If one wished to identify the true masters of corruption in Illinois, it would not be the petty thieves, numerous though they be; it would be those who originated the political networks that dominate state politics. Perhaps the most infamous of these dark masters is the Chicago mayor Richard J. Daley, who created a patronage army, estimated at more than 25,000 city jobs, for which he had nearly absolute authority over who was hired and who was fired. This control over city employment enabled him to reward supporters, punish opponents, and direct city employees to carry out political tasks. Backed by his patronage army, he ruled Chicago with an iron fist – or as close to it as one gets in a democracy – from 1955 until he died in office in 1976.

But one should also celebrate his son, Richard M. Daley, who governed Chicago between 1989 and 2011. Daley Jr did not have the absolute control of his father, but he was still surprisingly dominant – and no one could figure out how he was doing it. By the time Daley Jr took office, several US courts, including the US Supreme Court, had intervened directly in Chicago's corrupt politics. Patronage was made illegal. Specifically, it was illegal for city employees to carry out political work on government time; it was illegal to punish city employees for failing to carry out political orders; it was even illegal to take political loyalty into account when awarding public sector jobs.

So how was Daley able to run Chicago politics? The answer, it turned out, was the private sector. In the 1990s, Daley outsourced various city services – winter snow removal, asphalt paving, and so on – to private trucking companies. In 2004, a newspaper investigation blew the lid off the scheme. Many companies had been hired with no-bid contracts; the contracts were handed out to friends and political insiders; in many cases the trucks sat idle all day, because the main objective of the programme was politics not public services. A good portion of the $40m that the city spent on the trucks each year went to Daley's relatives, his friends and supporters, and especially to a political slush fund that enabled Daley to win elections and keep city politicians toeing the line (channelled, oddly enough, via the 'Hispanic Democratic Organization' – the Illinois equivalent of Huey Long's deduct box). There were forty-six indictments for the hired trucks scandal, most resulting in conviction.

Somehow, though, the prosecutors never got Daley himself, and to this day he has many supporters in Chicago. Even Blagojevich has his defenders. The speaker of the Illinois House of Representatives – who, according to Thomas Gradel and Dick Simpson, authors of a book on corruption in Illinois politics, continues to operate a statewide patronage network – also remains popular. Why?

Here is a hint: Illinois is one of the most unequal states in the United States. By some measures it is within the fifteen most unequal states; by measures based on the income share of the top 1 per cent, it falls within the top ten. As the United States as a whole is quite unequal, that is saying something; if Illinois were a country, it would be more unequal than Nicaragua.

Now why would that matter?

To answer that question, I call on Andreas Papandreou, a brilliant economist with a thriving academic career in the United States who decided he wanted to rule Greece.

The champagne socialist

Andreas Papandreou was born in Greece, but fled to the United States after the king's soldiers beat him up, dislocating his jaw. In the United States, he flourished, soon gaining impeccable middle-class credentials: a doctorate in economics from Harvard University, an American wife, an affair with a woman he met at his dentist's office, another American wife, and by 1956, a teaching position at the University of California. Eventually, he was offered the chancellorship of the University of California at Santa Cruz.

But Andreas's father, Georgios, had become a key figure in Greek politics, so there was always a strong link to home. In 1961, elections were held in Greece. Andreas's father led the opposition to the royalist conservative party. Andreas was caught up in the excitement, and returned to Greece to follow his father around on the campaign trail. The election was rigged, and Georgios lost. Andreas was bitterly disappointed; apparently he had been so caught up in politics he was dreaming of a political career himself. 'Don't you see,' he said to his wife. 'There's no way they'll let me get ahead in this country. They'll just cut me down!' He vented his outrage on his contacts in Washington, after the US Embassy sent a Christmas message lauding the Greek people who 'believe as we do in personal freedom'. The Panglossian nature of American Christmas cards is a long-standing tradition, but Andreas was having none of it. He waved the message in people's faces in Washington, calling it an 'unbelievable performance'.

Somewhat miraculously, a serious of street demonstrations convinced the Greek establishment to rerun the election, and this time, Georgios won. Andreas, still angry at the Americans, decided to ditch his US passport and campaign for office in Greece. He was full of idealism. When campaigning, he sounded a bit like a professor trying his hand at politics. He called the return of Greece to democracy a 'moment of world creation' and said 'it is worth freeing ourselves from all pettiness … to empower the new, uncorrupted forces, the only ones who are able to become the authentic agents of renewal and change'. Helped by his famous name, he won a seat in parliament in February 1964. His father, also victorious at the polls, remained prime minister.

Very quickly, however, it became clear that something was wrong. The king was nervous about the Papandreous' political movement, and for good reason – the last middle-class rebellion in the country, in the 1920s, had nearly resulted in the abolition of the monarchy. The king and various military officers made repeated requests to the United States to be allowed to carry out a military coup; the United States, which maintained a large military presence in the country, said no. The king and army released a report that included some trumped-up evidence that could be used to charge Andreas with treason. The king then forced Georgios to resign and arranged a new government, headed by the royalist conservative party. This action provoked even larger demonstrations; some half a million people took to the streets of Athens. The Egyptian ambassador called it 'a prerevolutionary crowd'. A group of military officers approached the Americans asking for coup permission.

At that point, Georgios called off the uprising and attempted to back down, possibly because he had had a mild heart attack. Andreas, young and full of passion, wanted to push for true democracy at all costs. He tried to encourage further mass mobilisations against the king. Astonishingly, Georgios then cut a deal with the king behind his son's back, while Andreas was on holiday in Italy. Andreas found out only when the deal was made public. 'The room swam around me,' he recalled. He immediately rang his father: 'I have heard that you offered … [the king] your support. Is it true?' His father said, 'don't rush to conclusions'. 'We were together last night,' Andreas said. 'Nothing was said about this. We talked for four hours. I had no hint.' Georgios said: 'do what you want', and hung up.

Andreas's relationship with his father had always mixed resentment and awe. When Andreas was young, his father had been absent, having taken up with the glamorous Greek actress Kiveli. But his father was also a heroic figure – one of Andreas's earliest memories was seeing Georgios come home from the hospital in bandages after a royalist assassination attempt. At one point, perhaps hoping to get attention, Andreas had acted out, flunking the fifth grade. His father had brought Andreas to his office and gave him a stern talking-to. Andreas finished his next school year first in his class.

Bewildered and enraged by his father's deal with the king, Andreas first attempted to turn Georgios's own political party against him. But he then thought better of it, and called off the rebellion – despite having lured forty legislators to his side. The family feud did not appease the king. He sent a palace envoy to the Americans asking if a coup would now be acceptable. Again, he was told no. But on 1 March 1967, three US Embassy officials walked out of a lecture Andreas was giving; the walkout was widely taken as an indication that from the US point of view, Andreas was fair game if the monarchy wished to arrest him. His wife Margaret wrote: 'we were shouting, but our words were heard only by us, echoing our desperation'. In April, the American ambassador helpfully informed Andreas that some people were calling him a 'walking corpse'. Andreas somehow maintained his composure, and said, with strained dignity, that he would some day make a comeback, and when he did, he would be 'a "difficult friend" of America, but a friend'.

And then, at 2.20am on 21 April, Andreas was awakened by gunshots. He looked out the window; the house was surrounded by soldiers holding rifles with bayonets fixed. Reaching the third floor, the army men found Andreas's son. They put a gun to his head. 'Where is your father?' they asked. 'I don't know,' said Andreas's son, heroically but dangerously. 'Here I am!' yelled Andreas, jumping down to the terrace from his hiding place on the roof, injuring his knee in his haste.

A few months later, once the generals had solidified their power, they released Andreas. He visited the US Embassy, thanked the US ambassador for his help in getting him out of jail, and promised that he would renounce all political activities. A few minutes after making it safely to Paris, Andreas held a press conference, angrily denouncing the United States and pledged to set up a resistance movement from exile. Like the military regime that deposed Perón's wife in Argentina (and for that matter, the revolutionary government in Iran), the Greek generals banned miniskirts – in the name of Orthodox Christianity rather than Catholicism or Islam, of course. They also, again like Argentina, rolled back public education, closing 2,500 primary schools – an economically costly but time-honoured technique for sapping people power.

On untaxability

Who had supported the coup? It was hard to say. Ironically enough, the plan for the coup turned out to have been based on a NATO contingency scheme to respond to Soviet invasion, but of course there had been no such invasion, and NATO had not ordered the coup. It later emerged that the chief of the army had, at the king's urging, undertaken the logistical preparations needed to implement the NATO plan, including some 1,000 personnel changes. Thus, the king had inadvertently made the coup possible. But the king did not actually launch the coup, and indeed, attempted a failed counter-coup a few days later. The United States was quick to support the new Greek military regime, but there is no evidence the United States had wanted the coup either – indeed, for years the United States had been playing whack-a-mole with the coup plots arising from the monarchy and military. It appears that a group of junior military officers, noting the opportunity provided by the NATO plan preparations, had simply seized their moment.

Still, all coups tend to need support, especially if the new military regime is to last – and this one lasted. A member of the US National Security Council wrote that 'the leading businessmen of Greece form a small coterie, unused to competition with each other, highly protected by tariffs and special deals from foreign competition, and quite alarmed at the prospect an earnestly modernizing government might open up the Greek economy to more competition, domestic and foreign'. He concluded: 'it seems to me that the real heat of the current struggle reflects this underlying clash of interests'.

He was talking about the intense political opposition to the Papandreous. A Greek-American businessman by the name of Tom Pappas, who had been awarded a government monopoly on purchases of petroleum for the Greek market, was one of the leaders of this opposition. Andreas Papandreou had attempted to remove Pappas's monopoly. Pappas had fought back, helping to bribe legislators to switch to the royalist conservative party. Then, after the coup, when the new Greek military regime opened diplomatic relations with the United States, it was Tom Pappas who showed up in Washington, making the initial contacts.

While it is tempting to imagine a conspiracy, Pappas probably only got involved with the junta after the coup. Indeed, he was not the only rich Greek who eagerly cosied up to the generals. In 1968, the head of the junta, speaking before the Shipowners' Union, said: 'tell us what you want us to do. I can assure you that the government will grant your wish.' The shipowners, delighted, made him the union's honorary president. Soon, there was a love-in between the generals and the shipping industry. The Greek government implemented a revised 'tonnage taxation' scheme, which meant that no matter how much profit the shipping companies earned, they would be taxed on how much their ships weighed. At a stroke, this measure drastically reduced the taxes on shipping. Partly because of these tax advantages, a surprisingly large portion of the global shipping industry relocated to Greece. Indeed, by the early 1970s, Greece – a small country and not a particularly wealthy one – controlled about 15 per cent of the world's shipping capacity.

Of course, the Greek shipowners were not the first rich people in the world to gain a few favours by supporting an authoritarian regime. But most of these rich people tended to lose these advantages when democracy returned and taxes went up. The Greek shipowners turned out to be different; they proved to be all but untaxable. Following the restoration of democracy in the 1970s, one of the first laws the new government passed was to increase taxes on shipping. But the tonnage taxation system was retained, which meant that the level of effective tax on Greek shipping profits remained at a derisory 1 per cent. Then, somewhat puzzlingly, this seemingly unfair system spread around the world, including to the world's richest countries – beginning with the Netherlands, which adopted tonnage taxation in 1996. Today, nearly all major shipping economies use the system of tonnage taxation.

Why did that happen? Unlike Greece in the late 1960s and early 1970s, many of these countries, including the Netherlands, were democracies known for egalitarianism and lots of social welfare spending. In the main, it appears that the shipping industry's power came from the fact that the industry's capital was so mobile. The shipowners were the polar opposite of Louisiana's landlords – ships travel the world as a matter of course; ships are one of the most mobile forms of capital investment imaginable. This extreme mobility made it hard for governments to tax shipping profits; if they did, the industry would relocate elsewhere. And thus, once Greece had reduced the tax burden on shipping to next to nothing, the rest of the world was forced to follow suit, or face the relocation of their shipping industry to Greece.

Low taxes, it must be said, did produce a boom in Greek shipping. As early as the 1970s, as much as 10 per cent of Greece's labour force was employed in shipping or a related occupation. By 2010, shipping constituted about 7.5 per cent of the country's economic output (against 0.2 per cent for the UK, for instance). In 2011, the shipping sector earned roughly 12 per cent of all the profits in the entire Greek economy.

Yet these profits were essentially untaxable. Which was going to pose a very big problem for anyone hoping to share the wealth.

Greek destiny

At first, no one was worried about the untaxability problem. The Greek economy was booming. Between the mid-1950s and the late 1970s, Greece's pace of economic growth averaged close to 7 per cent annually, with inflation of less than 2 per cent – not quite the breakneck pace of Japan at the time, but not far off either. Then, in the mid-1970s, the Greek military regime demonstrated its incompetence by losing catastrophically to Turkey in a conflict over Cyprus. A new group of officers overthrew their hapless colleagues, and ushered in a return to civilian rule. Happily, the Argentine standoff did not apply: unlike Argentina's landlords (or Louisiana's plantation owners), Greek shipowners – though by this point famous worldwide for their opulence – had little reason to oppose the return to democracy. Their wealth, after all, was nearly untaxable.

With the military regime gone, Andreas Papandreou returned to Greece. The political party he had founded, the Panhellenic Socialist Movement, promised to close US military bases, take Greece out of NATO, hold a referendum on leaving the EU, and to share the wealth. In Greek, its initials were PASOK – 'PASOK in government, the people in power', was one textbook-populist slogan. Andreas still looked and sounded a bit academic, but he was fast on his feet. In a debate, his opponent supported EU membership by saying that 'Greece belongs to the West.' Quick as a flash, Papandreou shot back: 'I'd prefer that Greece belong to the Greeks.' In the first election following the return to democracy, the Panhellenic Socialists did not do well. By the second election in 1977, however, the party had become, in effect, the official opposition. By the third election, in October 1981, Andreas won handily, campaigning on a slogan of 'change'.

Papandreou then promptly reneged on his promises to withdraw from NATO and the EU. He negotiated a few US military base closures, but let the Americans keep the key facilities. His bigger problem was his promises to share the wealth. There was a lot of concentrated wealth in Greece. But that wealth was mobile; if Andreas tried to tax the shipowners, they would simply move their operations elsewhere.

And so Andreas engaged in share-the-wealth politics on a spectacular scale.

Papandreou's machine

Just after the election, Papandreou handed out government jobs to between 3,000 and 4,000 Panhellenic Socialist party members. Greeks, not slow to spy an opportunity, joined the party in droves. In 1980, the Panhellenic Socialist Party had 75,000 members; by 1984, 220,000 members. To satisfy those new members, in 1983, the government passed a law eliminating competitive examination requirements for many public sector jobs, so positions could be staffed based on political loyalty. A 1984 law made civil service hiring requirements almost completely ad hoc and disconnected pay from performance. Thus Andreas could hire anyone he wanted, and pay them well; public employees were soon, on average, making almost twice the average private sector wage. The proportion of Greeks working directly for the government rose from 8.5 per cent in 1976 to 10.1 per cent in 1988.

Admittedly, that is not a huge increase; and it was not an

enormous government workforce by European standards. But the civil service was only the tip of the iceberg. The government passed laws to gain control of trade unions (in 1982), agricultural associations (in 1983) and associations of merchants, craftsmen and tradesmen (in 1987), and flooded these associations with party members. Shortly after taking office, Papandreou also nationalised forty 'problematic companies'. These companies then became a ready source of jobs and contracts for political supporters. By 1984, as many as nine out of ten socialist party members had a professional connection with the public sector – whether through direct employment, a temporary job or a contract with a government-owned entity. By the end of the 1980s, the proportion of Greeks working directly or indirectly for the state was approaching 20 per cent. After that, the increase tapered off. But it did not decline: as recently as 2009, the figure was 22 per cent.

Papandreou also engaged in populist economics – spending without taxing. Instead of financing his generosity with inflation, as in Argentina, Andreas went for debt. Usually, a country's budget deficit rises in bad economic times and falls in good times. The Greek budget deficit just went up and up, from about 4 per cent in 1981, to 6 per cent by 1985, to 14 per cent by 1990. As a result, over the course of the 1980s, the national debt increased by four times. Of course, the good times could not last for ever. As early as 1991, the OECD issued a report wondering how on earth Greek deficits could have 'reached the levels they have without triggering a financial crisis'.

But the end did not come until almost two decades later, after the global financial crisis. Andreas had by that time long since passed away (like the elder Daley, he died in office; he was so dominant in Greek politics that when he was on his deathbed, the government was effectively paralysed). George Papandreou, Andreas's son and Georgios's grandson, was running for prime minister against an opponent who was attempting to spend his way to re-election.

Not to be outdone, George promised to spend even more money, including a €3bn stimulus package (about $2.5bn today). 'There is money,' George promised, infamously. And indeed, in Greece there had always been money; the problem was that the Greek state could not get its hands on it.

Ironically, when the crash came, Greece's fiscal situation had arguably improved from Andreas's day. But Germany insisted that Greece repay its debts at the most inopportune time imaginable. George Papandreou did not help matters, blaming previous Greek governments for lying about the size of the budget deficit – which helped fuel the panic in debt markets. Eventually, Greece was forced into a default that outdid even Argentina's. Its economy contracted by more than 40 per cent, the harshest downturn in Europe since prewar Germany.

In 2012, I was having a drink at a bar near Syntagma Square in Athens with a few friends when I noticed something puzzling: about thirty people were queueing for the bathroom. Eventually, I realised why: the streets were full of people taking part in a riot (the post-crisis austerity measures provoked a lot of riots), and they needed toilets. It was the most decorous crowd of rioters I have ever seen. Admittedly I was in the queue for the bathroom rather than out dodging tear gas. But Greece is still very obviously a rich and civilised country. Life expectancy for men is seventy-eight years; eighty-three years for women – a bit better, in fact, than the United States.

That said, rich countries are not supposed to have major problems with political patronage; they are not supposed to default on their sovereign debts. Perhaps to avoid cognitive dissonance, after the Greek default, Morgan Stanley Capital International announced it had downgraded Greece back to 'emerging market' status. So far, no other rich democracy has replicated Argentina's fall. But Greece has taken the largest step in that direction.

The Greek trap

In modern-day Greece (and Illinois), there is little sign of a classic Argentine standoff – the Greek shipowners, although they had cosied up to the country's military rulers, did not oppose the return of democracy. The Daleys, though corrupt, were no dictators. But even in countries and regions with 'post-materialist' politics, where people no longer vote along class lines, if the level of inequality is high the spectre of distributive politics tends to appear. Sometimes via patronage or machine politics; sometimes via the half-hearted wealth sharing of populist economics. In Illinois, for instance, inequality has not become a headline political issue, and yet share-the-wealth politics has taken off regardless.

This relationship between inequality and distributive politics, including both outright vote buying and more subtle patronage politics, has been shown to hold true in locations ranging from major US cities to the states of southern India. In some of the world's most egalitarian countries, scholars have been unable to find any evidence of this kind of politics whatsoever. Sweden, for instance, progressed from being an egalitarian nation of small farmers to an egalitarian service economy. The Swedes do not even have a word for machine politics, having never really needed one; when Swedish newspaper stories cover this issue in other countries, they usually have to define it.

This kind of politics can arise even in well-governed countries. Good governance is the almost talismanic force that protects us from most of the political events we have read about in this book. I mentioned earlier that good governance is a country's main defence against violent political instability. In fact, good governance – democratic accountability, the rule of law, the effectiveness of the civil service, protection of individual rights and civil liberties – correlates with just about any desirable social indicator you might care to mention. Longer life expectancies, higher incomes, higher average levels of education, greater self-reported happiness, and pandas for every child.

Perhaps not pandas; but just about anything else desirable. Unfortunately, while there is broad agreement on the all-but-magical powers of good governance, no one is quite sure where good governance comes from (appropriately enough for a piece of near-magic). Still, many would say that a large middle class plays a key role. In the United States of Huey Long's day, for instance, the Progressives made great strides in cleaning up political corruption in many US cities, nearly eliminating vote-buying (although not patronage). Scholars have found that a large middle class correlates with less political corruption, lower risks of political violence and stronger democracy. As Aristotle put it over two millennia ago: 'Thus it is manifest that the best political community is formed by citizens of the middle class, and those states are likely to be well administered, in which the middle class is large.'

All of which makes the story of modern Greece a puzzling and worrying one. During the 1980s, Greece was rapidly getting richer (at the peak, the average Greek citizen was just about as wealthy as the average Japanese citizen). And yet, even as the Greek middle class was growing, Andreas Papandreou was developing his patronage machine. Greeks were not fooled about how he was winning votes; and many of them, especially middle-class Greeks, did not like it. By 1985, in well-off neighbourhoods of Athens, the Panhellenic Socialists were taking in only a bit more than half the vote share they had achieved in 1981. But the country was highly unequal, social benefits were limited, and in the end he won more support through patronage than he lost. At the time, the bottom 40 per cent of the Greek population received less than 10 per cent of national income – a proportion lower even than Mexico, Colombia or Brazil today. Hence there were lots of people who could be motivated by the offer of a government job – and especially by the offer of pensions and healthcare, the kind of perks that a public-sector job typically provides.

Let us call it the 'Greek trap'. It involves high inequality, populist economics, a lack of trust in establishment politicians, patronage, machine politics, and at times, populism. It is a trap because political and economic turmoil tend to feed on each other, as has been the case in Greece. Once a country is in, it is hard to get out. The Greek trap is not destiny; not all unequal countries fall into it. But Greece did, obviously. So did Thailand and post-Perón Argentina. Illinois is, at the very least, close to the edge. According to one survey, only 28 per cent of Illinoisans trust their state government (under the circumstances, a remarkably high figure). Politicians in the 'steals but delivers' mould have been popular, especially in Chicago; the state embraced populist economics so eagerly that by the summer of 2017 its unpaid debts exceeded $10bn, and Illinois's credit rating was downgraded to one notch above junk.

In the world of political risk analysis, the well-governed 'advanced economies' of North America and Western Europe have traditionally occupied a blank space on the map. In most of the world, there is a market for insurance that protects investors against the risks of political violence or sovereign default. In advanced economies, that market is all but non-existent. These countries do not elect populist presidents, vote to leave political unions, have restive regions suddenly announce their secession, or default on their sovereign debts. Until, suddenly, they do. In February 2017, I received the first request of my career for a political risk report on the United States. Not such a blank space any more.

Our Blade Runner future

I mentioned in the introduction that the wheels had been coming off for some time. For both the US and UK, risk and governance indicators have been trending in the wrong direction for at least a decade. Nobody paid much attention until the political upsets of 2016, and then they decided the world was ending. Francis Fukuyama, who famously asserted the 'end of history' in the 1990s, recanted in 2016, saying the world was no longer safe for liberal democracy. To this recantation he added, in an interview: '[Trump] said at one point that the mainstream media is the enemy of the American people, which is something we haven't heard from a leader, you know, really since Joseph Stalin.' At the closing banquet of Oxford Analytica's annual conference, which I attended in the autumn of 2017, a former prime minister of Finland offered a spirited defence of globalisation. He identified three years that were turning points in modern history: 1945, 1989, and – you guessed it – 2016, when the globalisation system went into decline.

These comments are a little extreme. The US, UK and even Greece are still well-governed places. I know a few people who voted for Trump or Brexit; none of them were voting to end liberal democracy. These comments were, to my mind, political comments rather than political risk comments. In other words, the commentators were trying to demonstrate just how bad the opposition's programme for the country was, rather than making a serious evaluation of the risk of instability.

At that same conference, I had the opportunity to join a panel discussion on political risk. The other panellists were risk managers at companies doing business in volatile places, from Afghanistan to Yemen. The reaction of these panellists to the idea of rising political risk in the US and UK was a bit blasé. For someone accustomed to doing business in Afghanistan, the events of 2016 were underwhelming. Nobody died; nobody needed to be evacuated; nobody was thrown in jail for political reasons; nobody even lost all that much money (aside from the devaluation of the UK pound and Mexican peso).

Indeed, from the point of view of the scholars who came up with the Argentine standoff theory, we have nothing to worry about. According to Carles Boix, for instance, wealth is increasingly mobile and therefore untaxable. We have come a long way from the world of 1940s Argentina (or Louisiana), where wealth was overwhemingly based in land. Falling costs of transportation and communication have made it possible to relocate a business just about anywhere, so more and more industries are developing something like the untaxability enjoyed by Greek shipping. The tax rate on corporate profits in the world's richest countries has fallen from an average of more than 45 per cent in 1980 to 25 per cent today (and shows every sign of continuing to fall). If we are worried about the standoff, that is arguably a good thing. If the rich are untaxable, they will have no reason to oppose democracy. Daron Acemoglu and James Robinson write that while democracy was at one time 'pro-majority, even possibly pro-poor … for those who expect democracy to transform society in the same ways as British democracy did in the first half of the twentieth century, it may be a disappointing form of democracy'. Essentially, it is a Blade Runner future – a world of extreme inequality in which democracy is controlled by the rich, the poor are powerless, and probably, everyone is pursued by android replicants.

That sounds like a great future, at least for makers of androids. But I doubt it is as sustainable as theory would suggest. The case of Thailand, for instance, suggests that even in economies where wealth is mobile, something very much like a standoff can occur. And even if populism does not correlate directly with inequality, inequality leads to lower political participation – which gives populists a ready pool of non-voters to mobilise.

In this book, we have covered a lot of social science research on the causes of political instability, and some of history's greatest moments of political turmoil. So: are we now fated to repeat that history? Or do the advances in governance since World War II mean that the fluttering of today's populists will produce only the lightest of breezes instead of the political hurricanes of the past?

As I have noted, the global financial crisis and the austerity that followed, both of which discredited mainstream political parties, gave populists a once-in-a-lifetime opportunity in 2016. As the shock of the crisis recedes, so should the populist surge. I do not think any country is yet condemned to repeat Argentina's decline – even Greece could, I believe, recover rapidly. That said, I think the challenges are more fundamental than a few unexpected polling outcomes. Some countries are heading towards a trap they will have a hard time escaping. Hence, I present the following points as a handy guide to assessing whether your own nation is doomed, along with some suggestions on how we might avoid the repetition of some of history's more unpleasant (although exciting) moments.

1. Think beyond the win

Most people, when discoursing upon the politics of saving the nation, come almost immediately on to the topic of getting the opposition out of power. In the United States, political polarisation has become so intense that many of my friends and acquaintances can no longer pass the 'screen test' – if the president appears on television or the internet, they become so annoyed they cannot watch. During the Obama years, that was true for some friends from my youth (I grew up in South Dakota and Indiana, both states that went for Trump in 2016 by large margins). The reactions of my more left-leaning friends to Trump's administration have been no less extreme.

Consider, though, the histories of Thailand and Argentina. Throwing Perón and Thaksin out of office, and even into exile, did not save those nations. One might well argue those were pyrrhic victories. It is hard to think about the politics of one's own country from a political risk perspective, rather than a partisan perspective. But generally speaking, who is in government is only a part, and usually not the largest part, of the doomed/not-doomed question.

Indeed, when all anyone can talk about is throwing the bums out, that is probably a sign something more fundamental is wrong.

2. Crazy politics does not mean crazy people

In her memoir, Hillary Clinton mentions that she and Bill re-read Eric Hoffer's classic, *The True Believer*, and gave out copies to her senior staff, during the 2016 campaign. I get it; the book, as I have mentioned, claims that mass movements attract desperate, frustrated losers. Imagining Trump's followers in that light was probably deeply satisfying for the Clintons. But, as we have seen, efforts to explain political events as incidents of collective insanity have turned out to be, in retrospect, wrong. Revolutions emerge neither from the madness of crowds nor from personal frustrations so extreme they produce violence. Indeed, the portrait of politics in *The True Believer* is very nearly the opposite of what makes mass movements effective. Hoffer pins the Russian Revolution, for instance, on a mass movement of failed individuals, living in a landscape of collapsed social structures and desperate to escape the consequences of their own poor choices, who were easy prey for Lenin's doctrine. As we have seen, the Russian Revolution was nothing like that; it turned on the people power of the most upwardly mobile of Russian workers, who became powerful not because of the collapse of social structures but because their increasingly effective community organisations, notably labour unions, helped them to overcome the weakness of crowds.

I do not want to deny anyone the right to call the opposition 'lunatics'; that is one of the most cherished of all democratic freedoms. But counting up the number of crazy people is not a good way to assess the risks to the nation.

3. Politics is a community sport

Instead of worrying about alienated, frustrated individuals, worry about frustrated groups. Politics is a community sport. We vote out governments that have failed to manage the nation's economy well, rather than voting with our wallets; we participate in politics when we think our community is suffering, not when we are in personal distress. It appears that in 2016, aggrieved communities across the US and UK voted for Brexit and Trump. Perhaps some of these votes involved racism or intolerance. But recent research has shown that these communities also had measurable grievances: they had been negatively impacted by globalisation; workforce participation had declined; they had experienced a dispropor-tionate number of deaths due to opioid use. Some people in these communities were doing well; others were doing badly; it appears that living in such communities made these people more likely to vote populist whatever their personal circumstances.

Some said 2016 was a class war. As the *New York Times* journalist Nate Cohn put it, in a now-famous tweet: 'How to think about this election: white working-class voters just decided to vote like a minority group. They're >40% of the electorate.' I am not entirely sure the class label fits; the Trump voters I know personally are college-educated, they just happen to live in struggling commu-nities. In fact, some studies have found that relatively better-off members of the 'working class' were more likely to vote for Donald Trump. Which would make sense: as we have seen, it is often the better-off members of aggrieved communities (like those Russian workers) who are the first to mobilise.

Many of the factors that produced the surprises of 2016 were ephemeral – FBI Director James Comey's untimely decision to announce new evidence regarding Clinton's emails; Boris Johnson's decision to join the 'out' campaign. In my view, the mobilisation of aggrieved communities has been going on for years. In Europe, aggrieved social groups caused a major upset in the 2014 European Parliament elections, turning parties of the populist right into the largest blocs in the European Parliament for both the UK and France. Elections where turnouts are low (like those European Parliament elections, in which less than 37 per cent of eligible Britons voted) tend to be good bellwethers of mobilisation, because a relatively small but determined group can make a difference. In a similar vein, in the United States, the populist-right Tea Party movement had been throwing its weight around for years, especially in low-turnout congressional primaries.

Mobilisation politics is not, of course, the only force that produced the populist upsets of 2016. Many habitual voters, voting on the issues, also voted for populists – religiously observant white Americans tended to vote for Trump, for instance. Still, whether the polarisation of today's politics escalates is going to depend a lot on mobilisation politics. Struggle stories (especially involving community decline and unfair treatment), a sense of group identity and opportunities to impact politics turned millions of non-voters into Brexit voters. If these communities continue to feel they have a political problem that can be addressed through political action, they are likely to continue to mobilise.

4. Volatile politics is good for populists

Of course, mobilisation politics is not universally a bad thing. Bringing new voices into politics often seems like a step forward for social justice. Average attendance at town hall meetings held for the general public by US members of the House of Representatives rose from below fifty people to more than 280 in 2017; it is heart-ening to see Americans taking such an interest in their democracy. Perhaps the group that has mobilised most dramatically following Trump's election has been women – first in the women's march (perhaps the largest single-day demonstration in US history), and then in a broad campaign against sexual harassment. Many people would celebrate this kind of mobilisation, which indeed may be necessary to produce substantive political reform. Going back in history, democracy in Europe was once only for the rich; before that, hereditary aristocracies ruled. Surely, those who mobilised the middle class in democratic movements in Europe were heroes rather than villains. Of course, getting from point A to point B in European politics involved the French Revolution. Even if the end goal is laudable, there are more and less pleasant ways to get there.

One of the most significant dangers of mobilisation politics is that it tends to polarise society. As we have seen, people's decisions to take political action turn on their belief that their social group has a political problem. Hence mobilisation of one social group tends to lead to mobilisation by others. The mobilisation that brought about Brexit brought more young people to the polls one year later – now convinced they had a political problem. Donald Trump's victory appears to have convinced many American women their problems are not personal, but political. Mobilisation, as we have seen, begets mobilisation in response, in a cycle that can escalate. After Thaksin helped to turn rural voters into a force in Thai electoral politics, the yellowshirts one-upped him by taking to the streets; the redshirts responded by pouring into the centre of Bangkok – and things went downhill from there.

Volatile politics is also the sea in which populists swim. Populists often come to power by mobilising politically disaffected non-voters; populists can gain from economic turmoil, which discredits the parties in power; populists can thrive in a polarised environment, because they find it easy to pick up support from across the political spectrum. Greece's sovereign default led to a victory by the populist left, which then formed a coalition government with a party of the populist right. That move astounded most commentators, but Juan Perón would have understood.

More broadly, populists tend to campaign, as we have seen, against a broken political system that prevents the people from getting their way. It is probably easier to win votes with such claims when they contain a grain of truth – as they surely did for Huey Long in the 'feudal state of Louisiana', for instance. For different reasons, today's populists have found it easy to make similar claims. In US politics, money buys a lot of influence, which was a key issue for the left-populist campaign of Bernie Sanders. In the UK (and other European countries), the governance of the European Union has been seen as something of an elite project over which the voting public has had little control. Quite possibly, one symptom of such 'democratic deficits' is declining trust in political leaders – which has been shown to correlate strongly with populist voting. Without political reforms in both the United States and Europe, populist claims about broken systems are likely to continue to win votes.

5. The rich are dangerous

Ordinarily, dull politics could have no better friend than the rich. Conservatives tend to like things just as they are, with perhaps a dash more polo and foxhunting. And yet, as I mentioned, the most comprehensive study of failures of democracy since 1980 found that interventions of the rich were a more frequent cause of failures than uprisings of the poor.

Most people's idea of the Argentine standoff probably involves someone like Huey Long – the ravening terror-beast of a trust-funder's fever-dreams; an active promoter of class warfare. But in the modern day, such campaigns tend to be paper tigers. The statistics on democratic failures since 1980 indicate that such campaigns are only rarely a genuine threat to democracy; the research on sharing the wealth suggests that such campaigns almost never produce significant changes in the income distribution.

The version of the standoff that has in recent years proved far more dangerous is more prosaic: the rich respond to the chronic pain of taxation, the incessant tiny thefts by the Average Joe, by turning against democracy. It is the standoff's inherent irony. Democracy and inequality make poor travelling companions because, under certain circumstances, the milquetoast thing to do is to soak the rich. That is to say, in highly unequal countries, redistribution can appeal to the person who votes out of civic duty; the average (voting) Joe. The kind of politician who brings about a dangerous standoff might well be thoughtful, mild-mannered, even professorial – a politician, in short, much like Barack Obama, whose Affordable Care Act, colloquially known as Obamacare, was the most redistributive piece of US legislation in three decades. Obama paid for healthcare for the poor with taxes on the rich – including taxes on high-cost health plans, taxes on healthcare companies, an 0.9 per cent payroll tax and a 3.8 per cent tax on investment income.

Many people on the populist right did not like Obamacare, fearing that their own healthcare would suffer. But the reaction of the American rich to the threat of redistribution has been little short of hysterical. The journalist Jane Mayer has documented close to $1bn in political donations raised in forums organised by two billionaire industrialists, the Koch brothers. I know the Argentine standoff is not supposed to apply in the United States, thanks to untaxability; but then the Koch brothers' wealth, tied up in US-based heavy industry, is not very mobile.

Reasonable people could disagree about whether this programme is inherently anti-democratic; arguably, it is a just a clever political strategy the Kochs thought of first (and which the US Democratic Party is now racing to counter). And yet historically, these kinds of political obsessions by the rich have not led in a good direction. Spending lots of money to win local government elections – as the Kochs have done, and as Thaksin did in Thailand – is nobody's idea of a pleasant way to spend one's free time, and suggests a rather desperate quest for political influence. I would sleep more easily if the Kochs (and other billionaires) would get some different hobbies. The Argentine standoff has not been an issue in rich countries for decades. But then again, for most of that time, inequality was at historic lows. Now that inequality has risen again, how lucky do we feel?

6. Progressives are also dangerous

The closing banquet of Oxford Analytica's conference was held in the spectacular setting of Blenheim Palace, with the audience in black tie. After the Finn finished his speech, a colleague's wife, a woman with populist sympathies, said: 'that was like a speech given at Versailles just before the French Revolution'. 'And here we are, eating cake,' I said, wittily. 'You just don't get it,' she said. 'You in here are the 10 per cent. The 90 per cent of people out there *want* the end of your globalisation system.'

She had a point. The well-meaning people in Blenheim Palace – mostly experts on geopolitics – were trying to plot a way to save globalisation and liberal democracy. But they were not really thinking about whether anyone else shared those goals. The political scientist Cas Mudde made a similar point. He noted that the rise of far-right populism was one of the most studied topics in European political science. And yet, he did not know of a single scholar who was sympathetic to the populists; all of them studied populism as a problem to be eradicated.

Progressives have always suffered from this tendency. Ambitious, high-achieving members of the educated middle classes struggle constantly to improve themselves; and very often they take that struggle out into the world. But progressive world-saving schemes have a chequered history. In Huey Long's day, the Progressives strayed into areas, most infamously eugenics, where their science was wrong. Books on eugenics became bestsellers; at agricultural fairs there were 'fitter family' and 'better baby' competitions.

This obsession with improving the gene pool led Progressives to advocate legislation requiring forcible sterilisation of inmates of mental institutions. Eventually, more than thirty US states passed such laws. It was the forefront of science; but eventually, Adolf Hitler would demonstrate that this line of thinking led societies to a place they did not want to go.

Progressive ideas were not only vulnerable to bad science. The policies that Progressive era experts recommended tended, inevitably, to be good for the experts themselves. Perhaps the most dramatic example was the power grab by the highly educated that produced the so-called 'fourth branch' of government, the regulatory agencies. In the modern day, regulatory agencies have gained powers beyond the dreams of even the most ambitious Progressives of Huey Long's era. In countries with independent central banks, for instance, experts set policy almost without interference from elected political leaders. And yet, the science of even these most exalted of experts often fails, as economists at central banks did, catastrophically, in the run-up to the global financial crisis. The highly educated are themselves an interest group, and their expert recommendations – even when delivered based on genuine expertise – can be wrong, and are rarely disinterested. As the historian Shelton Stromquist pointed out, the Progressives liked to play down class warfare, but in the end, they were fighting a class war, on their own behalf. My dinner companion was making a similar point: while professing to want to save the world, we were really thinking of saving our world. It is perhaps the original sin of progressivism.

It tends to fall to middle-class progressives to salvage political stability when society becomes polarised or democracy comes under threat. But these efforts can go wrong. In a worst-case scenario, the educated middle class can end up mobilised against the traditional middle class or the poor. That happened in the messy aftermath of the Iranian revolution, when Ali Shariati's dream of a utopian

Islamic revolution turned into something authoritarian. The middle class ended up opposing the poor in Greece and Argentina during the 1980s; and perhaps most dramatically, in modern-day Thailand. That is a bad scenario for stability.

At their best – for instance, in the United States in the 1920s – progressives make lots of cross-class alliances. That can be difficult; it is hard to imagine modern progressives partnering with labour unions. Progressives have tended to brand those who voted for Brexit and Trump as lunatics; or at the very least fools who were prey for unscrupulous populists. That kind of thinking is not a promising start for any kind of cross-class campaign. It also ignores most of the research on the causes of instability. Mobilised groups of the politically disaffected are not sheep waiting to be led; they are active participants in shaping struggle stories and group identities that enable them to mobilise. They take action because they believe they can make a difference – and in 2016, they were right.

7. Watch for hard choices

Which leads me to my last point in this handy guide: watch for hard choices, and if you see one coming, panic and sell everything. I was listening to Boston's public radio station recently, which played an interview with a journalist who won the National Book Award for her book on Putin's Russia. She said that when Trump was elected, Barack Obama and Hillary Clinton should have declared a state of national emergency and invalidated the election. A hard choice to be sure.

When societies become polarised, hard choices tend to creep on to the political agenda. All too often, after a populist victory, the next election pits populist against populist instead of populist against centrist. Citizens may be forced to choose between sacrificing economic progress or sacrificing a bit of democracy; like the citizens of Argentina during the country's long decline, they may be faced repeatedly with a menu of bad options. Such hard choices tend to be costly to stability. Sometimes, mobilised groups get so angry with each other that they start breaking things in their squabbles; or things really get out of control and they burn the place down.

You know what? I am going to finish the book with a sex scene.

Paris in springtime

It started with horny students. The authorities had decreed that college dormitories were to remain sex-segregated. Who were they kidding? This was Paris. *In the springtime.* As the trees budded in 1967, so many male students invaded a women's dormitory at the University of Nanterre that the efforts of both the police and fire departments were required to extract them. There were scandalous reports of 'free copulation'. Hoping to make an example, the authorities expelled nearly thirty students. But the amorous *étudiants* could not be held back. In January 1968, a government minister turned up at the Nanterre campus to find obscene graffiti covering the walls, including an enormous portrait of a phallus. As the minister walked by, a student by the name of Daniel Cohn-Bendit stepped out of the crowd. Cohn-Bendit complained loudly that in a recently released ministry white paper there was 'not one word on the sexual issues of youth'. Very likely, the minister thought he was being made the butt of a joke. Cohn-Bendit persisted, underlining the vital importance of coeducational dormitories. The minister lost his temper: 'with a face like yours, no wonder you have these sexual problems. I suggest you jump in the pool.'

'Now there's an answer,' Cohn-Bendit replied, 'worthy of Hitler's youth minister.'

It turned out that Cohn-Bendit, soon to be known to the world as 'Danny the Red', had more than sex on his mind. He was an amateur philosopher; and his philosophising had a lot to do with revolution. As Cohn-Bendit would later explain, Lenin's idea of a 'revolutionary vanguard', a small cadre leading the people in a mass uprising, was obsolete. A revolutionary's job, he claimed, was to create provocative situations, and let chaos do the rest. 'The movement's only chance is the disorder that lets men speak freely,' he told Jean-Paul Sartre. When rumours arose that Cohn-Bendit might be expelled or deported, some thirty to fifty students occupied the campus sociology building. The police were called in, whereupon Danny the Red's rather unorthodox theory of political uprisings proved surprisingly accurate. Just as the police were man-handling the struggling students, classes were let out for lunch, and roughly 1,000 of their classmates suddenly arrived on the scene. The situation was out of control. There was a near riot; windows were broken; cars overturned. The police fled the campus.

Even in France, students do not usually attack police. But in 1968, tensions were high. President Charles de Gaulle had taken power a decade earlier, by dubious means (with fears of a coup rising, de Gaulle had been given not only the presidency, but a free hand to rewrite the French Constitution). By 1968, de Gaulle was well into his second seven-year presidential term, and although he was no dictator, he was hardly a model democrat; his regime repeatedly and archaically prosecuted individuals who insulted the 'honour' of the presidency.

On Valentine's Day 1968, in support of the coed movement, France's national students' union organised male invasions of women's dormitories in universities across the country. This time it was the American men at the Cité Internationale Universitaire de Paris who were the last to withdraw from the ladies' lodgings – whether due to extreme amorousness or a light hand taken against foreign students was unclear. By March, some 500 students were engaging in regular demonstrations and sit-ins in Nanterre; by April, Cohn-Bendit was leading, while claiming not to lead, a protest movement uniting socialists, anarchists, anti-war protestors, and students who wanted coed dorms; by May, the movement had relocated from the suburban Nanterre campus to the Sorbonne.

On 3 May 1968, the police were sent in to arrest the students at the Sorbonne. The authorities overdid it, rounding up more than 500 students and closing the Sorbonne campus for the first time in the institution's 700-year history. The six-hour violent confrontation between students and police that followed spilled over into the Latin Quarter. And that was just the beginning. By 7 May the national students' union and parts of the teachers' union were supporting the protestors. On 10 May protestors built barricades on the Boulevard St Michel, chopped down trees, overturned parked cars, and pulled up paving stones from streets. Police charged in at 2.15am; the battle raged until 6.00am; students hurled Molotov cocktails; some 400 people were injured. As the violence took place in the centre of Paris, thousands of people witnessed these events. Because it was France, there were debates about which philosopher had inspired the uprising. Some said the students were disciples of Marcuse. 'None of us have read Marcuse,' said Cohn-Bendit.

By the middle of May, industrial labour unions had joined the uprising. There was a march of roughly 1 million people in Paris; the railway, airline and road transport unions went on strike; by 20 May all truck transport and mail delivery in Paris had stopped. By this point, the government had lost control of most universities (which were occupied by students and teachers) and much of the Latin Quarter. Paris came to a standstill. A student recalled: 'Paris was wonderful then. Everyone was talking.' On the wall of the occupied Sorbonne, graffiti read: 'the more I make revolution, the more I feel like making love'. The political scientists at the Sciences Po wrote, more desperately: 'Girls! Don't drive men to alienation! Give yourselves to the revolution!' A few places remained bastions of normalcy. A Sri Lankan student at the Cité Internationale recalled that the 'Belgian and Swiss houses, the cleanest, quietest, and most prudish of the compound, remained undisturbed'.

The protestors did not agree what they stood for – the red flag of communism and the black flag of anarchy flew together – but they agreed what they stood against: de Gaulle. 'I am not interested in metaphysics,' Cohn-Bendit told Sartre, 'I am not really interested in whether there can still be a revolution in advanced capitalist societies … The aim is now the overthrow of the regime.' By the end of May, about two-thirds of the French workforce had gone on strike. Charles de Gaulle asked some philosophical questions of his own. For instance, to his interior minister: 'Can you guarantee me, Fouchet – can you really guarantee me that there is no possibility of the forces of order being overcome by the uprising?' History does not record the answer de Gaulle received, but he may not have liked it. 'I have decided to leave,' de Gaulle said, and fled Paris by helicopter, ostensibly to his country home, but then vanished along with his personal papers and effects. It appeared the students would get their coed dorms and topple the French government in the process.

And then, a few hours later, de Gaulle turned up at the French military command in Germany. Presumably he was seeking the support of the army; apparently, he got it. (According to some accounts, de Gaulle was about to abdicate but the head of the army bolstered his nerve.) On 30 May, de Gaulle returned to France, and announced that new elections would be held.

That was when the truly unexpected occurred. In the elections, the leftist parties suffered a crushing defeat, losing almost half their parliamentary seats; de Gaulle's conservative right gained an absolute majority. De Gaulle thus remained comfortably in power. He banned demonstrations and shut down far-left publications. The student leaders were offered book contracts; the paving stones of the Latin Quarter were covered in asphalt to prevent anyone else throwing them at police; Cohn-Bendit was exiled from France for a decade; the dormitories were made coeducational; and people came to remember the May 1968 rebellion, not as it was – something astonishingly close to revolution – but as being all about student sex.

And so, if you are one of those who lost hope during 2016, take heart. Even the most extraordinary political events can be followed by a rapid return to the status quo. Famously, two months before the Paris uprising, a *Le Monde* editorialist wrote: 'France is bored.' After a brief flirtation with revolution, French citizens voted to go right back to being bored.

I must admit, I do not think we are going to escape our current predicament as easily as France in the 1960s (if you call that easy). I think high levels of inequality will pose ongoing challenges for stability, as will the effort to forge a stronger Eurozone, even if things get better in the near term. But the foundations are strong in most countries, and democracy has survived shocks in the past – it even survived Huey Long. The historical patterns covered in this book will influence our future, but we determine it.

Acknowledgements

For years I have been telling my successful friends: 'nice house, but you'll be first up against the wall when the revolution comes!' Ha, ha, they would say, but their eyes were not laughing. Imagine my surprise when along comes the revolution and it is a revolution of the populist right. How awkward!

My rich friends have been gracious in victory. Not only did they provide their comments and feedback on early drafts of this book, they also in many cases hosted me in their homes; although frankly they were not using many of those spare rooms anyway. Their graciousness has made me reconsider the need for certain post-revolutionary programmes that I had been discussing with Bernie Sanders and Jeremy Corbyn. Among the friends and colleagues who helped in the writing of this book – presumably without a thought that if they did so, things might go better for them if the revolution did indeed come to pass – were Meysam Ahmadi, Mark Blyth, Jeff Colgan, George Matthew Flory, Johanna Hanink, Jill Hedges, Mo Henderson, Jeff Lang, Dan Lefkovitz, Eric Patashnik, Felipe Rojas Silva, Laurence Williams, Marvin Zonis, and my parents, Judy and Peter Wilkin. My agents, Sally Holloway of Felicity Bryan Associates and George Lucas of InkWell Management, not only ensured the book saw print but contributed several of the best lines. I must also express my heartfelt appreciation to the Watson Institute for Public Policy and International Affairs at Brown University, which partly funded the writing.

I asked a panel of academic reviewers to look at each chapter from a specialist's perspective. The reviewers were: Kevin Hewison, Weldon E. Thornton Emeritus Distinguished Professor of Asian Studies, University of North Carolina at Chapel Hill; Cesar Martinelli, Professor of Economics, George Mason University; William G. Rosenberg, Professor Emeritus of History, University of Michigan; Jacquelien van Stekelenburg, Professor of Social Conflict and Change, Vrije Universiteit Amsterdam; and Ghoncheh Tazmini, Associate Member, Centre for Iranian Studies, SOAS, University of London. Professor Rosenberg was particularly generous with his insights. The demands of a readable narrative meant that I was not always able to take their good advice; any remaining over-simplifications or outright errors are my own. Look to the sources in the next section (including their own works) for more nuanced views.

Above all others, I must thank two people. My editor, Ed Lake at Profile, turned the manuscript from yet another dreary whine about the end of the world into an entertaining romp through the end of the world. My partner, Carrie Nordlund, supported me through another year of the writing rollercoaster. Lastly, I would like to thank the readers of *Wealth Secrets* who sent me their comments (particularly those from Africa and the Middle East, for whom a guide to success in a world of rent-seeking seemed to go over a treat). That kept me going.

Notes

Introduction

Before we begin, a housekeeping note. Throughout the text, I have updated historical monetary amounts to their modern purchasing power equivalent ('roughly equivalent to X dollars today'). Unless otherwise noted, I have done so using exchange rates from the Penn World Tables and the conversion tool maintained by Measuring Worth:

Robert C. Feenstra, Robert Inklaar and Marcel P. Timmer, 2015, 'The Next Generation of the Penn World Table', *American Economic Review*, 2015, pp. 3150–3182. www.ggdc.net/pwt/ (accessed 30/10/2017).

Samuel H. Williamson, 2017, 'Seven Ways to Compute the Relative Value of a U.S. Dollar Amount, 1774 to Present', *MeasuringWorth*, 2017. www.measuringworth.com/uscompare/ (accessed 30/10/2017).

In the introduction, I say that Che Guevara's death disproved his own theory of revolution. To be fair, he appeared to know that Bolivia was a lost cause, and his theory of revolution was more complex than his propaganda about apples and trees. That said, he had also just failed to spark a revolution in the Congo.

I conducted some background interviews in Thailand, but in the main, for quotes and biographical details in this book, I have relied on general histories and the popular media. It is hard to make a living as a writer, so I have tried to namecheck the authors on whom I drew most heavily in the text. For those I have forgotten, at least they are mentioned in these notes.

Chapter 1

In medieval times, of course, the animal of choice for Thai kings was not the dog, but the elephant; especially the white elephant, which symbolised royal power. Indeed, the power of feudal states in Southeast Asia was measured in elephants. When kingdoms lost wars, they handed over their tame elephants to their conquerors; when vassal kings came to pay tribute, they kept up appearances by riding an elephant; in lists of rich people's possessions, the elephants always came first. The greatest war elephants had names known even to their enemies. One ancient inscription reads: 'I fought Lord Sam Jan's elephant, Mas Moan by name, and beat him. Lord Sam

Jan fled.' Europeans living in the region estimated that by the 1600s the Thai king controlled at least 3,000 tame elephants; other sources said 5,000.

Perhaps the most famous battle of Thai history took place on elephants in the 1500s. The ancient Thai account of the battle describes in elaborate detail how a Thai prince known as Naresuan challenged his Burmese rival to an elephant duel and cut him down. The ancient Burmese account, by contrast, states that the Burmese prince was randomly shot by a stray bullet and propped up by another soldier; at just that moment Naresuan happened to ride by and, not realising what had happened, ran away in terror from the Burmese prince's dead body. (There is a marvellous movie of the Thai version, called *The Legend of King Naresuan*, released in 2007.)

From elephants to poodles. Most of the material on Foo Foo comes from the popular media, as well as the leaked birthday party video (as of this writing, easily accessible on YouTube by searching for 'Thai princess birthday' – but not safe for work). The quote from the US ambassador is from WikiLeaks. The book on Tongdaeng is:

His Majesty King Bhumibol Adulyadej, *The Story of Tongdaeng: Biography of a Pet Dog*, Bangkok, Amarin, 2002.

Foo Foo died in 2015, having achieved the rank of lieutenant general, and was cremated after four days of Buddhist rites.

The median voter theorem was made famous by:

Anthony Downs, 'An Economic Theory of Political Action in a Democracy', *Journal of Political Economy*, 1957, pp. 135–150.

It is based, believe it or not, on a theory of where it is optimal for businesses to locate:

Harold Hotelling, 'Stability in Competition', *The Economic Journal*, 1929, pp. 41–57.

My comments about the ways voters differ from the average citizen in the US and UK are based on:

'Voter Turnout Demographics', *United States Elections Project*. http://www. electproject.org/home/voter-turnout/demographics (accessed 30/10/2017).

Voter turnout in British elections and EU referendums:

'Who Makes it to the Polling Station', *The Economist Blog*. http://www.economist. com/blogs/graphicdetail/2016/06/daily-chart-16 (accessed 30/10/2017).

There is an extensive literature on this topic, and some sources claim that these voter characteristics are specific to advanced economies. In some emerging markets, for instance, poor people may be more likely to vote than rich people – which could be a result of machine politics, but there are many theories. See, for instance:

Kimuli Kasara & Pavithra Suryanarayan, 'When Do the Rich Vote Less Than the Poor and Why? Explaining Turnout Inequality Across the World', 2015, *American Journal of Political Science*, pp. 613–627.

The main sources for the narrative on Thaksin's rise are:

Federico Ferrara, *Thailand Unhinged: The Death of Thai-Style Democracy*, Singapore, Equinox Publishing, 2011. An opinionated book that, while by no means pro-Thaksin, emphasises the ugly, anti-democratic side of the yellowshirt movement.

Kevin Hewison, 'Thaksin Shinawatra and the Reshaping of Thai Politics', *Contemporary Politics*, 2010, pp. 119–133. Hewison provided a critique of an early draft of this chapter, for which I am grateful.

Kevin Hewison, 'Class, Inequality and Politics', in *Bangkok May 2010: Perspectives on a Divided Thailand*, Singapore, Institute of Southeast Asian Studies, 2012.

Andrew MacGregor Marshall, *Kingdom in Crisis: Thailand's Struggle for Democracy in the Twenty-First Century*, London, Zed Books, 2015.

Pasuk Phongpaichit & Chris Baker, *Thailand's Boom and Bust*, Chiang Mai, Silkworm Books, 1998.

Pasuk Phongpaichit & Chris Baker, *Thaksin*, Chiang Mai, Silkworm Books, 2010. The primary source for the biographical material on Thaksin, and much of the narrative about the redshirt/yellowshirt standoff (up to the late 2000s).

Amar Siamwalla & Somchai Jitsuchon, 'The Socio-economic Bases of the Red/Yellow Divide', in *Bangkok May 2010: Perspectives on a Divided Thailand*, Singapore, Institute of Southeast Asian Studies, 2012, pp. 64–71.

B. J. Terwiel, *Thailand's Political History: From the 13th Century to Recent Times*, Bangkok, River Books, 2011. A very readable history, and the source for the notes on elephants above.

Mark R. Thompson, 'People Power Sours: Uncivil Society in Thailand and the Philippines', *Current History*, 2008, pp. 381–387.

Of all the social science covered in this book, populism is perhaps the most controversial topic. Until 2016, populism was largely of interest to scholars of Latin America. Now, top-notch talent from around the world is on the case; but there are as of yet few points of consensus. There are at least four literatures on populism, which do not yet do a good job of talking to each other. The first is on populism in Latin America, which has a very long history. Then there is the study of the populist right in Europe, beginning in the 1980s, which contains a lot of statistical research. There is also a large literature on the US populist tradition, which stretches back to Andrew Jackson – a populist president before the term 'populism' was invented. Finally, there is the new literature launched by the events of 2016, and everyone from economists to sociologists has piled into the fray. There is a huge amount that is still unknown; indeed, there is basic disagreement on what populism is. Are some candidates and parties populist? Or is populism a 'frame', a type of political discourse that is adopted even by mainstream candidates (like Roosevelt)? How can populism be measured? Is someone populist or not-populist, or are there degrees of populism?

The definition of populist ideology that I use comes from Cas Mudde, whose focus is European populism:

Cas Mudde, 'The Populist Zeitgeist', *Government and Opposition*, 2004, pp. 541–563.

Cas Mudde, *Populist Radical Right Parties in Europe*, Cambridge, Cambridge University Press, 2007.

Cas Mudde & Cristobal Rovira Kaltwasse, *Populism: A Very Short Introduction*, Oxford, Oxford University Press, 2017. If you are new to populism, you could start with this book. It is, as the title promises, very short. That said, Mudde and his frequent collaborator Kaltwasse do not dumb things down.

Two recent books on populism have been published that are more oriented towards the general reader. I did not end up using material from them for this book, so if you are interested in further reading, everything will be new:

John B. Judis, *The Populist Explosion: How the Great Recession Transformed American and European Politics*, New York, Columbia Global Reports, 2016. A journalistic account, well-written but with a tendency to jump to conclusions.

Jan-Werner Müller, *What is Populism?*, Philadelphia, University of Pennsylvania Press, 2016. Makes a provocative argument on why the populist right is inherently anti-democratic. I am not sure I agree, but it is worth reading.

We will come back to populism, with more sources, in chapter 4.

The extraordinary Banharn appears in:

Yposhinori Nishizaki, *Political Authority and Provincial Identity in Thailand: The Making of Banharn-buri*, Ithaca, New York, Cornell Southeast Asia Program Publications, 2011.

With some background from:

Elin Bjarnegård, 'Who's the Perfect Politician? Clientelism as a Determining Feature of Thai Politics', in Dirk Tomsa & Andreas Ufen (eds), *Party Politics in Southeast Asia: Clientelism and Electoral Competition in Indonesia, Thailand and the Philippines*, Abingdon, Routledge, 2012.

The explanation of how 'steals but delivers' politics works is from:

Luigi Manzetti & Carole J. Wilson, 'Why Do Corrupt Governments Maintain Public Support?' *Comparative Political Studies*, 2007, pp. 949–970.

Before I decided to sell out and become a consultant, I wanted to be an academic. My one contribution to scholarship is on the topic of economic voting. Hence it is a topic dear to my heart. The explanation of the impact of the economy on politics comes from:

Anne Case & Angus Deaton, 'Mortality and Morbidity in the 21st Century', *Brookings Papers on Economic Activity*, 2017, pp. 397–476. The famous study that linked economic despair to substance abuse in rural America.

Michael S. Lewis-Beck & Mary Stegmaier, 'The VP-function Revisited: A Survey of the Literature on Vote and Popularity Functions After Over 40 Years', *Public Choice*, 2013, pp. 367–385. The primary source for the section on economic voting.

Sam Wilkin, Brandon Haller & Helmuth Norpoth, 'From Argentina to Zambia: A World-wide Test of Economic Voting', *Electoral Studies*, 1997, pp. 301–316. An acceptable effort.

And on the impacts of the economy on the stability of democracy:

Manuel Funke, Moritz Schularick & Christoph Trebesch, 'Politics in the Slump: Polarization and Extremism After Financial Crises, 1870–2014', *Center for Economic Policy Research Discussion Paper*, 2015. A statistical analysis showing that financial crises, throughout history, have led to gains for the far right.

Stephan Haggard & Robert R. Kaufman, *Dictators and Democrats: Masses, Elites and Regime Change*, Princeton, Princeton University Press, 2016. We will hear more from these authors in chapter 4.

Ellen Lust & David Waldner, *Unwelcome Change: Understanding, Evaluating, and Extending Theories of Democratic Backsliding*, Washington, DC, USAID, 2015. A good non-technical summary of current research on democratic breakdown.

Jurgen Möller, Alexander Schmotz & Svend-Erik Skaaning, 'Economic Crisis and Democratic Breakdown in the Interwar Years: A Reassessment', *Historical Social Research*, 2015, pp. 301–318. Argues, somewhat against the grain, that economic crises did not in fact lead to the prewar rise of fascists in Europe (even today, the debate rages on).

Jacopo Ponticelli & Hans-Joachim Voth, 'Austerity and Anarchy: Budget Cuts and Social Unrest in Europe, 1919–2008', 2012. https://econ-papers.upf.edu/papers/1342.pdf (accessed 31/10/2017). Statistical tests showing a link between austerity and political turmoil.

Hans-Joachim Voth, 'Tightening Tensions: Fiscal Policy and Civil Unrest in Eleven South American Countries, 1937–1995', 2012. https://ssrn.com/abstract=2012620 (accessed 31/10/2017).

I also mentioned Martin Wolf's calculations on austerity:

Martin Wolf, 'Economic Origins of the Populist Surge', *Financial Times*, 27 June 2017.

Austerity poses economic dangers as well as political dangers:

Mark Blyth, *Austerity: The History of a Dangerous Idea*, Oxford, Oxford University Press, 2013.

Chapter 2

Every generation reinvents the Russian Revolution, partly because of the availability of new material, but partly because histories of the revolution – as with this book – inevitably reflect today's politics as much as they do what happened in Russia. During the Cold War, revolutionary histories were deployed either to support the US anti-communist agenda or oppose it. Writing with sympathy for the rising workers were historians such as Victoria Bonnell, Sheila Fitzpatrick and Leopold Haimson; writing with animosity for the Bolsheviks was Richard Pipes. Then the 1990s brought an end to the Cold War, as well as the opening of the Soviet archives. Orlando Figes produced the first postmodern history of the revolution – in which none of the master narratives matter, individual stories carry the day, and the only consistent theme is chaos. In 2017, the 100th anniversary of the revolution, a new set of histories arrived. In these tellings, Lenin became a master political manipulator and an agent of German interests.

The sources for the Russian historical narrative of the chapter are:

Edward Acton, *Rethinking the Russian Revolution*, 2010, London, Bloomsbury Academic. Used for the notes on the 'underground universities'.

Orlando Figes, *A People's Tragedy: The Russian Revolution, 1891–1924*, New York, Penguin, 1996. The primary source for my revolutionary history, including the farcical telling of the Bolshevik takeover and the biography of the worker Kanatchikov. It is also a major source for biographical material on Lenin (although see below). If you read one history of the Russian Revolution, I would suggest it is this one. It is a long book, but the bizarre story of the Bolshevik takeover is far from the most extraordinary one in it. Rasputin, Trotsky, cannibalism? It is all here.

Sean McMeekin, *The Russian Revolution: A New History*, London, Profile, 2017. My favourite of the new 2017 histories. Comprehensive, balanced and demonstrates how much the revolution was a creation of German foreign policy.

Richard Pipes, *Russia Under the Old Regime*, London, Penguin, 1974. Used for a couple of items of background on czarist Russia.

Richard Pipes, *The Russian Revolution*, New York, Alfred A. Knopf, 1990. Marvin Zonis once told me that 'every country analyst falls in love with the country they cover', something that is certainly true of most historians of the Soviet Union. Somehow, Pipes managed to avoid it, or perhaps he fell in love with czarist Russia. Used primarily for a few biographical details of Lenin.

John Reed, *Ten Days that Shook the World*, New York, Penguin, 1977. A notoriously pro-Bolshevik eyewitness account of the rebellion. Used for some of the details in the opening scene.

Michael Broadbent's comment on the czar's wine appears in:

Michael Broadbent, *Michael Broadbent's Pocket Vintage Wine Companion: Over Fifty Years of Tasting Three Centuries of Wine*, London, Pavilion Books, 2007.

For the rise of the workers:

Victoria E. Bonnell, 'Radical Politics and Organized Labour in Pre-Revolutionary Moscow 1905–1914', *Journal of Social History*, 1978, pp. 282–300. Also includes some material on the worker Kanatchikov (famous for his autobiography).

Victoria E. Bonnell, *Roots of Rebellion: Workers' Politics and Organizations in St Petersburg and Moscow, 1900–1914*, Berkeley, University of California Press, 1983.

Sheila Fitzpatrick, *The Russian Revolution*, Oxford, Oxford University Press, 2008. Although it is a comprehensive history of the revolution, I used it mainly for the sections on the rising workers.

Leopold Haimson, *Russia's Revolutionary Experience, 1905–1917: Two Essays*, New York, Columbia University Press, 2005. The main source for the rising workers section, the Lena Goldfields massacre and the workers' struggle stories.

Diane Koenker & William G. Rosenberg, 'Skilled Workers and the Strike

Movement in Revolutionary Russia', *Journal of Social History*, 1986, pp. 605–629. Rosenberg provided a critique of an early draft of this chapter, for which I am grateful.

Deborah Pearl, *Creating a Culture of Revolution: Workers and the Revolutionary Movement in Late Imperial Russia*, Bloomington, Slavica, 2015. The source for the communist folktales. A number of these tales referenced the French Revolution. For instance, one noted that the French, 'the most intelligent of foreign peoples', were the first to overthrow their own 'czar'.

S. A. Smith, *Revolution and the People in Russia and China: A Comparative History*, Cambridge, Cambridge University Press, 2008.

And for biographical material on Lenin:

Nikolay Chernyshevsky, *What is to be Done?*, Ithaca, Cornell University Press, 1989 (1863). The book by Lenin's hero. It really is a bad book, but astonishingly influential.

Robert Payne, *The Life and Death of Lenin*, New York, Simon and Schuster, 1964. A bit dated, and some claims have been supplanted by new information. The main source for the role of Lenin's mother.

Robert Service, *Lenin: A Biography*, Cambridge, Harvard University Press, 2000. An excellent biography of Lenin drawing on Soviet archival material. The main source for biographical details I used in the chapter.

One of the great defects of Lenin's character exposed by Service's biography is that he seemed to place no value on human life – oddly, for a man pursuing a utopian vision of society. From exile, he exhorted the revolutionary contingents, saying they 'must arm themselves as best they can (rifles, revolvers, bombs, knives, knuckle dusters, sticks, rag soaked in kerosene for starting fires, ropes or rope ladders, shovels for building barricades, pyroxylin, cartridges, barbed wire, nails against cavalry etc. etc.)'. His violent ideas, gleaned primarily from books and his own imagination, included defeating Cossack cavalry by removing paving stones to break the horses' legs, and attacking policemen by throwing homemade acid at them. At one point during the 1905 uprising, Lenin almost had a fit, when he felt that the members of the Bolshevik Party in Russia were showing insufficient interest in violent acts. ('I see with horror, for God's sake with real horror, that there has been talk about bombs for more than a year and yet not a single bomb has been made!')

After Lenin took power, he did not change his spots. Here was his advice on incentivising the troops: 'We'll advance 10–20 kilometres and hang the kulaks, priests, landed gentry. 100,000 rubles prize for each one of them that is hanged.' Here was Lenin on economic policy: 'The peasant must do a bit of starving so as to relieve the factories and towns from complete starvation.' And here was his advice on winning hearts and minds: 'An example must be demonstrated ... Hang (and make sure that the hanging takes place in full view of the people) no fewer than 100 known kulaks, rich men, bloodsuckers. Publish their names. Seize all their grain from them.' He continued, in the manner of a gang boss from a work of fiction: 'Telegraph receipt and implementation. Yours, Lenin. (P.S.) Find some truly hard people.' The writer Maxim Gorky became a close confidant of Lenin's but was repelled by this aspect of

Lenin's character. Gorky said of Lenin: 'in general, he loved people: he loved them with abnegation. His love looked far ahead, through the mists of hatred.' Lenin appeared to realise that what he was advocating was wrong, but it did not stop him. He once told Gorky: 'one must break heads, pitilessly break heads, even if, ideally, we are opposed to all violence'.

The comment on Political Risk Services' track record is from:

Marvin Zonis, Dan Lefkovitz, Sam Wilkin & Joseph Yackley, *Risk Rules: How Local Politics Threaten the Global Economy*, Chicago, Agate, 2011.

The main point of the chapter, of course, is to address the question of why ordinary people decide to get involved in politics. The primary sources for the discussion of people power are:

Stephen G. Brush, 'Dynamics of Theory Change in the Social Sciences: Relative Deprivation and Collective Violence', *The Journal of Conflict Resolution*, 1996, pp. 523–545. Describes how our understanding of mass political action has changed since Gurr's influential book.

Jeff Goodwin & James M. Jasper (eds), *The Social Movements Reader: Cases and Concepts*, Hoboken, Wiley-Blackwell, 2014. Used for material on the intellectual history of rebellions.

Ted Robert Gurr, *Why Men Rebel* (Fortieth Anniversary Edition), Abingdon, Routledge, 2016 (2011). Still a classic, and perhaps due for a re-evaluation, now that 'people power' has become so much more important in rebellions (e.g., the Arab Spring).

Gustave Le Bon, *The Crowd: A Study of the Popular Mind*, New York, Dover Publications, 2002 (1895). The classic on bewitching crowds that Lenin repurposed as a how-to guide.

Karl Marx, *The Communist Manifesto*, Moscow, Progress Publishers, 1969 (1848). Used for some quotes on how the young Marx thought about revolutions.

Suzanne Staggenborg, *Social Movements*, Oxford, Oxford University Press, 2011. A textbook covering the current state of social movements research.

Jacquelien van Stekelenburg & Bert Klandermans, 'Individuals in Movements: A Social Psychology of Contention', in *Handbook of Social Movements Across Disciplines*, New York, Springer, 2010, pp. 103–139. Van Stekelenburg provided a critique of an early draft of this chapter, for which I am grateful.

Jacquelien van Stekelenburg & Bert Klandermans, 'The Social Psychology of Protest', *Current Sociology Review*, 2013, pp. 886–905. Together with the chapter cited immediately above, a good summary of current research on a 'bottom-up' view of mass movements – looking at the decisions of individuals who decide to join these movements.

Martijn van Zomeren & Aart Iyer, 'Introduction to the Social and Psychological Dynamics of Collective Action', *Journal of Social Issues*, 2009, pp. 645–660. Another good summary of research on individual decision-making in mass movements.

There is also a quote on Brexit. Nearly all the Brexit material in this book is from:

Tim Shipman, *All Out War: The Full Story of Brexit*, London, William Collins, 2016.

I then talk about collective action frames (or struggle stories). For this section, the sources are Brush (1996), Staggenborg (2011) and van Stekelenburg & Klandermans (2013), all cited above, as well as:

Jack A. Goldstone (ed), *Revolutions: Theoretical, Comparative and Historical Studies*, Belmont, Wadsworth/Thomson Learning, 2002. (Mainly the introduction by Goldstone himself.)

Thomas F. Pettigrew, 'Samuel Stouffer and Relative Deprivation', *Social Psychology Quarterly*, 2015, pp. 7–24. Together with the next two sources, an excellent summary of both the intellectual history of, and current research on, relative deprivation.

Heather J. Smith & Thomas F. Pettigrew, 'Advances in Relative Deprivation Theory and Research', *Social Justice Research*, 2015, pp. 1–6.

Heather J. Smith, Thomas F. Pettigrew & Silvana Bialosiewicz, 'Relative Deprivation: A Theoretical and Meta-Analytic Review', *Personality and Social Psychology Review*, 2012, pp. 203–232.

Tom R. Tyler, 'Psychological Models of the Justice Motive: Antecedents of Distributive and Procedural Justice', *Journal of Personality and Social Psychology*, 1994, pp. 850–863. Somewhat arbitrarily selected as a representative of the link between injustice and collective action. There is a large literature on this subject; the same point is also made in Goldstone, 2003, and Staggenborg, 2011, both cited above.

I mentioned that Lenin's economic policies were 'magical thinking'. He tried to shut down markets, which is very hard to do – efforts to restrict supply tend only to raise prices, and once prices rise high enough there will almost certainly be someone who finds a way around whatever restrictions have been imposed. Hence arresting the bagmen was not going to work. In the modern day, efforts to control abuse of narcotics by making drugs illegal tend to have the same effect – raising the price so much that suppliers are willing to break the law. That said, the Soviet Union did make an extraordinary effort to change human nature in such a way that markets would no longer operate. As an economist, I am sceptical that such an effort could ever work; but the remarkable early economic progress of the Soviet Union suggests that somehow, for a time, it was achieved. A remarkable book on the Soviet methods:

Jochen Hellbeck, *Revolution on My Mind*, Cambridge, Harvard University Press, 2009.

At the end of the chapter, I mentioned how Lenin divided up property. That material is from:

Walter Scheidel, *The Great Leveler: Violence and the History of Inequality from the Stone Age to the 21st Century*, Princeton, Princeton University Press, 2017.

We will be hearing more from Scheidel in chapter 5. I also quote:

Hannah Arendt, *On Revolution*, London, Faber and Faber, 1963.

And I quote from a lecture by the political scientist Jack Goldstone. You can see the lecture online at:

Jack Goldstone, 'A World in Revolution: The Inevitable Backlash against Global Elites', *Watson Institute for International and Public Affairs at Brown University*, 2017. http://watson.brown.edu/events/2017/jack-goldstone-world-revolution-inevitable-backlash-against-global-elites

I make a brief mention of why the collective action problem does not doom voting in democracies. As far as I know, the first mention of this insight is:

Gordon Tullock, *Toward a Mathematics of Politics*, Ann Arbor, University of Michigan Press, 1967.

Here are a couple of papers arbitrarily selected as good summaries of the extensive literature on why people vote, the first looking at overall turnout and the second looking at decisions by individual voters:

André Blais, 'What Affects Voter Turnout?', *Annual Political Science Review*, 2006, pp. 111–125.

Ching-Hsing Wang, 'Why do People Vote? Rationality or Emotion', *International Political Science Review*, 2013, pp. 483–501.

The comment that Lenin's excesses opened a space for the popular radical right – the subject of the next chapter – is based on:

Philip Morgan, *Fascism in Europe, 1919–1945*, London, Routledge, 2003.

Chapter 3

For better or worse, the United States and Iran are now inextricably linked. After the Allies got involved in Iran during the Second World War (deposing the Shah, who was flirting with the Axis powers) Roosevelt offered to step in, hoping to promote the country's development. 'I was rather thrilled with the idea of using Iran as an example of what we could do by an unselfish American policy,' he wrote. 'We could not take on a more difficult nation', plagued as it was by 'the worst form of feudalism'.

But things did not go as planned. 'Feudal' Iran was a lot more complex than Roosevelt had imagined; in 1905 and 1906 the country had undergone the first constitutional revolution in the Middle East, and enjoyed a brief flowering of democracy. Inconveniently for US policy, democracy came again to Iran in the late 1940s and early 1950s, in the form of the remarkable Mohammad Mossadeq, backed by a middle-class uprising. He managed to seize power from the Shah following extensive protests in Tehran. Mossadeq was tall, stooped and passionate to the point of caricature, engaging in fits of public weeping and fainting; during one memorable speech he ripped an arm from his chair to wave it for emphasis. The Shah had attempted to deal with Mossadeq by putting him in prison, but Mossadeq (like Lenin) had many friends in high places which made him difficult to get rid of.

The Americans did not like Mossadeq. Mossadeq's democratically-elected coalition government included the Communist Party, which was funded by the Soviet Union.

Worse yet, Mossadeq nationalised the oil industry. He had good reason to do it: the Shah had cut a deal with Anglo Iranian Oil Corporation (today, British Petroleum) that helped make him the richest man in the country but resulted in nearly all British Petroleum's profits going to Britain. Naïvely, Mossadeq imagined that the Americans, as champions of democracy, would back his rebellion. After overthrowing the Shah, he spent forty days in the United States, asking for loans and aid.

Unfortunately, the Cold War was by then in force, and the United States could not see beyond the communists. Instead of aiding Mossadeq, the Americans decided to eliminate him. In a joint Anglo-American operation, the CIA operative Kermit Roosevelt was dispatched to Iran with a slush fund of some $1m (about $8.9m today) and orders to find someone willing to back a coup. On 19 August a chanting crowd supported by half a dozen Sherman tanks and American money advanced on Mossadeq's house. The crowds were partly religious; because the communists in Mossadeq's coalition were atheist, many Shia leaders had also turned against Mossadeq, and (ironically enough) found common cause with the American effort. Three of the tanks positioned to defend the house were destroyed after two hours of gunfire. Mossadeq escaped in his pyjamas over a garden wall.

The United States then helped the Shah suppress democracy, became his main foreign financial backer, and helped him create a secret police force. Mossadeq was placed under permanent house arrest and died of cancer in 1965. Kermit Roosevelt published a rather self-congratulatory book describing the affair, and thus Iran would for ever be America's problem – and vice versa. During the Islamic revolution, the rebels were certain the United States would launch another coup; it has since emerged that the US national security advisor, Zbigniew Brzezinski, had indeed asked for a coup to be carried out against the new Islamic regime, apparently more or less on his own initiative; but both the US ambassador and the ranking US general in Iran at the time had said it would be impossible.

There is one upside to this unhappy relationship: after the Iranian revolution, many members of the Iranian intelligentsia attempted to flee to the United States; a few of them made it. As a result, one can find any number of superb English-language books on the Iranian revolution (and numerous other aspects of Iranian history and society).

In contrast to the Soviet Union, Iran's archives are not open – so even though the sources are good, there is much disagreement among them, on matters both important and trivial (was Khomeini travelling in a green Beetle or a black Beetle? How much money did Kermit Roosevelt take to Iran? Was middle-class involvement in the revolution all smoke and mirrors, in an operation masterminded by Khomeini?). The definitive history of the Iranian revolution has yet to be written. Still, there are many excellent first drafts to choose from.

Because of Iran's difficult history with the United States, I have made some vocabulary choices some may find surprising. For instance, I refer to the 'Shia clergy' rather than the more commonly used Arabic term. By doing so, I hope to make things easier on Western readers and avoid words that have become politicised.

The sources I used for my history of the revolution (and the above comments on the US–Iran relationship):

Ervand Abrahamian, *Iran Between Two Revolutions*, Princeton, Princeton University Press, 1982. An academic text, very good on the policies of the Shah's government; used also for some details on Khomeini and Shariati.

Michael Axworthy, *Revolutionary Iran: A History of the Islamic Republic*, Oxford, Oxford University Press, 2013. Both this book and Buchan are very readable texts with lots of journalistic detail.

James Buchan, *Days of God: The Revolution in Iran and Its Consequences*, New York, Simon & Schuster, 2012. Together with Axworthy, 2013, Milani, 1994, and Abrahamian, 1982, the main sources for my historical narrative.

Mohsen M. Milani, *The Making of Iran's Islamic Revolution*, Boulder, Westview Press, 1994.

Mansoor Moaddel, *Class, Politics, and Ideology in the Iranian Revolution*, New York, Columbia University Press, 1993. Used primarily for demographic information.

Roy Mottahedeh, *The Mantle of the Prophet*, Oxford, Oneworld, 2000. Sometimes, when doing research, I find a book that I intend to dip into and instead end up reading cover to cover. This is such a book. It interweaves a few life stories of persons known to the author and thus humanises the Iranian revolution. I used it primarily for background on the Shia clerics; also for some episodes on Khomeini's rise to power.

John D. Stempel, *Inside the Iranian Revolution*, Lexington, Kentucky, Clark Publishing, 2009.

Zonis, Lefkovitz, Wilkin & Yackley, 2011, cited in chapter 2. The book contains a chapter on the Iranian revolution, which explains how weak governance undid the Shah, the 'world's most powerful man'.

For biographical material on Khomeini I relied on:

Arshin Adib-Moghaddam, 'Ayatollah Ruhollah Khomeini: A Clerical Revolutionary?', introduction to *A Critical Introduction to Khomeini*, Cambridge, Cambridge University Press, 2014, pp. 1–18. The volume is one of the few authoritative works on Khomeini in English.

Mojtaba Mahdavi, 'The Rise of Khomeinism', in *A Critical Introduction to Khomeini*, Cambridge, Cambridge University Press, 2014, pp. 43–68. Contends that Khomeini adopted a lot of Shariati's ideas.

Amir Taheri, *The Spirit of Allah: Khomeini and the Islamic Revolution*, Bethesda, Adler & Adler, 1986. This book is the main source I used for journalistic detail on Khomeini's life. It is a well-written and engaging book. That said, there are lots of errors: Khomeini's wife's age, the number of guerrillas killed, the publication dates of Khomeini's main works. So, take some of the biographical details with a grain of salt.

Khomeini's love poetry comes from Taheri, 1986, cited immediately above, and an article in the *New York Times*, 'Mullah as Mystic'. For the biographical essay on Shariati the primary source was:

Ali Rahnema, *An Islamic Utopian: A Political Biography of Ali Shariati*, London, I.B. Tauris, 2014.

In the section on the determinants of revolutionary success, I mentioned some classic theories of revolutions:

Samuel P. Huntington, *Political Order in Changing Societies*, New Haven, Yale University Press, 1968.

Theda Skocpol, *States and Social Revolutions: A Comparative Analysis*, Cambridge, Cambridge University Press, 1979.

Charles Tilly, *From Mobilization to Revolution*, Reading, Massachusetts, Addison-Wesley, 1978.

Another classic text, which looks at the patterns of history appearing in revolutions:

Crane Brinton, *The Anatomy of Revolution*, New York, Vintage Books, 1952.

For a summary of current research on revolutions, see Goldstone, 2003, cited in chapter 2. Or for a shorter version:

Jack A. Goldstone, *Revolutions: A Very Short Introduction*, Oxford, Oxford University Press, 2014. The shortlist of factors common to successful revolutions is also from this source (although I have reduced the list from five factors to four).

For more on today's 'all-singing all-dancing' models of revolutions, see:

Jack A. Goldstone, 'A Global Model for Forecasting Political Instability', *American Journal of Political Science*, 2010, pp. 190–208.

And also the official website: Lockheed Martin. World-Wide Integrated Crisis Early Warning System. http://www.lockheedmartin.com/us/products/W-ICEWS.html (accessed 30/10/2017).

Another central point of the chapter is how right-leaning uprisings achieve success. I focus especially on the radical anti-democratic right, of which the most successful (if that is the right word) movements in history have been the fascists. The sources for the section on fascism are:

Morgan, 2003, cited in chapter 2.

Robert O. Paxton, *The Anatomy of Fascism*, New York, Penguin, 2004. A superb and very readable book, including material on fascist antecedents, such as the KKK. If Khomeini had known of it, he might have contemplated the history of a Romanian right-populist movement, the Legion of the Archangel Gabriel, a Christian fundamentalist group that appealed to Romanian peasantry with sharp green uniforms, patriotic Christian banners and anti-Semitism. But the Legion was unable to achieve a Christian revolution. In the late 1930s, the Romanian king arrested and then killed the Legion's leader. When the Nazis occupied Romania in the early 1940s, the Legion (which had lots of fascist ideas) made a comeback; however, with the approval of the Nazis, Romania's dictator first curtailed the movement, and when that did not work, crushed it bloodily.

Nicos Poulantzas, *Fascism and Dictatorship: The Third International and the Problem of Fascism*, London, Verso, 1979. A marxist account of fascism.

Lastly, I included some comments on the role of emotion in politics. I could not find a good review article, so apologies for citing several articles for a short section:

Antoine J. Banks, 'The Public's Anger: White Racial Attitudes and Opinions Toward Health Care Reform', *Political Behaviour*, 2014, pp. 493–514. On the link between anger and prejudice.

James N. Druckman & Rosie McDermott, 'Emotion and the Framing of Risky Choice', *Political Behaviour*, 2008, pp. 297–321. On the link between anger and risky choices.

John Garry, 'Emotions and Voting in EU Referendums', *European Union Politics*, 2014, pp. 235–254. On failing to consider economic consequences when voting under the influence of emotion (it is not just Brexit).

Barbara A. Gault & John Sabini, 'The Roles of Empathy, Anger, and Gender in Predicting Attitudes Toward Punitive, Reparative, and Preventative Public Policies', *Cognition and Emotion*, 2000, pp. 495–520. On anger and making political choices that punish others.

Leonie Huddy, Stanley Feldman & Erin Cassese, 'On the Distinct Political Effects of Anger and Anxiety', in *The Affect Effect*, Cambridge: Cambridge University Press, 2007. Also on the link between anger and risky choices.

George E. Marcus, W. Russell Neuman & Michael MacKuen, *Affective Intelligence and Political Judgment*, Chicago, University of Chicago Press, 2000. On the link between anger and information-seeking (and many other topics).

Nicholas A. Valentino, Ted Brader, Erik W. Groenendyk, Krysha Gregorowicz & Vincent L. Hutchings, 'Election Night's Alright for Fighting: The Role of Emotions in Political Participation', *Journal of Politics*, 2010, pp. 156–170. On anger and voter turnout.

Two articles that make the argument – somewhat going beyond the mainstream scholarly view – that emotion is a key driver of political participation:

Erik W. Groenendyk, 'Current Emotion Research in Political Science: How Emotions Help Democracy Overcome its Collective Action Problem', *Emotion Review*, 2011, pp. 455–463.

Nicholas A. Valentino, Krysha Gregorowicz & Erik W. Groenendyk, 'Efficacy, Emotions and the Habit of Participation', *Political Behaviour*, 2009, pp. 307–330.

I also referenced the famous book by Daniel Kahneman:

Daniel Kahneman, *Thinking Fast and Slow*, New York, Farrar, Straus and Giroux, 2011.

Van Stekelenburg & Klandermans, 2010 and 2013, cited in chapter 2, were also used for this section.

The definitive work on the Shah losing his marbles:

Marvin Zonis, *Majestic Failure: The Fall of the Shah of Iran*, Chicago, University of Chicago Press, 1991.

Chapter 4

From this point in the book, inequality becomes important. A couple of notes about inequality. First, in the modern day, no country is entirely equal. Even in the most egalitarian countries on earth, the top 10 per cent of the population takes home more than 20 per cent of the national income, and the distribution of wealth is usually far more unequal than that. For background on why this is the case, I suggest this remarkable book:

Carles Boix, *Political Order and Inequality: Their Foundations and their Consequences for Human Welfare*, New York, Cambridge University Press, 2015. It turns out that hunter-gather societies were egalitarian, but in surprisingly unpleasant ways.

A second note. When I refer to inequality in this book ('country A is more unequal than country B ... ') I am referring to the Gini coefficient for income, and the data, unless otherwise noted, are from:

UNU-WIDER, *World Income Inequality Database* (WIID3.4), 2017. I have selected the latest high-quality survey from each country. Using this approach, post-2010 data are available for about ninety countries worldwide.

I mentioned that economists enjoy attempting to puzzle out why Argentina declined so precipitously. A good place to start if you are interested in this research is the volume titled *Argentine Exceptionalism*. This paper provides a summary:

Rafael Di Tella, Edward Gleaser & Lucas Lach, 'Exceptional Argentina', in *Argentine Exceptionalism*, Cambridge, Harvard University Press, 2014.

Believe it or not, the United States attempted to intervene in Argentina's politics as well. The portly Spruille Braden, whose family had a large stake in some Chilean copper mines, was the US ambassador to Argentina when Perón burst on to the political scene. Braden decided, somewhat amazingly, to campaign against him personally. He went on a lecture tour through Argentina's major cities, denouncing Perón as he went. In Buenos Aires, he managed to pull a well-dressed crowd of some 5,000 people, waving handkerchiefs and shouting his name. It must have been exciting. And, compared to America's efforts in Iran, it was an admirably democratic approach.

At least, up to a point. As the election approached, Braden launched his main attack, the *Consultation among the American Republics with Respect to the Argentine Situation*. Dubbed the 'Blue Book', the pamphlet, in effect, claimed that Perón was a Nazi and an anti-Semite. (To this day, the pamphlet is a source of confusion about Perón's politics.) Most of the pamphlet was outright fabrication. Perón did have a wealthy supporter who was a German émigré, said to have links with the Nazi Party. That fact would have been worth investigating; but the Blue Book largely ignored that point and focused on slander.

It also backfired completely. Perón changed his campaign slogan to 'Braden or Perón'. Put that way, it was not much of a choice; most Argentines did not want to be governed by the United States. Even though the entire political spectrum unified against Perón, he sailed to victory. Perhaps, if Braden had never become involved, Perón would have lost, and Argentina's history would have been very different.

The sources for my historical narrative, and the above comments, are:

Jill Hedges, *Argentina: A Modern History*, London, I.B. Tauris, 2011. Hedges provided a critique of an early draft of this chapter, for which I am grateful.

Joseph A. Page, 1983. *Perón: A Biography*. New York: Random House.

David Rock, *Argentina, 1516–1987: From Spanish Colonization to Alfonsin*, Berkeley, University of California Press, 1985.

All three books are excellent, and to a degree, cover much of the same territory regarding Perón (it is difficult to say much about modern Argentine history without talking about Perón). Hedges's book is, of course, the most up to date. She has also just released a biography that provides the most comprehensive English-language treatment of Evita available:

Jill Hedges, *Evita: The Life of Eva Perón,* London, I.B. Tauris, 2016.

My historical narrative also includes a few items of colour from this short but brilliant review article:

Michael Greenberg, 'A Descamisada Diva', *Boston Review*, 1 December 1996, pp. 33–37.

And from this article:

Natalia Milanesio, 'A Man Like You: Juan Domingo Perón and the Politics of Attraction in Mid-Twentieth-Century Argentina', *Gender & History*, 2014, pp. 84–104. Perón was something of a sex symbol, evidently; a group of Argentine women attended his 1946 presidential rallies, chanting 'we want sons by Perón'.

One main point of the chapter is to return to the topic of populism, initially broached in chapter 1. For an introduction to Latin American populism, a good place to start is a textbook, *Populism in Latin America*. My comments regarding Perón's populism (for instance, that he was the 'purest' populist) are based on these two chapters in that textbook:

Michael L. Conniff, introduction to *Populism in Latin America* (Second Edition), Tuscaloosa, University of Alabama Press, 2012.

Joel Horowitz, 'Populism and Its Legacies in Argentina', in *Populism in Latin America* (Second Edition), Tuscaloosa, University of Alabama Press, 2012, pp. 23–47.

There are many studies showing that inequality and personal economic distress do not impact populist voting; and that populist voting instead turns on values issues. A somewhat arbitrary selection from this literature:

Ronald F. Ingelhart & Pippa Norris, 'Trump, Brexit and the Rise of Populism: Economic Have-Nots and Cultural Backlash', *Harvard Kennedy School Faculty Research Working Paper Series*, 2016. This paper was very influential in showing that the 2016 shocks were more related to values and policy than personal economic distress.

Eric Kaufmann, 'Trump and Brexit: Why it's Again NOT the Economy, Stupid', *British Politics and Policy Blog*, 2016. http://blogs.lse.ac.uk/politicsandpolicy/trump-and-brexit-why-its-again-not-the-economy-stupid/ (accessed 31/10/2017).

Chi-Mei Luo, 'The Rise of Populist Right-wing Parties in the 2014 European Parliament: Election and Implications for European Integration', *European Review*, 2017, pp. 406–422. Though focused specifically on the 2014 election, it is a good summary of recent research, including (unsuccessful) efforts to find links between economic distress and populist voting in Europe.

I mentioned that there have been many studies showing that the distress of communities does lead to populist voting. A selection from this new but growing literature:

Yann Algan, Sergei Guriev, Elias Papaioannou & Evgenia Passari, 'The European Trust Crisis and the Rise of Populism', *Brookings Papers on Economic Activity*, 2017.

David H. Autor, David Dorn & Gordon H. Hanson, 'The China Syndrome: Local Labor Market Effects of Import Competition in the United States', *American Economic Review*, 2013, pp. 2121–2168. As far as I know, this was the paper that started it all – the first paper showing a link between community distress and populist voting, after which a river of corroborating evidence has followed.

David H. Autor, David Dorn, Gordon H. Hanson & Kaveh Majlesi, 'Importing Political Polarization? The Electoral Consequences of Rising Trade Exposure', *MIT Working Papers*, 2016, pp. 1–62. Applies the same approach to the 2016 US presidential election.

Sascha O. Becker, Thiemo Fetzer & Dennis Novy, 'Who Voted for Brexit? A Comprehensive District-Level Analysis', *Warwick University Working Paper*, 2016.

Italo Colantone & Piero Stanig, 'Global Competition and Brexit', *Bocconi University Working Paper*, 2016.

Italo Colantone & Piero Stanig, 'The Trade Origins of Economic Nationalism: Import Competition and Voting Behavior in Western Europe', *Bocconi University Working Paper*, 2017.

Christian Dippel, Robert Gold & Stephan Heblich, 'Globalization and its (Dis-) Content: Trade Shocks and Voting Behavior', *National Bureau of Economic Research Working Paper*, 2015.

Jeff Guo, 'Death Predicts Whether People Vote for Donald Trump', *Washington Post Wonkblog*, 4 March 2016.

See also entries on 538.com by Ben Casselman ('Stop Saying Trump's Win Had Nothing to Do With Economics') and Jed Kolko ('Trump Was Stronger Where the Economy Is Weaker').

The supply–demand framework for understanding populism appears in many sources, including:

Luigi Guiso, Helios Herrera, Massimo Morelli & Tommaso Sonno, 'Demand and Supply of Populism', *Center for Economic Policy Research Discussion Papers*, 2017, pp. 1–65. This remarkable paper attempts to perform a statistical analysis of populist supply and demand simultaneously – an ambitious undertaking, and as far as I am aware, the first such attempt. The authors find that nearly all of the populist vote in

Europe comes from mobilising people who would not otherwise have voted, which accords with the literature on Latin American populism. The authors also contend they have found evidence of a large impact of individual economic distress on populist voting. I am sceptical; their indicator of economic distress includes elements of group identity; the study covers so many countries and years that the analysis could be picking up group distress. That said, if it were corroborated, it would be a very interesting finding.

Wouter van der Brug & Meindert Fennema, 'What Causes People to Vote for a Radical-Right Party? A Review of Recent Work', *International Journal of Public Opinion Research*, 2007, pp. 474–487. A good summary of current research (and disputes) regarding populist-right voting in Europe.

The comment on populist rule-breaking political behaviour is based on:

J. Eric Oliver & Wendy M. Rahn, 'Rise of the Trumpenvolk: Populism in the 2016 Election', *Annals of the American Academy of Political and Social Science*, 2016, pp. 189–206.

I then discuss 'populist economics' – which does not, in fact, have much to do with populism. The original papers that talked about populist economics are:

Rudiger Dornbusch & Sebastian Edwards, 'Macroeconomic Populism', *Journal of Development Economics*, 1990, pp. 247–277.

Jeffrey D. Sachs, 'Social Conflict and Populist Policies in Latin America', *International Center for Economic Growth Occasional Papers*, 1990, pp. 1–39.

I mentioned the link between inequality and populist economics. A somewhat arbitrary selection of papers on this link:

Stefania Albanesi, 'Inflation and Inequality', *Journal of Monetary Economics*, 2007, pp. 1088–1114.

Fahim A. Al-Marhubi, 'Income Inequality and Inflation: The Cross-Country Evidence', *Contemporary Economic Policy*, 2000, pp. 428–439.

Roel M. W. J. Beetsma & Frederick van der Ploeg, 'Does Inequality Cause Inflation? The Political Economy of Inflation, Taxation, and Government Debt', *Public Choice*, 1996, pp. 143–162. Discusses inequality and inflation, but also the link between inequality and high government debt.

Andrew Berg & Jeffrey Sachs, 'The Debt Crisis: Structural Explanations of Country Performance', *Journal of Development Economics*, 1988, pp. 271–306. On the link between inequality and debt defaults.

Raj M. Desai, Anders Olofsgård & Tarik M. Yousef, 'Democracy, Inequality, and Inflation', *American Political Science Review*, 2003, pp. 391–406.

Jaejoon Woo, 'Social Polarisation, Industrialisation, and Fiscal Instability: Theory and Evidence', *Journal of Development Economics*, 2003, pp. 223–252. On the link between inequality and high deficits.

I then move on to talk about the intellectual history of explanations of why governments run up deficits. Two articles on this intellectual history:

Brian Snowdon, 'The Influence of Political Distortions on Macroeconomic Performance: The Contributions of Alberto Alesina', *World Economics*, 2004, pp. 91–136.

Brian Snowdon & Howard R. Vane, 'The New Political Macroeconomics: An Interview with Alberto Alesina', *The American Economist*, 1999, pp. 19–33.

The statistics comparing inequality, taxation and government spending in Argentina and Europe are from:

Edwin Goñi, J. Humberto López & Luis Servén, 'Fiscal Redistribution and Income Inequality in Latin America', *World Development*, 2011, pp. 1558–1569.

And the new explanations of why countries run deficits:

Alberto Alesina & Allan Drazen, 'Why are Stabilizations Delayed?', *The American Economic Review*, 1991, pp. 1170–1188.

Alberto Alesina & Roberto Perotti, 'The Political Economy of Budget Deficits', *Staff Papers (International Monetary Fund)*, 1995, pp. 1–31.

César Martinelli & Raúl Escorza, 'When are Stabilisations Delayed? Alesina-Drazen Revisited', *European Economic Review*, 2007, pp. 1223–1245. Martinelli provided a critique of an early draft of this chapter, for which I am grateful.

Sometimes, voters are, in fact, poorly informed about policy (a point I de-emphasise in the text). But that is not because they are foolish: it is because it is not rational for them to pay a lot of attention to politics. See, for instance:

César Martinelli, 'Would Rational Voters Acquire Costly Information?', *Journal of Economic Theory*, 2006, pp. 225–251.

The unhappy ending for Argentina in the 1980s and early 1990s is from Hedges, 2011, and Rock, 1985, cited above, as well as:

Jennifer Adair, 'Democratic Utopias: The Argentine Transition to Democracy Through Letters, 1983–1989', *The Americas*, 2015, pp. 221–247.

Sarah Muir, 'On Historical Exhaustion: Argentine Critique in an Era of "Total Corruption"', *Comparative Studies in Society and History*, 2016, pp. 129–158.

Osvaldo Soriano, 'Living with Inflation', in *The Argentina Reader: History, Culture, Politics*, Durham, Duke University Press, 2002, pp. 481–487.

But the real point of the chapter, one might say, is the Argentine standoff. The theory has caused a lot of controversy since it was first put forward nearly fifteen years ago (one fun experiment is to try explaining the theory to your rich friends at a dinner party, and seeing how they react). At first, the theory was intended to explain democratisation – why some countries become democracies and others do not. The idea was that dictators and monarchs, fearing revolutions, would offer democracy as an alternative; but only if their country was egalitarian enough that they did not expect to be taxed excessively. So in Russia and Iran, which were highly unequal, the czar and Shah hung on until the revolutions came – they were never going to permit democracy. In the United States, by contrast, the founding fathers had little fear of democracy, because income was evenly distributed.

This idea was put forward by Daron Acemoglu and James Robinson (famous for *Why Nations Fail*) and it attracted a lot of attention – and controversy. The historical case studies, especially of England, appeared to confirm the theory. But there is an enormous political science literature on the causes of democratisation. This new theory appeared, rather cheekily, to slice through all that detailed analysis to base democratisation on a simple economic foundation. Carles Boix added to the excitement by, roughly at the same time, coming up with his own theory linking inequality and democratisation and including extensive statistical tests supporting his claims.

More than a decade of research has cast doubt on the standoff as a theory of democratisation. Perhaps the theory holds under very specific conditions – at certain levels of income, or where wealth is based in land. But overall, inequality does not appear to impact whether countries democratise; to take just one example, South Africa, perhaps the most unequal country on earth (for which data are available), is a democracy. That said, the theory has done better as an explanation of why democracies fail. Distributive conflict has, as I noted in the main text, been confirmed as a major contributing factor in many democratic failures. Still, it is important to keep in mind that the impact of inequality does not appear to be all that large; it seems that political factors are more important in determining whether democracies fail – inequality may push democracies in the direction of failure, but probably not that hard.

The original Argentine standoff books, and more recent updates from the same authors:

Daron Acemoglu & James A. Robinson, *Economic Origins of Dictatorship and Democracy*, Cambridge, Cambridge University Press, 2006.

Daron Acemoglu, Suresh Naidu, Pascual Restrepo & James A. Robinson, 'Democracy, Redistribution, and Inequality', in *Handbook of Income Distribution*, Volume 2B, Amsterdam, Elsevier, 2015, pp. 1886–1960.

Carles Boix, *Democracy and Redistribution*, Cambridge, Cambridge University Press, 2003.

Carles Boix, 'RMDs', *Comparative Democratization*, 2013, pp. 12–15.

The most comprehensive effort to test the theory, using both statistics and cases:

Haggard & Kaufman, 2016, cited in chapter 1.

A somewhat arbitrary selection from the many articles that critique elements of the theory. I selected these because they advance alternatives:

Eduardo Alemán & Sebastián M. Saiegh, 'Political Realignment and Democratic Breakdown in Argentina, 1916–1930', *Party Politics*, 2014, pp. 849–863. A spirited critique of the standoff theory as an explanation of Argentina's hard political choices.

Christian Houle, 'Inequality and Democracy: Why Inequality Harms Consolidation but Does Not Affect Democratization', *World Politics*, 2009, pp. 589–622. Statistical tests showing that inequality prevents the strengthening of democracy, but does not prevent countries becoming democracies in the first place.

Christopher Reenock, Michael Bernhard & David Sobek, 'Regressive Socioeconomic Distribution and Democratic Survival', *International Studies Quarterly*, 2007, pp. 677–699. Statistical tests showing that inequality per se is not the best predictor of the onset of distributive conflict.

· Dan Slater, Benjamin Smith & Gautam Nair, 'Economic Origins of Democratic Breakdown? The Redistributive Model and the Postcolonial State', *Perspectives on Politics*, 2014, pp. 353–374. Statistical tests showing that political factors are most important in determining democratic breakdown.

In an excellent recent book, Ganesh Sitaraman, an advisor to US Senator Elizabeth Warren, apparently unaware of this controversy (or perhaps seeking to avoid it), derived a very similar theory based on the history of US democracy. That book is the source of the quotes from the US founding fathers, as well as the historical US inequality statistics:

Ganesh Sitaraman, *The Crisis of the Middle-Class Constitution: Why Economic Inequality Threatens our Republic*, New York, Alfred A. Knopf, 2017.

The explanations of why the average Joe might not want to tax too heavily are from:

Alberto Alesina & Edward Glaeser, *Fighting Poverty in the US and Europe: A World of Difference*, Oxford, Oxford University Press, 2004.

Alessandro Lizzeri & Nicola Perisco, 'Why Did the Elites Extend the Suffrage? Democracy and the Scope of Government, with an Application to Britain's "Age of Reform"', *Quarterly Journal of Economics*, 2004, pp. 707–765. This article also advances an alternative theory of democratisation.

Chapter 5

If you fall in love with Huey Long, and it is hard not to, he has inspired a great work of fiction – a book that has twice been made into a movie:

Robert Penn Warren, *All the King's Men*, San Diego, Harcourt, 2001 (1946).

That (unsympathetic) book won the Pulitzer Prize, so did a (sympathetic) biography, over two decades later by Harry Williams. Long's personality and story are so remarkable, it is almost inevitable he would attract the A-list talent. Both books remain excellent, and relevant, reads.

There is also quite a bit of Huey Long material on YouTube. You can, for instance, see several speeches and his drunken press conference – at least in part. The sources for the story about Long's carousing include the press conference video, a few articles in the popular media (including a *New York Times* article that explains in detail how to make the 'Ramos gin fizz'), and the main texts I consulted to produce my much-abbreviated tale of Long's rise:

Alan Brinkley, *Voices of Protest: Huey Long, Father Coughlin and the Great Depression*, New York, Vintage Books, 1982. Puts Huey Long in context with other populists of his day. It is a good book, although I mainly relied on the other sources listed here.

William Ivy Hair, *The Kingfish and His Realm: The Life and Times of Huey P. Long*, Baton Rouge, Louisiana State University Press, 1991. Drier than the other sources, but by far the best at explaining the Louisiana context that gave rise to Long.

Richard D. White Jr, *Kingfish: The Reign of Huey P. Long*, New York, Random House, 2006. The most recent biography of Long, it updates a few details based on newer information.

T. Harry Williams, *Huey Long*, New York, Alfred A. Knopf, 1969. The classic.

For the background on the 'feudal state of Louisiana' I relied on the above sources, as well as:

William Ivy Hair, *Bourbonism and Agrarian Protest: Louisiana Politics 1877–1900*, Baton Rouge, Louisiana State University Press, 1969.

Towards the end of the book, I mentioned that economics is almost never destiny. Economic factors do influence political outcomes – the phenomenon of economic voting, for instance, has a measurable impact on which candidate wins office. But such economic factors are almost always dominated by political factors. For instance, in determining who wins elections, economic voting tends to be less important than the political skill of the candidates, how long the opposition has been in power, the issues at stake, and so on.

There is one notable exception, where economics dictates a country's political destiny: the link between oil wealth and the absence of democracy. Even the richest and most stable oil-rich countries – Qatar, the UAE or Kuwait, for example – tend to show little sign of transitioning to democracy. Indeed, in recent decades, the annual chance that any given country with an oil-dominated economy will do so has been effectively nil. That said, it has not been precisely nil: there are at least three countries in history that have done it (one could say four, after US invasion brought democracy to Iraq). Norway, for instance, is oil-rich but also stable, prosperous and democratic. Usually the Norwegian case is explained away by referring to the fact that the country was already a stable democracy at the time the oil really started flowing. Venezuela is another democracy, but might be the exception that proves the rule: it has recently descended into demagoguery and chaos (one might put Iraq in a similar category). The other oil-rich country that has become a democracy is Trinidad and Tobago, and basically, there is nothing wrong with Trinidad and Tobago. It is not rich, but nor is it poor. It is known for good beaches, birdlife, a raucous carnival season, religious and ethnic diversity (35 per cent of South Asian origin, 35 per cent African, the remainder largely mixed-race), and for being a somewhat miraculous exception to the general rule about oil and democracy.

Why does the rule exist in the first place? There are lots of different theories, but one of the most influential is that – like landlords – oil barons tended to create an extreme version of the Argentine standoff. Oil wealth is, of course, based in land; it is therefore extremely easy to tax. Hence people who are getting rich from oil will tend to be very leery of democracy.

For more on the 'oil curse':

Jeff D. Colgan, *Petro-Aggression: When Oil Causes War*, Cambridge, Cambridge University Press, 2013.

Ellis Goldberg, Erik Wibbels & Eric Mvukiyehe, 'Lessons from Strange Cases: Democracy, Development, and the Resource Curse in the U.S. States', *Comparative Political Studies*, 2008, pp. 477–514. This article attempts to explain Louisiana politics from a resource curse perspective. It is sort of a through-the-looking-glass view; Huey Long becomes a petro-oligarch, when in fact he spent most of his career attempting to tax Standard Oil's refining operations and failing. Still, it is fascinating.

In the main text of the book, I mentioned the long-standing antipathy of landlords to democracy. The classic texts I cite are:

Samuel P. Huntington, *The Third Wave: Democratization in the Late Twentieth Century*, Norman, Oklahoma, University of Oklahoma Press, 1991.

Barrington Moore Jr, *Social Origins of Dictatorship and Democracy: Lord and Peasant in the Making of the Modern World*, Boston, Beacon Press, 1966.

The rest of the discussion is based on Acemoglu & Robinson, 2006, and Boix, 2003, both cited in chapter 4, and:

Charles Tilly, *Coercion, Capital and European States, A.D. 990–1992*, Hoboken, New Jersey, Wiley-Blackwell, 1992.

I picked up the quote from Aristotle in the classic:

Seymour Martin Lipset, *Political Man: The Social Bases of Politics*, Baltimore, Johns Hopkins University Press, 1981. Although firmly in the 'people are deluded' school of political thought, it is provocative and a good read.

The discussion of the Progressive movement is based on:

Steven J. Diner, *A Very Different Age: Americans of the Progressive Era*, New York, Hill and Wang, 1998.

Thomas C. Leonard, *Illiberal Reformers: Race, Eugenics and American Economics in the Progressive Era*, Princeton, Princeton University Press, 2016. Focuses on how the Progressives went too far.

Michael McGerr, *A Fierce Discontent: The Rise and Fall of the Progressive Movement in America, 1870–1920*, Oxford, Oxford University Press, 2003. Together with Leonard, cited immediately above, the main source for the material in the section.

Shelton Stromquist, *Re-inventing 'The People': The Progressive Movement, the Class Problem, and the Origins of Modern Liberalism*, Urbana, Illinois, University of Illinois Press, 2006. Argues, in effect, that the original sin of the Progressive movement was its inability to acknowledge that it was acting in its own (middle-class) interests – a point I take up in the concluding chapter.

Charles Tilly & Lesley J. Wood, *Social Movements, 1768–2012* (Third Edition), Boulder, Colorado, Paradigm, 2013. The source of the comment on the usual tactics of social movements.

Lest the above sources be tarred by association, I should mention that the paragraph about how stressful it is to be middle class is my own invention.

When Roosevelt at last enters the picture, the details on him are from the above sources and:

H. W. Brands, *Traitor to His Class: The Privileged Life and Radical Presidency of Franklin Delano Roosevelt*, New York, Doubleday, 2008.

The material on how hard it is to share the wealth is based on a large literature. A few representative articles, selected somewhat arbitrarily:

Walter Korpi, 'Power Resources and Employer-centred Approaches in Explanations of Welfare', *World Politics*, 2006, pp. 167–206. Claims that proportional representation leads to stronger unions, which makes countries more egalitarian.

Torsten Persson & Guido Tabellini, *Political Economics: Explaining Economic Policy*, Cambridge, MIT Press, 2000. A textbook that includes, among many other topics, a good review of different explanations for the differences in majoritarian and proportional representation systems.

Ronald Rogowski & Mark Andreas Kayser, 'Majoritarian Electoral Systems and Consumer Power: Price-Level Evidence from the OECD Countries', *American Journal of Political Science*, 2002, pp. 526–539. Contends that proportional representation countries are more egalitarian due to the greater voice of the poor.

Ronald Rogowski & Duncan C. MacRae, 'Inequality and Institutions: What Theory, History, and (Some) Data Tell Us', in *Democracy, Inequality, and Representation: A Comparative Perspective*, New York, Russell Sage Foundation, 2008, pp. 354–386. An excellent overview article; the edited volume in which it appears is a good place to start if you are interested in the details on this topic.

Scheidel, 2017, cited in chapter 2, contends that only political violence can achieve material changes in the distribution of income. The history of populists like Perón suggests otherwise; but I suppose it depends on your definition of 'material'. Perhaps if Perón had wished to make his changes stick, violence would have been necessary.

David Soskice & Torben Iversen, 'Electoral Institutions, Parties, and the Politics of Class: Explaining the Formation of Redistributive Coalitions', in *Democracy, Inequality, and Representation: A Comparative Perspective*, New York, Russell Sage Foundation, 2008, pp. 93–126. The source of the United States vs. Sweden comparison; contends that proportional representation countries are more egalitarian due to the greater voice of the poor (although for different reasons than Rogowski & Kayser, 2002).

The discussion of how the era of inequality was ended in the United States is based on:

Anthony B. Atkinson, *Inequality: What Can be Done?*, Cambridge, Harvard University Press, 2015.

Thomas Piketty, *Capital in the Twenty-First Century*, Cambridge, Belknap Press, 2014.

Sam Pizzigati, *The Rich Don't Always Win: The Forgotten Triumph Over Plutocracy that*

Created the American Middle Class, 1900–1970, New York, Seven Stories Press, 2012.

Kenneth Scheve & David Stasavage, *Taxing the Rich: A History of Fiscal Fairness in the United States and Europe*, Princeton, Princeton University Press, 2016.

Huey Long's role in ending inequality is analysed in:

Edwin Amenta, Kathleen Dunleavy & Mary Bernstein, 'Stolen Thunder? Huey Long's "Share our Wealth", Political Mediation, and the Second New Deal', *American Sociological Review*, 1994, pp. 678–702.

The point about how democracies adopt the policies that populist parties have used to rise to power was based on an Oxford Economics client note, written by Gabriel Stein. I also mentioned research on the 'representation gap', which for Europe is summarised in Luo, 2017; a similar theory for the United States is laid out in Oliver & Rahn, 2016. Both are cited in chapter 4.

There are lots of conspiracy theories regarding the death of Huey Long. Some say that Weiss was part of a conspiracy of the plantation caste; one witness claims that he overheard Weiss in a meeting of conspirators, and that he drew the proverbial short straw and was tasked with the assassination of Long. Others claim that he had intended only to talk to Huey Long, but one of Long's bodyguards, while scuffling with Weiss, accidentally shot Long – and then in the ensuing confusion, Weiss was also shot, and the bodyguards then tried to cover everything up. Yet another claim is that Long's bodyguards killed Huey Long deliberately and made Weiss into their scapegoat. The biographies of Huey Long I cite above give little credence to these theories, but who knows? If you would like to dig into some conspiracy theories yourself:

Eric Hodge, Phoebe Judge & Louise Schlemmer, *Criminal: Kingfish*, North Carolina Public Radio. http://wunc.org/post/criminal-kingfish/ (accessed 30/10/2017).

Chapter 6

Matilde (not her real name) lives in a slum on the outskirts of Buenos Aires. Matilde's neighbours like her. A lot. 'She is so good,' one says. Another chimes in: 'Matilde pays attention to every single detail. You can go and see her whenever you have a problem, any problem, medicine, she will get it …' One neighbour says she gets free birth control pills from Matilde. People come knocking on Matilde's door any time of day, asking for a driver's licence, a plot of land on which to build their shack, the water truck (there is no running water in the slum), to avoid a ticket issued by the police, or a job in local government. One grateful woman says: 'That's the reason why, if my mother can help with anything, she will be there, with Matilde.' 'Helping Matilde in which sense?' asks Javier Auyero, a sociologist studying Matilde's slum. 'Attending a rally, because Matilde always needs people. Or when she organizes a festival, she always needs some people to help her in the organization.'

Matilde, it turns out, is a Peronist Party organiser. In the 1980s, she was the press secretary of the local Peronist Party, then the women's secretary, and eventually was elected a member of the city council. 'My passion is the people,' Matilde says. 'I take care of them as if they were my children.'

During the 1980s, the Peronist Party changed. Throughout Peron's reign, and up to his second coming, the core of Peronist organisational strength had been the labour unions. With the decline of the industrial workforce, however, union support was no longer an election-winning formula. Indeed, following the 1980s return to democracy, the Peronists lost to the middle-class Radical Party. They needed a new base of support. They found it in the urban poor. But this time, they did not lure the *descamisados* with rhetoric about the broken system; they lured them, rather, with machine politics.

In the 1983 elections, even though the Peronists lost the national vote, they won thousands of regional and local government positions. Eventually, they began to use these positions to award jobs to party activists. Soon, activists like Matilde were providing the kind of social welfare benefits that a government usually provides. A survey of 112 Peronist Party branch offices in greater Buenos Aires, for instance, found that 96 per cent engaged in some form of social assistance, such as food distribution, medical and legal services, and childcare.

Doing the job of government has produced political results. For years, Matilde's neighbourhood turned out a nearly 60 per cent vote share for the Peronist Party, in a city that habitually voted for the opposition. That required a lot of effort: in Argentina, ballots are secret (as in most modern democracies). Hence Matilde had to have a very good idea of who would vote Peronist, and make sure only those people got to the polls. It took a long time to get such a sophisticated network of machine politics up and running, but by the midterm parliamentary elections of 1987, the network was operating at a national level. By 1989, a Peronist president was in office. Eventually, the party won five consecutive national elections. There were downsides, of course. The party became known for corruption; people quickly figured out why it was winning. Middle-class support plummeted. By 1999, in the wealthiest district of Argentina, the Peronist vote share was just 9 per cent. But – as in Papandreou's Greece – even after losing the support of the middle class, the Peronists still won elections.

While the poor and uneducated usually are less likely to vote, in Argentina, they not only voted, they became part-time political organisers. The Peronist Party, once a union vehicle, became something else entirely. Many party activists embraced this change. As one put it: 'Peronism is about helping poor people, and that's what we are doing here ... That's what Peronism is all about.' Of course, Peronism had been about many different things to many different people; that was its populist genius.

Matilde embraces the new Peronism. 'When I first came to Villa Paraiso, I was so blonde, so delicate ... I didn't match with the environment,' she says. But there were children living in poverty, and her heart went out to them. 'I cleaned and washed them,' she says, 'I even removed lice from their hair, because kids were my passion.' Listening to Matilde, the sociologist Auyero is suddenly reminded of someone. The love for the poor, the working to exhaustion, the blonde hair (dyed blonde, it turns out). A female social worker at the government offices in Cospito confirms his suspicions. She refers to one Peronist activist as an 'Evita-type-of-blonde'. Later, she is even more direct: 'All of them want to be Evita.'

The above tale of machine politics is from:

Javier Auyero, *Poor People's Politics: Peronist Survival Networks and the Legacy of Evita*, Durham, Duke University Press, 2000.

Steven Levitsky, 'From Labor Politics to Machine Politics: The Transformation of Party-Union Linkages in Argentine Peronism, 1983–1999', *Latin American Research Review*, 2003, pp. 3–36.

The tale of machine politics in Illinois is from:

Thomas J. Gradel & Dick Simpson, *Corrupt Illinois: Patronage, Cronyism, and Criminality*, Springfield, University of Illinois Press, 2015.

If you google 'golden Blagojevich' you can find audio of the Illinois governor's comments. Needless to say, it is not safe for work.

The data on inequality in US states are from:

Estelle Sommeiller, Mark Price and Ellis Wazeter, 'Income Inequality in the U.S. by State, Metropolitan Area, and County', *Economic Policy Institute*, 2016. http://www.epi.org/publication/income-inequality-in-the-us/ (accessed 30/10/2017).

United Health Foundation. America's Health Rankings. http://www.americashealthrankings.org/explore/2015-annual-report/measure/gini/state/ALL/ (accessed 30/10/2017).

The sources for the narrative on Greece are:

Richard Clogg, *Preface to Greece in the 1980s*, London, Macmillan, 1983, pp. vii–xii.

David H. Close, *Greece Since 1945: Politics, Economy and Society*, London, Longman, 2002.

Stan Draenos, *Andreas Papandreou: The Making of a Greek Democrat and Political Maverick*, London, I.B. Tauris, 2012.

Stathis N. Kalyvas, *Modern Greece: What Everyone Needs to Know*, Oxford, Oxford University Press, 2015.

Vasilis Kapetanyannis, 'The Left in the 1980s: Too Little, Too Late', in *Greece, 1981–1989: The Populist Decade*, London, Macmillan Press, 1993, pp. 78–93.

Christos Lyrintzis, 'Greek Politics in the Era of Economic Crisis: Reassessing Causes and Effects', *Hellenic Observatory Papers on Greece and Southeast Europe*, 2011, pp. 1–25.

George Mavrogordatos, 'Civil Society Under Populism', in *Greece, 1981–1989: The Populist Decade*, London, Macmillan Press, 1993, pp. 47–64.

James Edward Miller, *The United States and the Making of Modern Greece: History and Power, 1950–1974*, Chapel Hill, University of North Carolina Press, 2009.

Yannis Palaiologos, *The 13th Labour of Hercules: Inside the Greek Crisis*, London, Portobello, 2014.

Takis S. Pappas, *Populism and Crisis Politics in Greece*, Basingstoke, Palgrave Macmillan, 2014.

Dimitri A. Sotiropoulos, *Populism and Bureaucracy: The Case of Greece Under Pasok, 1981–1989*, South Bend, University of Notre Dame Press, 1996.

Stavros B. Thomadakis, 'The Greek Economy: Performance, Expectations, and Paradoxes', in *Greek Paradox: Promise vs. Performance*, Cambridge, MIT Press, 1997, pp. 39–60.

Again, apologies for the large number of sources for a relatively short section. In contrast to Argentina, Iran, Russia and Thailand, no one has yet written a comprehensive English-language history of modern Greece. Hence there is no single source I can cite that covers everything. The biographical material on Papandreou is mostly from Draenos, 2012. The other main texts used for general history are Close, 2002, Kalyvas, 2015, and Miller, 2009. The machine politics is largely from Sotiropoulos, 1996, with a few details from Mavrogordatos, 1993. The economics and role of the shipowners are from Palaiologos, 2014, and Thomadakis, 1997.

I mentioned the view that Germany played a role in provoking the Eurozone crisis by forcing Greece to repay its debts at the worst possible time. That view is put forward in:

Erik Jones, 'Getting the Story Right: How You Should Choose between Different Interpretations of the European Crisis (and Why You Should Care)', *Journal of European Integration*, 2015, pp. 817–832.

The section on how machine politics works is based on Auyero, 2000, cited above, and:

Valeria Brusco, Marcelo Nazareno & Susan Carol Stokes, 'Vote Buying in Argentina', *Latin American Research Review*, 2004, pp. 66–88.

Susan Carol Stokes, Thad Dunning, Marcelo Nazareno & Valeria Brusco, *Brokers, Voters and Clientelism: The Puzzle of Distributive Politics*, Cambridge, Cambridge University Press, 2013.

Rodrigo Zarazaga, 'Brokers Beyond Clientelism: A New Perspective Through the Argentinian Case', *Latin American Politics and Society*, 2014, pp. 23–45.

On the relationship between machine politics and inequality, the above sources are used as well as:

Alberto Alesina, Reza Baqir & William Easterly, 'Redistributive Public Employment', *Journal of Urban Economics*, 2000, pp. 219–241.

Thomas Markussen, 'Inequality and Political Clientelism: Evidence from South India', *Journal of Development Studies*, 2011, pp. 1721–1738.

The Greek trap is my own invention. Most of the statistical relationships that produce it have been discussed earlier in the book. The link between machine politics and lack of trust, and between a lack of trust and populist voting, is covered in studies including:

Lenka Bustikova & Cristina Corduneanu-Huci, 'Patronage, Trust and State Capacity: The Historical Trajectories of Clientelism', *World Politics*, 2017, pp. 277–326.

Francis Fukuyama, 'Democracy and the Quality of the State', *Journal of Democracy*, 2013, pp. 5–16.

The remainder of the chapter is largely my own thoughts as an analyst. The comment that better-off members of the 'working class' were more likely to vote populist is based on:

Kai Arzheimer & Elisabeth Carter, 'Political Opportunity Structures and Right-wing Extremist Party Success', *European Journal of Political Research*, 2006, pp. 419–443.

Emma Green, 'It Was Cultural Anxiety that Drove White, Working Class Voters to Trump', *The Atlantic*, 9 May 2017.

The comment on the redistributive nature of Obamacare is from:

Anon., 'Democracy in America', *Economist*, 29 January 2014.

Mayer's exposé of the Koch brothers is:

Jane Mayer, *Dark Money: How a Secretive Group of Billionaires is Trying to Buy Political Control in the US*, Melbourne, Scribe, 2016.

On why Berlusconi entered politics:

Alexander Stille, *The Sack of Rome: How a Beautiful Country with a Fabled History and Storied Culture Was Taken Over by a Man Named Silvio Berlusconi*, New York, Penguin Press, 2006.

Mudde's comment about not knowing any academics who support the populist cause is in:

Cas Mudde, 'The Study of Populist Radical Right Parties: Towards a Fourth Wave', *C-REX Working Paper Series*, 2016.

And finally, the sex scene. The sources are:

Hervé Bourges & Daniel Cohn-Bendit, *The French Student Revolt: The Leaders Speak*, New York, Hill and Wang, 1968

Mattei Dogan, 'How Civil War Was Avoided in France', *International Political Science Review*, 1984, pp. 245–277. Civil war? Seriously?

A. Belden Fields, 'The Revolution Betrayed: The French Student Revolt of May-June 1968', in *Students in Revolt*, Boston, Houghton Mifflin, 1969, pp. 127–166.

Mark Kurlansky, *1968: The Year that Rocked the World*, New York, Random House, 2005.

Patrick Seale & Maureen McConville, *French Revolution 1968*, New York, Penguin Books, 1968.

And the closing comment about everyone remembering it as being all about student sex:

Chris Reynolds, *Memories of May '68: France's Convenient Consensus*, Cardiff, University of Wales Press, 2011.

Kristin Ross, *May '68 and Its Afterlives*, Chicago, University of Chicago Press, 2002.

Lawrence Jones, 'May '68 and Its Afterlives' (review), *Common Knowledge*, p. 361.

Index